THE EXPLODING POLITICAL POWER
OF PERSONAL MEDIA

THE COMMUNICATION AND INFORMATION SCIENCE SERIES
Series Editor: BRENDA DERVIN, The Ohio State University

Subseries:
Progress in Communication Sciences: Brant R. Burleson
Interpersonal Communication: Donald J. Cegala
Organizational Communication: George Barnett
Mass Communication/Telecommunication Systems: Lee B. Becker
User-Based Communication/Information System Design:
    Michael S. Nilan.
Cross-Cultural/Cross-National Communication and Social Change:
    Josep Rota
International Communication, Peace and Development:
    Majid Tehranian
Critical Cultural Studies in Communication: Leslie T. Good
Feminist Scholarship in Communication: Lana Rakow
Rhetorial Theory and Criticism: Stephen H. Browne
Communication Pedagogy and Practice: Gerald M. Phillips
Communication: The Human Context: Lee Thayer

THE EXPLODING POLITICAL POWER
OF PERSONAL MEDIA

Gladys D. Ganley

ABLEX PUBLISHING CORPORATION
NORWOOD, NEW JERSEY 07648

Copyright © 1992 by Gladys D. Ganley.

Printed in the United States of America

Library of Congress Cataloging-in-Publication Data

Ganely, Gladys D.
  The exploding political power of personal media / Gladys D. Ganley.
    p. cm.—(Communication and information science)
  Includes bibliographical references and index.
  ISBN 0-89391-756-7
  1. Mass media—Political aspects. 2. Mass media—Technological innovations. I. Title. II. Series
  P95.8.G35 1991
  302.23—dc20   91–34545
                                                      CIP

Ablex Publishing Corporation
355 Chestnut St.
Norwood, NJ 07648

To Ossie
For 35 fascinatingly unpredictable years

TABLE OF CONTENTS

ACKNOWLEDGMENTS

The author wishes to thank all of the people who helped to make this book possible. Special thanks go to the following people who reviewed and critically commented on specific chapters or the entire manuscript while it was in progress. They are not necessarily in agreement with the views expressed, for which the author is solely responsible, as is the case for any errors of fact or interpretation.

Robert Bigelow
Richard Bissell
Nancy Boulton
Benjamin Compaine
Oswald Ganley
John LeGates
Anthony Oettinger
Walter Wriston
Ezra Vogel

The author thanks those who contributed but preferred not to be mentioned.

Special thanks also go to the Program on Information Resources Policy of Harvard University which sponsored the early work on the political uses of audiotapes and videotapes by the author and her husband and has permitted some parts of that work to be included in Chapters 3, 4, and 9.

And very special thanks are extended to nearly 500 researchers, reporters and writers whose works are cited in this volume. It is they who have recorded for history the big moments and the small ones of the personal media revolution that is transforming the world around us.

PREFACE

Over the past few decades, many types of new electronic capabilities have become available and have been used to significantly alter the way we live, work, play, run our economies, make war, and protect ourselves against our enemies. In multitudes of large and small ways, they are also being used to alter the basis of political systems we have come to take for granted. To take advantage of the opportunities and to protect ourselves against the dangers these changes present, it is imperative to understand whatever we can about what has made them possible. This book attempts to contribute to that understanding by examining the political uses by "the people"—individuals and groups—of new personal electronic media.

The designation *personal electronic media* has been chosen because the media to be examined here include more than just the new "small" electronic media. For the purposes of this book, personal electronic media mean those media to which individuals and small groups have meaningful access and which they can use to acquire, create, store, and/ or disseminate information. To function as a personal medium, the technology must be one over which an individual can exert control, although the extent of that control will vary considerably. How widely depends on the capabilities of a given technology, as well as the possibilities in a given situation for circumventing traditional political restraints and economic controlling factors.

Personal media to be discussed here include the individual machinery and software that can inform or create alone, such as personal computers or videocassette or audiocassette recorders, and also media like the phone, facsimile machine, and linked computers that rely on telecommunications networks for transmission. They include those aspects of cable television, larger or institutional computers, satellite transmission, and broadcasting that are actually available for individual uses. They also include media such as radio and television sets and satellite dishes that provide information but do not, in themselves, permit its creation or further dissemination. Not discussed in this book are those personal media where the limits to individual participation have already been set by others.

This book is not designed to be a definitive product, but as one step on the road to understanding a largely uncharted and very exciting new era. The main emphasis has therefore been placed on an examination of what these new personal media are capable of doing that could be politically significant, and a presentation of the political acts that people have actually chosen to perform with them. The evidence presented is mainly a collage of information gathered by others which has been assembled to give a sense of the overall political changes that are occurring, and the place the uses of these media have assumed in global societies. From this assemblage of specific events, a glimpse can be caught of the broad destabilizing forces being exerted on existing political structures, and the role new personal media are playing in the erosion of some systems and the alteration or creation of others.

Only a few personal media have been singled out to show what, of political significance, individuals are capable of doing with them, and just a partial list of acts of a political nature that individuals have actually achieved with these media is given. The ways that individuals are beginning to be able to exploit capabilities formerly reserved to the mass media are restricted to a few examples. The locale of most kinds of events will be confined to one or to a few countries, but it can be assumed that all such events as are described here are, in one way or another, occurring globally.

Mass media reports, especially print media reports, have been chosen as a major source of information for this book for several reasons: they provide large numbers of examples as personal media history is literally being invented; they have a global sweep and are available fast enough to keep up with breakneck happenings; they put rapidly changing situations in some historical context by recording events as they take place; their range of coverage is diverse enough to include a wide variety of disciplines; and, as befits the topic of this book, such stories are often focused on individuals.

With a few exceptions, no reference has been made to the growing body of media-related social sciences literature, and no attempt has been made to place the material presented here in the context of those findings.

In an effort to concentrate attention on the capabilities of new personal media and the political acts performed with their assistance, much that is closely related has been rather ruthlessly excluded. Events involving personal media rarely operate alone, but are more often thoroughly intertwined with mass media events and with whatever else is occurring in a given society. The assessment of the actual importance of the influence of a new medium in a specific situation or in a very broad sense, or in comparison to the importance of other influences, is being conducted by many researchers, and for the most part this book attempts no such assessment. So as not to detract from the part played by those media controlled by individuals, the role of the mass media has been deliberately omitted, except in a limited number of instances, where they are performing as "personal media." The role of the mass media in the June 1989 Chinese "prodemocracy" movement was very important, for example, but in this work is deliberately given only cursory attention.

Political acts aided by new personal electronic media by no means form the center of the political universe, and this presentation of material out of context calls for reader caution. The generation of politically oriented acts accounts for only a tiny fraction of total new personal media uses, these machines being mainly employed for ordinary work and amusement. This does not, however, render insignificant their political uses, or potential for such uses. The prompt global adaptation of these new media to political acts, the variety of political acts being conducted with them, the ingenuity involved in carrying out these acts, the growing variety of available technologies and their interactive capabilities, and the actual political change which has already followed their uses, all sound a warning that something of very basic importance is happening.

It should be stressed that, with new personal media as elsewhere, motivation and receptivity are the real keys to any kind of meaningful political activity. While these new machines make new types of political events possible, such events will never occur without political motivation. And if they do take place, they will come to nothing unless they involve an appealing political message directed toward a receptive audience. Political messages can be sent across borders all day long, but if nobody cares or has the resources to do anything with them, such happenings are politically unimportant. Nor are more and faster necessarily better. Computers now generate many millions of pieces of mail for American political candidates, but a lot of them are tossed away as junk mail, unopened.

In the material presented here, it has been possible to show that vast new technological capabilities now exist, and that a wide variety of political acts can be and have actually been conducted. But only occasionally can the receptivity of the audience be seen, or the actual outcome determined. The most complete story presented is the earliest one—that of the 1979 Islamic revolution in Iran (Chapter 2). Here, the technologies used to deliver the Ayatollah Khomeini's political messages across national borders are known, the receptivity of his audience in Iran is known, and the political outcome—10 years of a new Iranian government under the Ayatollah—is known. This is a beautiful example of how these things can and do work. One is rarely treated to such a complete story. Much of what is presented here is thus fragmentary. What really went on, how far it extended, how it interacted with and was influenced by other things, and what its eventual importance was can often only be guessed at. But as these incidents are examined, and added up, it is possible to see, if not what actually happened, at least the potential for what might sometime happen. These combinations of incidents also make clear certain trends that are developing.

The structure of the book roughly follows the chronological advent of each new medium. That is, after a general introduction, the story progresses from events involving audiocassettes to those involving videocassettes, then to those involving personal computers, and then those involving facsimile machines. Chapters 9 and 10 describe ways in which videotape technology is allowing the individual to tap into the technological power of the mass media. Chapter 11 describes the gamut of technologies available to political candidates by 1988, and how they were employed in that year's U.S. election. That chapter also points to in-creased interaction by individuals with the mass media via satellite transmission. Chapter 12 demonstrates how far these technological possibilities have been extended in the 10 years between the 1979 Iranian revolution and the 1989 Chinese student pro-democracy movement. And Chapter 13 stresses the fact that the new political freedoms provided by new personal electronic media have also contributed to perhaps undesir-able political destabilization.

The massive changes resulting from the advent of new personal media, and from other new information technologies, are generally viewed by this author as positive. But such new power in the hands of millions of variously motivated people does give a certain amount of pause to even the most devout optimist.

While there are a few exceptions, the information on which this book is based substantially ends with 1989 and early 1990.

chapter 1

THE CHANGING PERSONAL MEDIA

Two events of great political importance occurred during the first weekend of June 1989. Iran's elderly leader, the Ayatollah Ruhollah Mousavi Khomeini, died, and the government of The People's Republic of China brutally crushed a student-led "pro-democracy" movement. The latter occurred in the presence of more than a thousand members of the foreign media who had assembled with their high tech equipment to cover the Sino Soviet Summit. The government of China slapped restrictions on foreign reporters and issued massive disinformation. But Chinese students within China and abroad responded by using personal electronic media—facsimile (fax) machines, personal computers, direct dial telephones, audiotapes and videotapes, as well as an academic computer network, the international mass media, and The Voice of America—to get information out of China, to pour information into China, and to spread information widely within China (Chapter 12).

In all this China excitement, remarkably little notice was taken of the Ayatollah Khomeini's death, and few grasped the parallel between Khomeini's 1979 Iranian takeover—using audiocassettes, dry copiers, the direct dial phone, and the international mass media—and the 1989 Chinese situation. Occurring just 10 years apart, the Iranian revolution and the student uprising bracketed a decade of collection, creation, copying, and communication of politically useful information by individuals on a scale without historical precedent. For the Chinese students had simply extended the pattern developed by Khomeini (Chapter 2) to include state-of-the-art technology, and continued what individuals and small groups all over the world have been doing as each new personal medium appears and rapidly spreads globally.

THE ELECTRONIC SCENARIO

The post-World War II period has been the scene of one big electronic revolution, with the accompanying machinery and software providing new information-fueled ways to do almost anything. This has transformed the world's economic bases, its financial activities, its currency exchanges, its social and cultural activities, its military, security, and intelligence operations, and the role of its mass media.[1] With changes so far-reaching, it hardly seems surprising that spin-offs would put new technologies in the hands of individuals. And yet, a look at the relative dearth of personal media which had formerly existed shows that what has happened in the last few years is actually some sort of a miracle. It is a change so basic that it could ultimately unsettle virtually all preceding political givens.

PRIOR LIMITS ON PERSONAL MEDIA

Until a few decades ago, the media were basically the mass media—the newspaper, magazine and book publishers, radio broadcasters, movie and record producers, and that post-World War II newcomer, television. Even in the most liberal democracies, because of the lack of technical means and/or prohibitive costs, individuals and small groups had few and quite laborious methods of expression, and the scope of these was sorely limited. In addition, repressive governments have always heaped political restrictions on top of technical and economic ones.

Under favorable political conditions, individuals have been able to write letters or draw posters or print and distribute a limited number of pamphlets for centuries. When the typewriter came along in the 1900s, these became easier to turn out, but copies that could be produced were still few in number. Books and articles could be written, but generally could not be widely dispersed without a publishing company. Ads could be placed if some mass medium would accept them. Hand cameras could take snapshots and, relatively recently, movie cameras recorded certain events, but film processing time and expense made the effort tedious. The telegraph and the phone, around since the last century, made it possible to send messages or call up another person. But telegrams and long distance calls were very expensive, and mainly reserved for emergencies or used sparsely as luxuries. Phone calls and telegrams also required the intervention of operators, and getting messages across national borders was time consuming and cumbersome. Relatively efficient telephone service has until recently been limited to only a few countries. Paintings have always required and still require exhibition in some public place to make a statement, so only a handful of artists have ever been "heard." Letters to newspapers and magazines were and still are printed on the whims of editors, and calls to radio (and TV) programs were and still are kept to segments of the MC's choosing. Some exceptions are individuals who have acquired station ownership or control over radio programs, and those involved in clandestine broadcasting.

Such limitations were relative, and individuals have always used whatever means were available to conduct important political acts throughout history. They have always found ways to create and distribute underground literature, the production of *samizdat* being one powerful example. And they continue to make good use of older media—leaflets, wall posters (as well as that new nonelectronic medium, the spray can)— mixing and matching them to get access to whatever best suits their purpose. But with some powerful exceptions, personal opinions have generally found smallish audiences which, of necessity, have often been local. Technological and financial constraints have normally meant that only governments, large organizations, and the mass media have had access to the means to produce and distribute substantial amounts of idea-containing materials. These they offered to—or pressed upon—the general public, whose participation from necessity was for the most part passive. When governments are repressive—and the vast majority still are—production and distribution may be limited to those things meeting government approval. In unfavorable political climates, access by the public to the mass media is almost always restricted, and the mass media themselves denied anything resembling free expression. Censorship of what is published and what is listened to, seen, or read has been, in one way or another, nearly universal.

THE PARADE OF NEW ELECTRONIC MEDIA

The possibilities for individuals to play a more active role began to change significantly when World War II ended, and the parade of personal electronic media started: Both TV sets and citizen's band radios (CBs) appeared in the 1940s.[2] So did the first monstrous computers. Small transistorized radios and reel-to-reel audiotapes came in the 1950s. Dry copiers, mainframe computers, audiocassettes, and reel-to-reel videotapes were added in the 1960s. Portable video recorders, video cameras and cassettes, direct-dial phones, a few personal computers and computer modems, and satellite reception dishes marched forth in the 1970s. And then desktop and laptop computers, personal fax machines, handheld camcorders, and cellular telephones joined the parade in the 1980s. Touch-tone phones, electronic pagers, laser and other printers, radar detectors, and telephone answering machines have all added their voices to the personal media cacophony. During the last decade and a half, just about every personal medium has also grown smaller, more portable, and at the same time more powerful.

The great friends of the people in this revolution have been miniaturization, mass production, and plummeting prices. First transistors in the 1950s, then silicon chips in the 1960s, increased the power, reduced the size, and brought the price of many new media within the range of the individual. The history of the computer alone is the history of personal media liberation: In 1946, the first electronic digital computer, ENIAC, weighed about 30 tons and used 18,000 large, heat-producing, vacuum tubes.[3] Transistors became available to replace vacuum tubes in the late 1940s and early 1950s. In 1953, there were only 50 existing computers, still occupying large rooms, costing at least $3 million each, and requiring the energy of electric locomotives. About this time, IBM estimated its best market at about 50 new (institutional) customers, which was already a five-fold increase over 1945 projections of "total world-wide sales of only ten units."[4] The silicon chip appeared in 1960, permitting power needs to fall, computer memory to rise, the computer to perform more diverse tasks, and the machinery to start getting smaller. This prompted *The Wall Street Journal*, during the 1960s, to make the breathtaking prediction that, by the turn of the century, computers in the U.S. might number as many as 220,000.[5] Nineteen seventy-six saw the first personal computer (the Apple) produced, and in the early 1980s, sales of desktop and then laptop computers skyrocketed. By 1989, computers had surpassed anything imaginable: U.S. computers numbered around 50 million, and the world's computers, double that figure, with expectations of 60 million desktops in the U.S. by 1992.[6]

Most of these are personal computers, and many personal computers can now do much of what it took large computers to do only a few years ago. Some laptops now weigh as little as four pounds—pocketbook models a pound or less[7]—and some can be had for under a thousand dollars. Most importantly, millions of computers have escaped institutional surroundings and are free to do individual biddings. Such biddings include producing desktop publications; preparing mass mailings from computerized mailing lists; logging on to various networks; accessing vast databases, electronic mail systems, and a wide variety of services; setting up and communicating with electronic bulletin boards; distributing facsimile copies; and communicating instantaneously with other computers locally, nationally, or internationally.

The new personal electronic media vary greatly in their capabilities, and the importance of each depends on the needs and the political environment of given individuals. In very restrictive situations, simple access to information and evasion of censorship are major problems, and the smallest achievements in this regard are of maximum importance. In countries with liberal governments, the importance of information acquisition recedes somewhat, and what is most desired may be the capability for creation and transmission.

The power of such personal media as computers is both enhanced and stayed by their ability or necessity to use telecommunications networks. While personal media decentralize communications and give control to individuals, telecommunications networks, even when privatized, are centralized and subject to control by the establishment or governments. What passes over these networks is also amenable to being tapped into or interrupted. Thus phone lines, while the most ubiquitous and often the handiest of the personal media globally, also number among the most politically vulnerable. Networked computers of individuals are also subject to the powers of other individuals, and, along with the networks of large organizations and governments, may fall victim to scourges such as computer "hackers" or "viruses" (Chapter 6).

The power of personal media is also available to governments and is readily used by intelligence agencies and the police against individuals as official countermeasures. But governments have always had such powers, and these new ones are merely relative. The important change is one of balance, and the scale, previously always tilted toward the government's side, has at least for the moment tipped toward the individual.

NEW PHYSICAL MEANS OF GETTING THINGS ACROSS BORDERS

Great friends of individuals in countries with restrictive governments have also been the post-World War II advent of quick, easy, and relatively inexpensive jet airline travel; the economic necessity for millions of migratory workers to transit national borders regularly; the widespread presence of smuggling and black markets, especially in countries with centralized economies; massive dependence by economies on international tourism; and vastly increased global exports and imports. All these conditions have led to the virtual collapse of customs systems, and to the creation of sieve-like borders through which massive amounts of personal media equipment, programming, and other information march daily. Legal restraints applied to traditional media like print matter have often not been extended to new forms of media, nor is it clear that, in practice, they ever can be. Even where such controls have been attempted, they have thus far been largely ineffective.[8] Partly this is because of their newness, and the failure of laws and institutional arrangements to keep up with them, but mainly it is because these and other new technologies have changed the way the world functions.

CHANGES IN GLOBAL TELECOMMUNICATIONS

In addition to new physical means of transport, the past few decades have brought vast new means of electronic transport. Much of the power of computers and other personal media to utilize information would be impossible without recent sweeping global telecommunications changes.[9] These changes were led by a transatlantic cable in the 1950s and communications satellites linked into a global INTELSAT system, first launched in the 1960s. These systems have since had continuous extensions and improvements. Along with an information revolution, the post-World War II period has also seen the emergence of more than a hundred newly independent nations, and some of these are among the most enthusiastic INTELSAT users. Many of the newly industrialized countries (NICs) have adopted information-intensive industries as the basis for their economies and are spending vast sums to put in place telecommunications improvements.[10] Even when installed for the needs and goals of governments, these facilities are available for the use of individuals whose needs and goals may be very different.

Such cables and satellites are now being supplemented by both national and transoceanic fiber-optic cables. Fiber-optics will further advance personal media uses, since they permit undistorted computer data and fax messages as well as video broadcast transmission. In December 1988, a transatlantic fiber-optic cable was completed, tripling the capacity of the in-place satellites and copper cables. Satellite phone capacity for the Pacific area was quintupled in the second half of the 1980s, and in Spring 1989, Asia was also linked to the U.S. by fiber-optics.[11] There is even consideration of laying a fiber-optic cable the length of the Soviet Union. While calls by businesses, governments, and the mass media still predominate, individuals are now firmly linked across borders by direct dial phones, fax machines, and computers.

Changes in telecommunications regulations around the world are also promoting the effective use of personal electronic media. In 1975, the U.S. ruling that non-phone company equipment could be attached to the AT&T system provided the liberation needed by PC, laptop, and fax machine users. Other changed regulations in various parts of the globe, and technological advances, have provided those services at phone-call prices and caused long distance call prices themselves to fall drastically. Lower prices and better facilities have meant that international phone calls have increased astronomically. For instance, in the decade between 1977 and 1987, calls from the U.S. to overseas rose to 4.7 billion minutes worth from

580 million minutes worth.[12] A considerable proportion of these calls are now fax calls, to deal with various languages, to transmit graphics, and to combine the speed of the phone with clarity.

CHANGES IN COMPUTER AND OTHER ELECTRONIC MEDIA LITERACY

Most people in the world over forty and multitudes who are younger have achieved whatever electronic media literacy they may possess on a mainly catch-as-catch-can basis. But, through access to an avalanche of such personal media in schools, work places, stores, banks, video game parlors, homes, and village squares, millions and millions of the world's children are now growing up electronically literate. As the sophistication of the machines increases, that of the population also increases. As this generation matures, and another follows it, and as skills mesh with new machines, anything we can now imagine and much that we cannot will become possible.

NEW PERSONAL MEDIA IN AN AGE OF POLITICAL UPHEAVAL

The advent of personal electronic media has coincided and is interacting with an age of massive political upheaval. The emergent political voice of more than a hundred newly independent countries, the ascendency of guerrilla and terroristic types of warfare, and an interest in direct action by a wide variety of groups globally are all being affected by new means of personal and mass communications. Cultural materials from the industrialized West—books, TV programs, records, videocassettes— spread quickly to developing and communist nations by means that are both legal and illegal. The astounding political changes since 1985 in the Soviet Union and some countries of Eastern Europe, although forced by economics, have no doubt been heavily influenced by new transglobal communications networks and the increasing access, even in closed societies, to new personal media (see Chapter 4).

THE INFORMATION REVOLUTION AND THE MASS MEDIA

The revolution in personal media has taken place alongside, and in concert with a revolution in the mass media. Just as the personal computer, the fax machine, and the video camera have become the people's version of electronic news gathering, personal media have become invaluable to reporters.[13] Broadcast TV, vast numbers of cable TV channels, videotape technology, real-time reporting by satellite, computerized newsrooms, and facsimile transmission of whole newspapers for computerized printing at distant locations have all served to provide individuals with more, and more timely, information. The *International Herald Tribune*, for instance, sells daily copies in 164 countries, obtaining information by satellite globally, compiling it by computers in the U.S., setting copy by computers in Europe, and transmitting it by satellite for printing in Asia.[14] Cable News Network (CNN) alone is seen in about 90 countries.[15]

Individuals all over the world have come to rely heavily on television for their information, even if they are tuning in illegally. An important adjunct to freedom of program choice is the home satellite dish.[16] In the information-deprived Soviet Union and Eastern Europe, smuggled or homemade dishes have long been used illegally to receive Western programming. But, like other smuggled personal media, such as the VCR, illegal dishes eventually became so widespread that, even before the opening of these areas to the West in the second half of 1989, some countries began allowing dishes to be brought in legally.[17] One of the very important political products of the satellite age is the availability of cross-border television. The broad satellite footprint across Europe, for instance, as well as neighboring country TV, often makes it impossible for individual nations to keep control over their citizens' television reception. Where TV programs themselves cannot be viewed, they have been regularly taped off the air and smuggled in on videocassettes from other countries. This was apparently quite important to the vast political changes that took place in the USSR and Eastern Europe in the latter part of the 1980s (see Chapter 4).

Private citizens in many nations are now also in a better position to be more critical of their mass media. Formerly so dependent on them for information, and thus forced to tolerate their excesses and deficiencies, individuals now have at least a few new options. If television programs don't meet their needs, they are turning to video, which is being substituted for TV in many countries where programming is rigidly controlled by governments.[18] If newspapers don't satisfy them, at least limited refuge can be taken in desktop publishing. For political advertising, there are now the options of computer bulletin boards and direct mailers in many countries.

Frustrations are not confined to government-controlled media. The mass media in the U.S., for example, have been using their own new information resources to change the way they do their reporting. Some of these changes are controversial. Instantaneous and massive reportage of terroristic events, a concentration on violent pictures, news sent from battlefields in real time, remote sensing images from space that may show military targets, statistically derived election results broadcast before poll closings, docudramatization mixing fact and fiction, and simulated news events acted out on videotape have all brought substantial criticism. Individual access to alternatives could bring changes in the way people, even in democracies, view the role of the mass media.

INTERACTION BETWEEN PERSONAL AND MASS MEDIA

One of the most fascinating consequences of the advent of personal electronic media is the merger now occurring between the individual and at least certain aspects of the mass media. The public is no longer just a passive recipient of mass media products but is steadily becoming, at least in a small way, a mass media actor. Videotape technology, especially, has made it possible for lobbyists, politicians, and members of special interest groups to ply television stations with free videotaped news releases. Hostage-taking terrorists have been especially adept at getting videos played as central parts of global television news programming. Cheap and light video cameras permit more and more amateurs to take on-the-spot, politically pertinent news footage, which the mass media are often happy to broadcast. Much of this is nonpolitical, but there are still concerns that it can contribute to nonobjective or distorted news reporting. And some of it could not be more political. Students supporting the 1989 Chinese uprising, for example, fed amateur videocassettes and news releases to both the Western mass media and to The Voice of America. Several of these new possibilities for individuals to interact with the mass media are discussed in Chapters 9 through 12.

INCREASED SATELLITE ACCESS

Among new tools being employed by politicians and beginning to be used by special interest groups is access to satellite television, and new types of uplinks, which can be used to relay videotaped materials to TV stations or be combined with purchased TV time. Uplinks have been made available by the advent of the mobile Ku-Band uplink truck and access to studio rental. While still relatively high, prices have now come within the reach of sufficiently motivated individuals and small organizations. TV time is especially available on cable stations, where demand for customers is high, prices are low, and specific audiences can be easily targeted. Candidates for political office made good use of these facilities in the 1988 election (Chapter 11), and as prices continue to fall, this is a new field that will probably be wide open.

POWER TO THE PEOPLE

From the moment of the appearance of new personal electronic media, individuals the world over have used them ingeniously, employing them in ways never designed for nor anticipated by their creators. Some of the greatest inventiveness has been among those who had been previously powerless and have now attained the means to do things that are forbidden. The result has been not just the conduct of political acts, of which there have been many. More importantly, these new media allow geographically distant groups with like interests to merge for common activities, and people around the globe to exert power against their governments, their societies, their institutions, and their employers.

Free people tend to think of more power to the people as "democratizing" and therefore desirable. And it is. But power to the people, even used in "good" causes, can also be critically, even fatally, destabilizing. As power has shifted to individuals and allowed them to play more of a role, it has enlarged the ways they can respond in both domestic and international times of crisis. The fate of individuals now falls more into their own hands, but it also falls more into the individual hands of others. As it strips away oppressions, power to the people can also strip away the protective devices put in place by institutions. Power to the people can mean, not just freedom, but also that nobody is in charge anymore, with as yet incalculable political consequences.

NOTES

1. For an overview of these sweeping changes, see: Oswald H. Ganley and Gladys D. Ganley, *To Inform Or To Control? The New Communications Networks*, Second Edition, Ablex Publishing Corporation, Norwood, NJ, 1989.
2. Amateur radio clubs have long existed. The Harvard Wireless Club, for instance, claims to have been around since 1909. ("Wireless Club. Tuning in To the World for 80 Years," *Harvard Alumni Gazette*, February 1990, p. 7.)
3. "Events That Helped Shape the Century," *The Wall Street Journal*, Centennial Edition (June 23, 1989), p. B12. (Article begins p. B9.)
4. Robert H. Hayes and William J. Abernathy, "Managing Our Way to Economic Decline," *Harvard Business Review*, July-August 1980, p. 71. (Article begins p. 67.)
5. Michael W. Miller, "A Brave New World: Streams of 1s and 0s," box, "Futures Past and Present," *The Wall Street Journal*, Centennial Edition (June 23, 1989), p. A-15.
6. See, for instance: William M. Bulkeley, "Computer Gurus Cast Their Eyes Toward Tomorrow's Hot Machines," *The Wall Street Journal*, Centennial Edition (June 23,

1989), p. A-15, and Richard Brandt with Deidre A. Depke, Geoff Lewis, Keith H. Hammonds, and Chuck Hawkins, "The Personal Computer Finds Its Missing Link. New Hardware and Software are Making Networks the Hottest Ticket in the Computer Industry," *Business Week*, June 5, 1989, pp. 120-128.

7. Maria Shao, "Beyond the Laptop: The Incredible Shrinking Computer," *Business Week*, May 15, 1989, pp. 134, 136.

8 These various points are discussed in detail for the videocassette recorder in Gladys D. Ganley and Oswald H. Ganley, *Global Political Fallout. The VCR's First Decade, 1976-1985*, Ablex Publishing Corporation, Norwood, NJ, 1987.

9 For a general discussion of changes in telecommunications, see: Oswald H. Ganley and Gladys D. Ganley, *To Inform Or To Control? The New Communications Networks*, Second Edition. Ablex Publishing Corporation, Norwood, NJ, 1989, pp. 211-219. For regulatory and legal changes, see: Carol L. Weinhaus and Anthony G. Oettinger, *Behind the Telephone Debates*, Ablex Publishing Corporation, Norwood, NJ, 1988, and *Toward a Law of Global Communications Networks*, Anne W. Branscomb, Ed., Longman, New York, 1986. For the broader significance of changed ways in which information is formatted and distributed, see: Anthony G. Oettinger, *The Information Evolution: Building Blocks and Bursting Bundles*, Program on Information Resources Policy, Harvard University, Cambridge, MA, August 1989.

10. Taiwan, for instance, has installed 22 phones per 100 people, and Hong Kong exceeds this number by more than 50 percent with 46 to 100 installed. South Korea, which 10 years ago had less than one phone per hundred people, had 16 phones per hundred in 1987 and is aiming for 40 per hundred by the year 2000. Newly installed systems, such as Korea's, are direct dial systems. ("Communications: Vital for Growth," *Far East Business*, May 1989, pp. 39-40.) The use of mobile radio phones, which not only perform as long distance walkie-talkies, but also obviate some telecommunications installation difficulties, is rapidly spreading. Every 10th phone in Hong Kong is a cellular one. For mobile phone use in the Asia-Pacific area, see: "Mobile Phones Sales Skyrocket in Asia," *Far East Business*, May 1989, p. 44. Some Pacific countries are just beginning to upgrade their phone systems. Indonesia, for instance, has only about .6 phones per hundred people, and Thailand 1.8 per 100. (Richard Borsuk, "Indonesia is Expected Soon to Award Big Contract to Improve Phone Network," *The Wall Street Journal*, January 26, 1990, p. A-98, and "Communications: Vital for Growth," p. 40).

11. Calvin Sims, "Fiber-Optic Calling to Japan Starts Today," *The New York Times*, April 18, 1989, pp. D-1, D-6. "Cable or Satellite: Which Way to Go?" *Far East Business*, May 1989, pp. 42-46.

12. To Japan alone, during this time, U.S. callers increased their calling time from 14 million to 175 million minutes, in parallel with Japan's emergence as an economic leader. The price of those U.S.-Japan calls fell from $6.34 in 1964 to $3.78 in 1989, and is expected to drop further. (Calvin Sims, "New Atlantic Cable Makes More Calls Possible," *The New York Times*, December 14, 1988, p. 1, and Calvin Sims, "Fiber-Optic Calling to Japan Starts Today," *The New York Times*, April 18, 1989, pp. D-1, D-6.) See also: John Burgess, "Americans Ring up Deficit of Phone Calls. Fees For Long-Distance Connections Add $2 Billion to Trade Gap," *The Washington Post*, February 17, 1990, p. C-1. For comments on the general expansion of phone calls, see: Trish Hall, "With Phones Everywhere, Everyone Is Talking More," *The New York Times*, October 11, 1989, p. A-1.

13. For some discussions of uses of personal media by reporters, see: Andrew Blake, "Byte by Byte, Technology Aids Reporters," *The Boston Globe*, July 3, 1988, p. 12. Gib Johnson, "The Compleat Reporter. With a Few Essentials, the Journalist is Wired to the World," *Washington Journalism Review*, May 1990, pp. 16-19. Tim Miller, "The Data-base Revolution. A Look at How Reporters are Making Use of a Powerful New Technology,"

Columbia Journalism Review, September/October 1988, pp. 35-38. For personal media uses by reporters during the 1989 crackdown on Chinese students, see, for instance: "In Beijing, A Month of Living Dangerously," *The New York Times*, June 25, 1989, Sec. 2, p. 29. This article contains reports by several U.S. TV anchors and correspondents on their uses of the walkie-talkie, the cellular and ordinary hotel phones as substitutes for TV uplinks, and the use of home camcorders in lieu of professional minicams.

14. Kenneth W. Dam, "Barriers to Integration," *InterMedia*, Volume 16, Nos. 4-5, Autumn 1988, p. 28. *The Wall Street Journal* does much the same thing, with news collected around the clock and transmitted by computer and facsimile for its U.S., European, and Asian editions. So does the *Financial Times* of London. See: Daniel Henninger, "Editing This Page: Modern Means, Traditional Ends," *The Wall Street Journal*, Centennial Edition (June 23, 1989), p. C-18, John Morton, "Newspapers By Satellite," *Washington Journalism Review*, October 1982, p. 42, and Clive Cookson, "Printing Under the Sun," *Financial Times*, June 5, 1990, p. 16. For the computerization of newsrooms, see: William R. Lindley, "From Hot Type to Video Screens: Editors Evaluate New Technology," *Journalism Quarterly*, Summer 1988, pp. 485-489.

15. "Ted Turner's CNN Gains Global Influence and 'Diplomatic' Role. In News-Starved Countries, the Atlanta Network Has Credibility Officials Lack," *The Wall Street Journal*, February 1, 1990, p. 1.

16. Even in the information-rich and censorship-free United States, about 2½ million of these dishes now supply information to rural people. Tracy L. Myrup, "Dishing it Out to the Farmers," *Washington Journalism Review*, December 1988, p. 14. Nick Ravo, "Scanning the Video Universe in Rural America's Backyards," *The New York Times*, August 9, 1989, pp. C-1, C-10. Calvin Sims, "Cost of Halting TV Signal Thieves," *The New York Times*, October 16, 1989, pp. D-1, D-6.

17. Colin McIntyre, "Eastern Bloc Joins Satellite Explosion," *The Hong Kong Standard*, May 16, 1989, p. 15. See Chapter 4 for discussions of satellite dishes in Eastern Europe and the Soviet Union.

18. Gladys D. Ganley and Oswald H. Ganley, *Global Political Fallout. The VCR's First Decade, 1976-1985*, Ablex Publishing Corporation, Norwood, NJ, 1987, p. 87.

chapter 2

THE AYATOLLAH AND THE TAPES[1]

The political uses of personal electronic media exploded on the scene when Iran's Ayatollah Khomeini employed audiotapes, the direct-dial telephone, and the dry copier to help carry out his 1979 revolution. His success in gaining and sustaining the political momentum to unseat Shah Mohammed Reza Pahlavi made Khomeini the leader of Iran's Shiite Islamic Republic until his death in June 1989. During this decade, the Ayatollah demodernized Iran, fanned the flames of Islamic fundamentalism, conducted a devastating war with Iraq which killed millions, further destabilized an already unstable Middle East and Persian Gulf area, held 50 American hostages captive for 444 days, assisted hostage-taking and bomb-wielding Shiite terrorists in war-torn Lebanon, and waged a relentless war of words against Israel, the U.S. and other Western nations, and his Sunni Muslim neighbors.

Although his goal was to lead his country backward to a purer time, the aged Khomeini's tenure reads like the most *avant garde* media menu. As the appetizer of his administration, the Ayatollah used the technique of capturing and holding hostages, and publicity ploys including videotapes of them, to manipulate governments via the world's mass media. As dessert, a few months before he died, the Ayatollah endangered free speech globally by issuing a death warrant for British writer Saloman Rushdie and all those associated with the publication of Rushdie's *Satanic Verses*. Khomeini succeeded in creating havoc among nations for 10 long years. That he did not succeed further seems mainly due to his excessively narrow view of what otherwise could have been a widely popular Muslim message.

BACKGROUND TO THE USE OF ELECTRONIC
PERSONAL MEDIA

Khomeini's successful bid for power hinged on his ability to combine those new media he then had available—the direct-dial telephone, the dry copier, and especially audiotape technology—with old, indigenous communications systems. Many of these latter operated orally or informally through mosques, bazaars, university students, and a variety of Islamic organizations.[2] The Ayatollah's genius lay in recognizing that, despite his antipathy to modernity, audiotapes were perfect for his situation. They not only permitted distant command, control and communications, but also allowed him to lead a vast Iranian population where adults were only about 32% literate.[3] Audiotapes could communicate his message better to more people than could the written word, and had the added appeal of permitting the intimacy of exhortation.

The Ayatollah Khomeini did not invent the political uses of audiotapes. Adolf Hitler used the first wire tapes to spread disinformation about his wartime whereabouts,[4] and the "Watergate tapes" destroyed the presidency of Richard Nixon. Since they first became available, such tapes and cassettes have also been employed throughout the Middle East, the Gulf region, and North Africa to circulate political plays and poetry, and have found a multitude of other political uses globally.[5] Audiotapes were used by other ayatollahs and clerics in Iran to disseminate politico-religious messages. Notably, audiocassettes were used to distribute the political lectures of the Iranian Revolution's martyred ideologist, Ali Shariati.[6]

In his pursuit of political power, the Ayatollah did not confine himself to personal electronic media. As in most recent political upheavals, mimeographed leaflets and posters, as well as dry copied materials, were also used abundantly to push forward the cause of the revolution. Mosque sermons were another means of spreading information. And when they were available to him, as during his brief stay in France in 1978-79, Khomeini also made use of the powers of the global mass media. The role of the international media was in any case quite strong. Shortwave broadcasts gave the Iranian people the information they could not get from their own media. There were about 19 foreign stations broadcasting in Persian in the 1970s, the most widely listened to being the BBC Persian and World Services. One Iranian political cartoon depicted a newscaster telling the audience, "And now for the domestic news, will you please turn to the BBC."[7]

TAPES IN THE PRELUDE TO THE IRANIAN REVOLUTION[8]

Khomeini began his active rebellion against Shah Mohammed Reza Pahlavi's regime in 1962, when he led a general strike against a ruling that court witnesses did not have to swear on the Koran. He vigorously opposed the Shah's 1963 White Revolution plan to modernize Iran, and especially his attempts to emancipate women and to nationalize lands held by Iran's Islamic clergy. Khomeini was first imprisoned by the Shah, then put under house arrest, and in 1964 was exiled from Iran to Turkey. While under house arrest, Khomeini was already taping his sermons and distributing them to "important religious centres," and shortly after he was exiled, "tapes of his declarations began to be smuggled from Turkey into Iran."[9] In 1965, the Ayatollah moved from Turkey to Najaf in Iraq. From then until 1978, when he left for France, he regularly sent tape recordings and pamphlets, with messages directed against the Shah, imperialism, and Zionism, covertly across the Iraq/Iran border. His works were smuggled into Iran mainly by sympathetic Iranian pilgrims who came to visit Iraq's chief Shiite shrines, which are in Najaf and Karbala. By 1967, a steady stream of the Ayatollah's messages flowed to his Iranian followers. In 1969, difficulties between the Iranian and Iraqi governments caused Iraq to severely limit the numbers of Iranians who could enter for several years, which cut down on Khomeini's communications. But in 1975, these contacts were restored when Iraq agreed to let in 130,000 Iranian pilgrims.

During the period of border restrictions, Khomeini used another option—that of sending messages to Iranians via Iraqi pilgrims attending the annual Hajj in Mecca. Unlike most Muslims, both Khomeini and Ali Shariati viewed the pilgrimage as a political opportunity. Some message against the Shah, Israel, Zionists, and Americans and other "imperialists" was sent to the Hajj nearly every year, and in 1973, Khomeini himself made the journey.[10] Under the influence of his arguments during the 1970s, discontentment with the Shah's regime grew among a large segment of the Iranian clergy, and this was reflected and perpetuated in their politically oriented sermons.

Within Iran, Khomeini's smuggled tapes and other messages met, not only with a receptive audience, but with Iran's extremely efficient albeit traditional underground communications system. Some 90,000 clergymen constantly communicated informally. Bazaar merchants, who were closely tied to the mosques, also had vast networks of informal communications. Post-1965, Islamic associations had rapidly multiplied, so that, by 1974, Teheran had some 12,300 of them. All of these groups had numerous ties with each other and with myriad groups within the universities. University students were extremely active in disseminating Khomeini's tapes and other messages. Seasonal migrants to the cities also took the latest fashions, which included political/religious audiocassettes, back to the villages with them.[11]

One description of the distribution of Khomeini's tapes says that, in the early days, they were smuggled to Qom through the mosque network, and that, "from there, they were taken to other cities, where enterprising and friendly bazaar merchants duplicated and sold them to the faithful."[12] Starting in 1976, "the middleman" was eliminated, with the mosque network passing the cassettes and other materials on to mullahs, who then delivered them to the people. Messages were not only delivered through the mosque system of informal communications, but regular religious occasions were used to distribute them. Besides the five daily prayers, weekly prayer meetings throughout Iran attracted huge congregations, and here Khomeini's taped speeches, and those by other important religious figures, were played to the gathering and further disseminated. The mosques sometimes also showed films of successful revolutions, which added to the political fervor.[13]

As a part of the general modernization and Westernization of Iran which Khomeini was opposing, the Shah had installed advanced broadcasting, print media, and telecommunications, and the latter included an up-to-date international direct-dial telephone system. Although the mass media were all strictly controlled by the Shah's government, personal media, many of them state-of-the-art for that time, were readily available to the Iranian people. Dry copiers and audiocassette recorders, as well as mimeograph machines, had been imported, and these were put to use in the huge antimodernization underground effort that developed in support of Khomeini.[14]

Perhaps because of the newness of the technologies and their unexpected uses in conjunction with known distribution systems, these dissident activities did not—until too late—draw the particular attention of the Shah's government. When such activities became too apparent to ignore, they had already been organized into a smoothly functioning operation. By then, the political situation was so tense that any effort at disruption resulted in more support for Khomeini.[15]

THE TAPES, THE DIRECT-DIAL PHONE, AND THE WESTERN MEDIA

By 1978, as Khomeini's messages became increasingly strident, attempts were made by the Shah to quiet him. Partly because of Iranian pressure on Iraq, Khomeini was forced to leave that country. But with the Shah's permission, the French government allowed Khomeini to move to France and, in October 1978, he made his residence there, just outside Paris.

When he sanctioned this change, the Shah obviously did not take the political significance of access to modern media into account. "This proved a foolish move," says one writer, pointing out that the change of country gave Khomeini better access to transportation and telecommunications facilities, and allowed him to get global mass media coverage for his statements.[16]

In France, the Ayatollah was also able to send messages into Iran instantly by the direct-dial phone system. The Ayatollah's messages and instructions were taped directly off the France-to-Iran long distance telephone, and thousands of copies made and distributed throughout Iran.[17]

At the time of the revolution, there were only about 500,000 phones in Iran, almost all in Tehran, but they were all automatic. A project was underway by some 30 contractors from various countries, coordinated by AT&T, to improve efficiency by combining Iran's civilian telecommunications with the separate military, railway, steel company, and radio and television telecommunications networks. As the revolution approached, some integration of civilian and military communications had been completed. A former AT&T official has said that all of Iran's long distance lines terminated in one building in Tehran, and that:[18]

> It would have been very easy to shut down the civilian communications and still keep the military, Savak [the secret police] and even the power companies and railroads all working.

Savak, this official said, "and probably military intelligence," monitored virtually every call, and had to know what was going on. But despite this fact:[19]

> there was never any attempt, on the part of the Shah or anybody else, to shut off the civilian network while keeping the military network going.

The reasons given for this lack of interference were the possibility of sabotage of military communications by revolutionaries within the telecommunications union, the easy availability of tapes and other dissident literature, which were "all over the place," and perhaps that President Carter had made aid contingent on a relaxation of censorship and human rights violations.[20] It can also be assumed that there were the usual tensions between the needs for communications security and those of the intelligence communities.

By 1978, Khomeini's basic message had become that there was no possibility of compromise with the Shah, and that "The Pahlavi dynasty must go."[21] While he was still in Iraq in August 1978, Ramadan, the holy month of Islamic fasting, occurred, and during this period the Ayatollah began to insist, via cassettes, that the monarchy be overthrown and to tell his followers to get ready to unseat the Shah. He asked the clergy to provide leadership, and exhorted the military to desert the Shah and join the revolution. On the 19th of August, a mysterious fire took place at the Rex cinema in Abadan and 410 people were killed, which caused tensions to rise even more against the Shah's government. Khomeini exploited this situation by giving taped instructions for organizing large protest demonstrations. Before departing Iraq for France, Khomeini also began to refer to the United States as "satanic" and to push the clergy to greater action. He told the clergy that Islam was a political religion, that Friday and festival prayers and the Hajj were all political events, and that propaganda, the students, and both violence and nonviolence were all legitimate tools for use in an Islamic revolution. Besides being given wide distribution, Khomeini's taped speeches were often played at the daily Ramadan services at sunset.[22]

From early November until the Shah was driven out of Iran in mid-January, Khomeini orchestrated revolutionary events from Paris by tape and telephone. He told students and others where to spread his messages and how to organize and carry out everything from small street processions to massive marches and demonstrations attended by millions. By the time of the arrival of the holy period of Moharram in early December, pro-Khomeini forces had reached a fever pitch, and as the period approached, stereo speakers were put on windowsills after curfew each night:[23]

> and filled the air with taped chants of 'There is no God but Allah' and 'Death to the Shah,' spaced out with tapes of machine-gun fire.

The Shah was forced to leave Iran on January 16, 1979, and Khomeini made his triumphant entry into Teheran on the first day of February. On that day, one of the first acts of Khomeini's new Islamic regime was to distribute a piece of taped disinformation saying that "the Shah [was] briefing his ranking commanders and calling for the armed forces to instigate prolonged civil war."[24] This tape was later analyzed by U.S. and British voice experts and found to be a forgery. But it had already served its purpose of discrediting and thus "disarming" the senior Iranian military.

THE NEW IRANIAN OPPOSITION
AND PERSONAL MEDIA

Audiocassettes continued to be used politically in Iran after the revolution, but now they also became useful tools for Khomeini's political opposition. By mid-1980, Iran's President, Abol Hassan Bani-Sadr, had been at odds for some months with Khomeini, among other things over the hostages being held in the American Embassy. In June, Bani-Sadr was passed a tape recording that revealed "a plan to undermine the president's authority."[25] Bani-Sadr responded by sending his own taped messages to his supporters, asking them to help resist the movement to oust him. However, the Islamic authorities, expecting trouble, thwarted the effort by cancelling prayer meetings to head off pro-Bani Sadr demonstrations. Bani-Sadr went underground, sending taped messages back to Khomeini in a reconciliation attempt, but no agreement could be reached, and Bani-Sadr was removed from the President's office. Still underground, Bani-Sadr allied himself with Massaud Rajavi, who had headed the Mujahedin in Khomeini's support but had, like Bani-Sadr, fallen from favor. The two fled to Paris, where they formed the National Resistance Council as an anti-Khomeini provisional government.[26]

During the period of upheaval in Iran following Bani-Sadr and Rajavi's departure, the Khomeini government attempted to crack down on the availability of political and Western music. Large numbers of audiocassettes, videocassettes, and records were confiscated, but this had little effect on available information. As had the Shah, Khomeini strictly controlled broadcasting and the press, but personal electronic media remained accessible privately and to individuals in government offices.[27] Among other new opposition acts, taped messages by Reza Shah II (the deposed Shah's son), Shapour Bakhtiar (the Shah's last prime minister), and Bani-Sadr were both direct-dialed and smuggled into Iran, and widely distributed throughout the country.[28]

Bani-Sadr remained in Paris, but in 1986, Rajavi moved to Iraq to lead Mujahedin resistance efforts by exiled Iranians against Khomeini. Putting Khomeini's teachings to use, he invited Western reporters in to view Mujahedin facilities and training and showed them videotapes of parading guerrilla battalions.[29]

EXPORTING THE ISLAMIC REVOLUTION

In a 1980 speech, the Ayatollah Khomeini expressed his determination to export his Islamic revolution.[30] Although he now headed a government, he still relied upon many of the information techniques and media that had served him so well as an individual. As early as 1981, "thousands of publications" were being exported to help him carry out his continued revolutionary intentions.[31] The Ayatollah also put together extensive programming for radio and television broadcasts which were transmitted all over the Persian Gulf region[32] and also into Muslim Soviet Central Asia.[33] This latter activity took on renewed importance when, from 1988 onward, political disturbances arose in Azerbaijan and other Muslim sections of the Soviet Union.[34]

Videocassettes were also routinely added to audiocassettes as political messengers and, by 1986, such revolutionary audiocassettes, videocassettes, leaflets, brochures, and books were "being distributed on a mass scale in all large Turkish cities."[35] In March 1987, Tunisia broke relations with Iran, accusing Khomeini of attempting to replace the government of then President Habib Bourguiba with a pro-Iranian fundamentalist Islamic regime. The Tunisian government claimed that a network, thought to be composed of members of the unofficial but tolerated Islamic Tendencies Movement, had been discovered plotting the overthrow of the Tunisian government, and that video, photocopying, and printing equipment had been confiscated. The group was accused of distributing pro-Khomeini literature in the mosques and universities that called for a Tunisian insurrection, and of attempting to infiltrate youth movements like the Boy Scouts. The Iranian Embassy in Tunis was called a recruiting center for the fundamentalist cause, and a distribution center for videocassettes and other forms of subversive propaganda. Some videocassettes, the Tunisian government claimed, gave instructions for building barricades and for starting fires in the course of street demonstrations. The Iranian Embassy was also said to be soliciting Tunisians to help create disturbances at the annual Mecca pilgrimage. To support these claims (which Iran denied), Tunisian officials showed samples of the "subversive" literature to reporters.[36] But some sources say that the accusations against Iran may have been just an excuse for Bourguiba to crack down on home grown fundamentalism.[37]

Because his political message was not palatable to the vast majority of

Muslims, who are not Shiites but Sunnis, or even to Arab Shiites, and probably also due to the distractions of the Iran/Iraq war, Khomeini was never very successful in exporting his revolution to other Muslim populations.[38] His greatest inroads appear to have been made with the Lebanese Shiites, the Hezbollah, who have given the United States so much grief with kidnappings and car bombings. This small group of militants is said to have been supported by the Ayatollah, and at least in part to have done his political bidding. Among other things, the Hezbollah have emulated Khomeini's political ploy of taking hostages and feeding videotapes of them to the global mass media (see Chapter 10).

When Khomeini died in June 1989, newer media—facsimile machines, personal computers, and computer networks—were being exploited in the Chinese "prodemocracy" movement, along with the direct dial phone and audio and videotapes. But it is the Ayatollah who beat the original path to political exploitation of personal electronic media. His rise to power on their strength will forever inspire political activists and worry established groups and governments.

NOTES

1. Among the references that follow, those that best put the use of new personal media in the context of other factors involved in the success of the Iranian revolution are: Majid Tehranian, "Iran: Communications, Alienation, Revolution," *InterMedia*, March 1979, pp. 6-12, and Annabelle Sreberny-Mohammadi, *The Power of Tradition: Communication and the Iranian Revolution*, Dissertation, Columbia University, New York, 1985. For the text of many of the Ayatollah Khomeini's statements, see: Hamid Algar, *Islam and Revolution. Writings and Declarations of Imam Khomeini*, Mizan Press, Berkeley, 1981.

2. Ervand Abrahamian, "Structural Causes of the Iranian Revolution," *MERIP Reports*, Number 87, May 1980, pp. 21-26. This source describes the wide influence of bazaar merchants over small retailers and rural manufacturers, as well as the clergy, which permitted them to play such a strong role in the revolutionary process (p. 24). See also: Annabelle Sreberny-Mohammadi, *The Power of Tradition: Communication and the Iranian Revolution*, Dissertation, Columbia University, New York, 1985. A shorter paper derived from this dissertation appeared as "Small Media for a Big Revolution: Iran," *International Journal of Politics, Culture, and Society*, Volume 3, Number 3, Spring 1990, pp. 341-371.

3. For literacy and other social and economic conditions in Iran at the time of the revolution, see Ervand Abrahamian, "Structural Causes of the Iranian Revolution," *MERIP Reports*, Number 87, May 1980, pp. 21-26, and Annabelle Sreberny-Mohammadi, *The Power of Tradition*, Dissertation, pp. 50-79, among others.

4. Victor E. Ragosine, "Tape Recording," *The Encyclopedia Americana*, Volume 26, Grolier Inc., Danbury, CT, 1982, p. 282. For a background on early German audiotape, see: Douglas A. Boyd, Joseph D. Straubhaar, and John A. Lent, *Videocassette Recorders in the Third World*, Longman, New York, 1989, pp. 30-31.

5. For uses of cassettes in the Arab world, see: Haifaa Khalafallah, "The Arab Cassette Culture. An Underground Response to Censorship," *World Press Review*, April 1983, p.

60. For political uses of audiocassettes globally, see Gladys D. Ganley and Oswald H. Ganley, *Global Political Fallout. The VCR's First Decade, 1976-1985.* Ablex Publishing Corporation, Norwood, NJ, 1987, pp. 8-16. Recording technologies have long been used in the Arab world, where illiteracy is high. Wax cylinders dating to 1909 have been found with recorded songs, poetry, travel experiences, and announcements of "sanitary regulations." ("Photo Led to Old Arabic Recordings," *Harvard University Gazette,* December 19, 1986, p. 1.)

6. Ali Shariati, an Iranian sociologist in constant conflict with the Shah's regime, was 44 when he was found dead in 1977, two years before Khomeini's takeover. He taught at the high school and the University of Mashad. His university courses, extremely popular with students, were revolutionary in content, and led to his dismissal. He moved to Tehran and became a much sought after lecturer. His Islamic courses in 1973 attracted 6,000 students, and his lectures were further spread in Iran and to students overseas by audiocassette and in mimeographed copies. His death at such a young age and from questionable causes made Shariati a revolutionary martyr, and during demonstrations, his picture was often carried along with Khomeini's. See: Nikki R. Keddie, *Roots of Revolution. An Interpretive History of Modern Iran,* Yale University Press, New Haven, CT, and London, 1981, pp. 215-216, 223. Asaf Hussain, *Islamic Iran. Revolution and Counter-Revolution,* Frances Pinter, London, 1985, pp. 78-79. William H. Forbis, *Fall of the Peacock Throne,* Harper & Row, New York, 1980, p. 147. Eric Hooglund, "Rural Participation in the Revolution," *MERIP Reports,* Number 87, May 1980, p. 5. (Article begins p. 3.) Ervand Abrahamian, "The Guerrilla Movement in Iran, 1963-1977," *MERIP Reports,* Number 86, April 1980, p. 10. (Article begins p. 3.)

7. Annabelle Sreberny-Mohammadi, *The Power of Tradition,* Dissertation, p. 163. See 129-132, 213-218 of this source for the role of broadcasting in the Iranian revolution.

8. See the following, as well as specific references:
Nikki R. Keddie, *Roots of Revolution. An Interpretive History of Modern Iran,* Yale University Press, New Haven, CT, and London, 1981, pp. 180-181, 207, 242-245, 251. Dilip Hiro, *Iran Under the Ayatollahs,* Routledge & Kegan Paul, London, Boston and Henley, 1985, pp. 55, 64, 68-69, 74-77, 83-87. John D. Stempel, *Inside the Iranian Revolution,* Indiana University Press, Bloomington, 1981, pp. 44-47, 109, 127, 174, 215. Asaf Hussain, *Islamic Iran. Revolution and Counter-Revolution,* Frances Pinter, London, 1985, pp. 61, 64, 71-72, 117, 124, 130. Majid Tehranian, "Iran: Communication, Alienation, Revolution," *InterMedia,* March 1979, pp. 6-12. Majid Tehranian, "Communications Dependency and Dualism in Iran," *InterMedia,* May 1982, p. 45. Hamid Mowlana, "Technology Versus Tradition: Communication in the Iranian Revolution," *Journal of Communication,* Summer 1979, pp. 105-110. Annabelle Sreberny-Mohammadi, *The Power of Tradition,* Dissertation, pp. 122-123, and "Small Media For a Big Revolution: Iran," *International Journal of Politics, Culture and Society,* Volume 3, Number 3, Spring 1990, pp. 357-358. William H. Forbis, *Fall of the Peacock Throne,* Harper & Row, New York, 1980, pp. 5, 7. Harry Anderson, "The End of the Khomeini Era," *Newsweek,* June 12, 1989, p. 40. Raymond H. Anderson, "Ayatollah Ruhollah Khomeini, 89, Relentless Founder of Iran's Islamic Republic," *The New York Times,* June 5, 1989, p. B-11. "Sword of Relentless Revolution. Ayatollah Ruhollah Khomeini: 1900-1989," *Time,* June 12, 1989, pp. 36, 38.

9. Annabelle Sreberny-Mohammadi, *The Power of Tradition,* Dissertation, p. 122, and Shaul Bakhash, *The Reign of the Ayatollahs. Iran and the Islamic Revolution,* Basic Books Inc., New York, 1986, p. 35.

10. Khomeini and Shariati urged their followers "to view the pilgrimage as a political rite." Martin Kramer, "Tragedy in Mecca," *Orbis,* Spring 1988, p. 237. (Article begins p. 231.)

11. Nikki R. Keddie, *Roots of Revolution. An Interpretive History of Modern Iran*, Yale University Press, New Haven, CT, and London, 1981, pp. 242-245. John D. Stempel, *Inside the Iranian Revolution*, Indiana University Press, Bloomington, 1981, pp. 4, 44, 311. Asaf Hussain, *Islamic Iran. Revolution and Counter-Revolution*, Frances Pinter, London, 1985, pp. 64, 117-118, 130. Majid Tehranian, "Iran: Communication, Alienation, Revolution," *InterMedia*, March 1979, pp. 6-12. Hamid Mowlana, "Technology Versus Tradition: Communication in the Iranian Revolution," *Journal of Communication*, Summer 1979, pp. 105-110. Annabelle Sreberny-Mohammadi, Dissertation, pp. 63, 96.

12. John D. Stempel, *Inside the Iranian Revolution*, Indiana University Press, Bloomington, 1981, p. 45.

13. Asaf Hussain, *Islamic Iran. Revolution and Counter-Revolution*, Frances Pinter, London, 1985, pp. 61-62. For taped political messages by the other ayatollahs, see Annabelle Sreberny-Mohammadi, "Small Media For a Big Revolution: Iran," *International Journal of Politics*, Culture and Society, Volume 3, Number 3, Spring 1990, p. 358.

14. For a description of the content and function of the various "leaflets, flyers, communiques, manifestos and other brief documents" produced and distributed in support of the revolution, see Annabelle Sreberny-Mohammadi, *The Power of Tradition*, Dissertation, pp. 194-211.

15. John D. Stempel, *Inside the Iranian Revolution*, p. 45.

16. Nikki R. Keddie, *Roots of Revolution. An Interpretive History of Modern Iran*, Yale University Press, New Haven, CT, and London, 1981, p. 251.

17. William H. Forbis, *Fall of the Peacock Throne*, Harper & Row, New York, 1980. p. 5. Asaf Hussain, *Islamic Iran...* p. 130. Sreberny-Mohammadi says that "Khomeini refused to talk on the telephone directly so international lines were used for tape-to-tape recording," and that "two tape machines were kept permanently running, recording his speeches and announcements and duplicating them for transmission or transportation to Iran." (*The Power of Tradition*, Dissertation, pp. 122-123).

18. "With AT&T in Iran," Hubert L. Kertz with Anthony G. Oettinger, Interview in *Seminar on Command, Control, Communications and Intelligence*, Incidental Paper, Program on Information Resources Policy, Harvard University, Cambridge, MA, Spring 1984, p. 4. (Article begins p. 1.) Mr. Kertz was President and Managing Director of AT&T subsidiary American Bell International, Inc. at the time of the Iranian revolution.

19. Ibid., p. 2.

20. Ibid, p. 3.

21. William H. Forbis, *Fall of the Peacock Throne*, Harper & Row, New York, 1980, p. 5.

22. John D. Stempel, *Inside the Iranian Revolution*, pp. 109, 127, 215, Asaf Hussain, *Islamic Iran*, p. 127.

23. William H. Forbis, *Fall of the Peacock Throne*, p. 7. See also: Asaf Hussain, *Islamic Iran*, p. 130.

24. John D. Stempel, *Inside the Iranian Revolution*, p. 174.

25. Dilip Hiro, *Iran Under the Ayatollahs*, Routledge & Kegan Paul, London and Henley, 1985, p. 178.

26. Hassan Dabdoub, "Slow-Motion Civil War," *The Middle East*, September 1981, p. 18. Hassan Dabdoub, "The Revolution Waiting in the Wings," *The Middle East*, December 1981, p. 12. Delip Hiro, *Iran Under the Ayatollahs*, p. 181.

27. VCRs were banned by the Khomeini government but have always been readily available on the black market. See: Gladys D. Ganley and Oswald H. Ganley, *Global Political Fallout. The First Decade of the Videocassette Recorder 1976-1985*, Ablex Publishing Corporation, Norwood, NJ, 1987, p. 40. For other references to personal media in Iran,

see pp. 8-9, 14, 22, 27, 66-67, 73, 80, 105-106, 120, and 130-131 of this reference. For specific references to VCRs in Iran, see pp. 22, 27, 40, 66-67, 80, and 120.

28. Majid Tehranian, "Communications Dependency and Dualism in Iran," *InterMedia*, May 1982, pp. 43-44.

29. Alan Cowell, "Exiled Iranians Press a Political Cause From Iraq," *The New York Times*, February 7, 1988, p. A-3.

30. Radio Tehran, March 21, 1980, FBIS Translation, March 24, 1980. Reprinted as "Documents. Khomeini: 'We Shall Confront the World With Our Ideology,'" in *MERIP Reports*, June 1980, pp. 22-25.

31. Majid Tehranian, "Communications Dependency and Dualism in Iran," *InterMedia*, May 1982, p. 44.

32. James A. Bill, "Resurgent Islam in the Persian Gulf," *Foreign Affairs*, Summer 1985, pp. 118-119. (Article begins p.108.) "Turkey Finds Iran is Behind Turmoil," from *Hurriyet*, reprinted in *Insight*, November 9, 1987, p. 33.

33. Delip Hiro, *Iran Under the Ayatollahs*, p. 291. Hiro also discusses the vulnerability of Gulf states to Iran's export of revolution. See pp. 334-341.

34. Thomas Weyr, "Dear Client" letter, *Research Recommendations*, March 7, 1988, p. 4. This source commented that "The Ayatollah's message is getting through and it is heard," that the "fundamentalist doctrine is making headway fast," and that the situation is "tailor-made for Iran-type extremism." Unrest in the various Muslim republics of the USSR steadily increased in the last years of the 1980s. At that time, videotapes of dissident activities were circulating in that republic. See, for example, Bill Keller, "A Once-Docile Azerbaijani City Bridles Under the Kremlin's Grip," *The New York Times*, February 18, 1990, p. A-18. (Article begins p. A-1.)

35. Martin Sieff, "Islamic March Tiptoes into Turkey," *Insight*, March 3, 1986, p. 32.

36. Michel Deure, "Tunisia Accuses Iran of Plotting Revolution," *United Press International*, March 27, 1987. (NEXIS).

37. Robin Wright, "The Islamic Resurgence: A New Phase?" *Current History*, February 1988, pp. 53ff. Alan Cowell, "Tunisia, Accusing Iran, Cracks Down on Dissent," *The New York Times*, June 22, 1987, p. A-10. "Tunisia and Iran: That's Enough," *The Economist*, April 4, 1987, pp. 29, 32.

38. Although Khomeini's interference was much feared in Islamic countries and his influence often felt, fundamentalist movements have not necessarily been directly attributable to the Ayatollah. (Robin Wright,"The Islamic Resurgence: A New Phase?" *Current History*, February 1988, pp. 53ff.) Turkey has developed home-grown fundamentalist material, including audiocassettes, in addition to that shipped in by Khomeini. (Robert Burns, "Turkey Sees Rise in Islamic Fundamentalism," *The Associated Press*, July 6, 1987, NEXIS.) Home-grown fundamentalist cassettes are also found in Egypt, where fundamentalists assassinated President Anwar Sadat in 1981 and where such preachers have huge followings. In the slums of Cairo, one cleric has about 300 best selling videocassettes of his sermons, and a cleric in Alexandria has become a millionaire from cassette sales of his TV broadcasts. (Joseph L. Galloway, with John Barnes and Giora Shamis, "Egypt is the Prize as the Threat to Mubarik Increases; A Flood of Radicalism in the Land of the Nile," *U.S. News & World Report*, July 6, 1987, p. 35.) See also William E. Farrell, "Keeping Tabs on the Mosques Can't Be Easy," *The New York Times*, September 13, 1981, p. D-5.

chapter 3

THE ADVENT OF THE VIDEOCASSETTE RECORDER AND PORTABLE VIDEO CAMERA*1

Videotape technology, like audiotape before it, gave individuals and small groups the power to choose, collect, copy, create and communicate information. But videocassettes and cameras also provide the additional impact of a picture, and put two other powerful media—world films and TV programming—under more control by ordinary people. Videocassettes, along with audiocassettes, launched the personal media assault against controls over information that most governments have insisted on having for centuries. Videocassettes have also made a good sized dent in the traditional economic domination of entertainment and other information enjoyed by large corporations, producers, distributors, and the mass media. The VCR's gifts to the people are numerous, but among the greatest of these is the power to elude government censors.

The VCR can stand alone, be run by a battery if necessary, and permits any kind of programming to be watched in perfect privacy. Because it need not be attached to a telecommunications network to be useful (it "is brought into the home by individuals, not signals"[2]), it is less vulnerable to government controls than are, for instance, phones, networked PCs, and facsimile. When used as a stand-alone, the VCR is probably, therefore, one of the most resilient political tools among the several new personal media.[3] It is a good guess that this machine played a heady role in the

* This chapter is based in large part on material included in Gladys D. Ganley and Oswald H. Ganley, *Global Political Fallout. The VCRs First Decade, 1976-1985*, Ablex Publishing Corporation, Norwood, NJ, 1987. Originally published as *The Political Implications of the Global Spread of Videocassette Recorders and Videocassette Programming* by the Program on Information Resources Policy, Harvard University, 1986.

radical policy shifts in the major communist countries in the late 1980s (see Chapter 4).

Like the computer, the videocassette recorder began as a huge monster, though only "about the size of a side-by-side washer-dryer," and in 1963 it still cost $30,000.[4] However expensive and big, the early VTRs and nonportable video cameras nevertheless transformed the television industry by allowing immediate use of footage without time consuming processing. Along with the satellite communications systems that made instantaneous transmission possible in the late 1960s and 1970s, this portable video equipment switched the world's TV diet from slightly stale news to global reportage routinely transmitted in real time or near real time.[5] While some cumbersome personal reel-to-reel models and some with one-hour cassettes had been around awhile, videocassette recorders became generally available to private individuals in 1976. In that same year, the portable video camera also first became generally available, even to news reporters. Like the VCR, cameras have steadily grown smaller, progressing from a heavy, bulky shoulder model to an extremely light hand-held one.

THE GLOBAL SPREAD OF THE VCR
AND ITS PROGRAMMING[6]

Almost as soon as VCRs became available, the machines, blank tapes, and programming (that were, and still are, heavily pirated) began pouring across the world's borders in substantial quantities. This process was strongly assisted by omnipresent black markets, huge labor migrations, well organized smuggling groups, corrupt customs officials, borders that were unprepared for jet age transportation and electronic communications, lack of legal and other institutional means to deal with new forms of goods and services, and a combination of unawareness and higher priorities by governments.

VCRs and programming thus became rapidly available, not only in the liberal democracies, but also in the USSR and Eastern Europe in the early 1980s. They began to appear in China just as it began its 1978 surge toward modernization, and by 1986, VCRs there numbered about 2 million.[7] Quickest and most copiously of all, VCRs and tapes spread into the Muslim nations of the Persian Gulf area—Saudi Arabia, Kuwait, Bahrain, the United Arab Emirates, Oman, and Qatar—where oil wealth had created large amounts of disposable income.[8] VCRs have been especially welcomed by the people where governments practice harsh censorship (much of the world) and/or where pictures and sound could help compensate for a high rate of illiteracy. VCRs have also been highly prized in areas where videocassette programming can be used to substitute for the absence of broadcast television and other forms of entertainment.

EVADING CENSORSHIP

Immediately upon becoming available, videocassettes began to be used very effectively all over the world, both to evade government restrictions on amusements and to acquire politically pertinent and other types of information. Pirated copies of both old and recently released movies with both political and nonpolitical themes spread with great speed into the remotest or most restrictive countries. Although the majority of videocassettes being peddled throughout the world are not "custom made" for political uses, programs made for entertainment can often serve this purpose. This is especially true if they depict lifestyles, consumer comforts, and freedoms that are lacking in the life of the viewer.

From the first, Soviets and Eastern Europeans have smuggled in a wide assortment of movies and TV shows that have been banned for ideological reasons (Chapter 4). Cuban viewers watch films like the anticommunist Rambo, while Pakistanis and Bangladeshis smuggle in banned Hindi films from India, and Indians watch equally banned Pakistani soap operas. Egyptians, who prefer their own programming, smuggle videocassettes of censored plays out of the country, reinsert the banned parts, and smuggle them back in again for viewing.[9] The videocassette recorder itself is smuggled into many countries to avoid high taxes, customs duties, and other economic barriers, as well as numerous political restrictions.

ACCESS TO TAPES THROUGH VIDEO CAFES AND PARLORS[10]

Restricted in the beginning to the elites who could afford a machine, VCRs and their programming have quickly found a wider audience. To compensate for leaving their families behind in order to earn remittances—now crucial to many developing country economies—migrant laborers pressure their governments to allow them to bring home VCRs, along with other consumer luxuries. The Persian Gulf region has thus long been a major distribution point for VCRs, which are taken from there to poorer nations by massive numbers of homeward-bound migrants. The same is true for Western European countries, which attract many millions of migrant workers.[11] Returning migrants who have acquired a

VCR and tapes often set up showings in home theaters, making money while offering shows at low prices.

Illegal video parlors in homes or small shops, charging mainly modest prices, have proliferated in many countries. In much of the developing world, where people can't afford a VCR, groups regularly meet in such parlors, in some type of improvised theater, or at the homes of friends to watch videos.[12] Home video parlors where Western or pornographic movies are shown for big money have been prevalent underground activities in Eastern Europe and the Soviet Union for several years (Chapter 4). In the late 1980s, even the Soviets capitulated to video, permitting "video saloons" or cafes with video to operate openly under the auspices of some official group such as a trade union. Many of these saloons are actually privately financed and simply operate "'under the roof' of an official sponsor." The videos permitted to be shown in these Soviet cafes are, amazingly, uncensored black market products.[13]

Video parlors and other places where videos can be watched communally are thus in place for use at the time of intense political troubles. China, for instance, which was on the brink of civil war in 1989 (Chapter 12), not only has impromptu video showings under illegal or quasilegal conditions, but in some instances video parlors have been actively encouraged by the Ministry of Culture. As Chinese peasants earned more money under the "responsibility" program, put in place during the late 1970s and the 1980s as part of the modernization effort, the government has sought to discourage them from migrating to the cities. Local amusements have thus been encouraged, and by 1985, in just five of China's provinces, 130,000 peasants were reported to be running "cultural businesses" instead of farming. This included operating video parlors, along with theaters, libraries, and game rooms.[14] How these parlors were used during the June 1989 political upheaval in China is unknown, and how these activities will fare under reimposed political restrictions in the aftermath of that upheaval is an open question.

THE "LIVING ROOM VIDEO"[15]

Video showings to groups in living rooms and other makeshift theaters has been a spontaneous, fairly apolitical, development globally. But the privacy and intimacy of a living room or other small gathering place lend themselves admirably to dissident political activity. A politically oriented video designed to be watched by a group in a living room setting is now therefore a specific genre. The "living room video" was an important instrument in maintaining information access during the 1986 people's revolution in the Philippines, which led to the ouster of President Ferdinand Marcos and the installation of President Corazon Aquino. After the 1983 assassination of Marcos's political opponent, Benigno Aquino, the Marcos government attempted to shut off outside news from the Philippine people. This action was quickly countered with a vigorous campaign by Filipinos abroad who used both massive mailings of clippings and videocassettes with disguised content carried into the country by travelers to supply U.S. and Japanese news reports. In one case at least, news tapes of the Aquino slaying were substituted for a pornographic movie to get it into the country. Videotaped documentaries composed of taped news materials were prepared and widely disseminated. The tapes were shown in multiple living rooms to many people, and spliced-together news reels were available as video rentals.[16]

The living room video has become the tool of candidates in U.S. election campaigns, serving as a focus for "watch parties" where votes and money are solicited (Chapter 11). Many individuals, including political candidates, lobbyists, and terrorists, using broadcast media resources, are now finding ways to have their "living room videos" delivered electronically (Chapters 9-11). Episodes of a racist talk show, "Race and Reason," produced by Tom Metzger for a California public access cable channel and placed on such public access channels across the U.S., can be watched directly or taped for later group viewings.[17]

Politically explosive television can now be easily taped from cross-border signals or carried on videocassettes from one country to another, often serving as ideal "living room videos." In the early 1980s, for instance, Saudi Arabia banned the U.S.-U.K. television production of "The Death of a Princess" and attempted to restrict its showing on the TV of some 25 countries. But the program, a docudrama that concerned the execution of a Saudi princess for adultery, was taped off the air in Great Britain, and cassettes of it were circulating in Riyad by the next morning.[18] In the late 1970s, Egypt banned a political play, "The Witness Who Witnessed Nothing." But, in their anger over Egypt's Camp David agreement with Israel, other Arab nations broadcast the cassettes on their (neighboring, watchable, and tapeable) television. In the Pacific Basin, a scheduled TV debate (later canceled) between leaders of Malaysia's Islamic political parties over who were believers or nonbelievers caused great anxiety among Malaysia's neighbors. At a time when the Ayatollah Khomeini was pushing for worldwide Islamic revolution, the debate was certain to be taped and smuggled to living rooms elsewhere, possibly causing political dissensions in other countries. Some taped-off-the-air messages have been destined to serve how-to political purposes. Pakistani army officers, implicated in a conspiracy to assassinate the late President Zia at a parade, were found to possess a model—a videocassette of the assassination of Egypt's President Anwar Sadat, taped from Western TV newscasts.[19]

VIDEO PRODUCTIONS AS ALTERNATIVE INFORMATION SOURCES

Lack of access to news and other information has inspired the production of videos as alternative media in a number of countries. Between 1981 and 1988, Solidarity used video documentaries, among other things, to keep itself alive, the *Los Angeles Times* points out.[20] Two Indian magazines, *India Today* and *Surya*, each produce 90 minute long monthly video magazines, one in English called "Newstrack," and another in Hindi called "Insight." These are designed to evade the restrictions imposed on other news media by the Indian government.[21] Palestinians in the Israeli Occupied Territories are recording happenings on videotapes as evidence of brutality by Israeli soldiers in their attempts to put down the Intifada uprising.[22] The use of videocassettes as alternative media is very strong in Latin America. In Brazil, Nicaragua, and El Salvador, more cameras and VCRs are sold together than is usually the case, because they are being used by various groups to produce alternative videos. Such "popular videos" are more prevalent in Brazil than in any other Latin American country, but they are also produced in Mexico, Brazil, Chile, Peru, Panama, Bolivia, Uruguay, El Salvador, and Nicaragua.[23] Pinochet's censorship of television in Chile prompted alternative programming—"documentaries, interviews, protest music and other information"[24] and banned movies—to be put on videocassettes and circulated. In addition, Chilean video production companies Teleanalisis and Vitel Noticias offered their subscribers monthly 40-minute cassettes of the news kept off of Chilean television.[25] Alternative videos can be used as a political put-down. In 1987, it was rumored that an anti-Gorbachev videocassette was circulating in the Soviet underground, featuring Raisa Gorbachev using an American Express Gold Card and spending extravagantly.[26] *Ogonyok*, a political weekly, produces video news magazines as an alternative to government-controlled television.[27] Extensive video "libraries" of their protest demonstrations and other political activities were prepared by Soviet minorities in Azerbijian and in the Baltics in the late 1980s.[28] In Poland, videotapes have been used for a variety of underground publishing since early in that decade (see Chapter 4).

Videos have become popular propaganda tools of guerrilla groups. Since 1980, the Farabundo Marti Front for National Liberation (FLNM) in El Salvador has been using home video cameras and VCRs in part to make propaganda cassettes of its activities. These are shown in village plazas to win peasant support, and are also sent to the United States for distribution to gain wider political sympathy. Similar videos have also been used in Nicaragua.[29] And in Afghanistan, the *mujahedin* rebels "shot hundreds of hours of videotape" and used it "to rally supporters."[30]

Some U.S. videocassettes also serve to provide alternative information. For instance, the International Freedom Foundation sold a 30-minute videocassette of pro-Nicaraguan-rebel slides that Lt. Colonel Oliver North had been refused permission to show at the summer 1987 Congressional hearings. And MPI Home Video brought out a 90 minute videocassette of the boiled-down North testimony, which he had presented during the Iran/Contra hearings.[31]

EVADING CONTROLLED TELEVISION

VCRs have been found useful in evading government messages. In many developing countries, government-furnished televisions set up in village squares are being diverted from developmental and other governmental messages to whatever videocassettes the villagers find more interesting. In numerous countries, people are simply tuning out government-controlled television programs, preferring to view from a wider and more personalized videocassette selection.

GOVERNMENT FAILURE TO CONTROL THE SPREAD OF VCRS AND CASSETTES[32]

From the very beginning, conflicting priorities have created a confused effort regarding the control of VCRs and their programming, even among authoritarian governments. While some concerns are regularly expressed, they have been mild considering the threat to vested interests. Access to uncensored videotapes has seriously undermined the interests of governments, who for centuries have obsessively controlled information. But, while many countries have instituted some sort of control mechanism, these have rarely appeared commensurate with real danger. Much more importantly, when controls have been applied, nowhere in the world have they proved to be effective.

When an information source falls within the traditional framework, or where the government controls the means of production and dissemination—books, newspapers, radio, and television, for example—are still vigorously censored. But video and audiocassettes, and the machines that play them, have, even in rigidly controlled countries, for the most part been subjected to only mild restrictions. There are many reasons for this lack of control. One is that, as something new and unexpected, VCRs and cassettes fall outside many laws and other traditional control mechanisms. Global smuggling has become universal, and these machines and tapes come in with all the other smuggled items. With increased travel and means of transport, the world's borders have largely become sieves, letting in, not only VCRs and other personal electronic media, but also illegal drugs and armaments. Black markets, which depend on illegal activities like smuggling, have become a mainstay of the economies of many countries. Powerful economic considerations of some sort are the usual things that appear to keep governments from cracking down politically. The desire of communist countries to control information, for instance, has for some years weighed strongly against the desire to keep up with the West technologically.

Perhaps most important, the countries of the world have yet to learn to deal effectively with any of the vast changes that have arrived in the wake of the new electronic technologies. Coping with the monumental shifts in industries, armaments, trade, finance, and other vital sectors brought about by the "information age" may also have pushed control of personal media to a low priority. VCRs can also be helpful to economies, for instance, by creating money-making opportunities in poor countries. Audiocassettes and videocassettes also seem to be considered by some countries as safety valves, permitting tightly repressed peoples to let off steam harmlessly.

VCRs and cassettes have thus spread all over the world rapidly, unplanned, and totally spontaneously. They have been met by an eager audience that was starved for entertainment and also often lacked means of expression or suffered severe restrictions of political freedom. Despite the VCR's destruction of former governmental monopolies on information in most countries, no government has been able or willing to stop them. It is not at all certain that, even given the will, VCRs and videocassettes would be stoppable under today's global economic and other conditions. VCRs and cassettes are already being actively used by very diverse groups for a wide variety of political purposes. There is every reason to believe that, in the future, the variety of these uses will be extended further. The breadth of possibilities for individual political uses of video technologies goes far beyond the stand-alone machine to activities involving telecommunications networks and interaction with the mass media. In addition to avalanches of often negative campaign ads placed on television, videos have become a popular means of expression by all manner of political factions. One of the most sensational videos during the prelude to the 1988 U.S. presidential election was an "attack video" released to the mass media by the campaign of Michael Dukakis. In the midst of a media controversy over whether fellow democratic candidate Joe Biden had committed plagiarism, a videotape was given to reporters that juxtaposed a scene of Biden participating in an 1987 political debate next to a scene from a 1986 British campaign commercial. In this way, Biden was graphically shown using statements almost identical to those used by British Labor Party leader, Neil Kinnock, a year earlier. The publicity following on the heels of this video abruptly ended the Delaware senator's bid for the presidency. The video's release was admitted by John Sasso, campaign manager to Michael Dukakis, who left the campaign as a result of his action.[33] The loss of Sasso's talents and the disruption of the campaign's momentum may have cost the Democrats the 1988 presidential election, and this video that backfired may well have altered U.S. history.

The capability for computer enhancement now exists that permits untraceable digital retouching of videotapes to change the time, place, and/or characters involved in a happening. Such equipment, which has been available since 1987, is still too expensive for individuals, but will no doubt be available some day soon, if this technology follows the usual pattern.[34] Acquisition of sometimes politically important videotape footage from private individuals and groups by the news media is a growing practice that could be democratizing but could also affect objective news reporting adversely.[35]

If VCRs and videocassettes had never done anything but alleviate the oppressions of censorship, they would have earned an important place in history. Their powers have not stopped there, but have extended in innumerable directions. Videotaped press releases, home made videotapes of hostages passed to the mass media by terrorist groups, and individual purchases of satellite and cable TV time to show specially prepared videos, are a few of the new means of individual political expression made possible by this medium. These subjects will be discussed in later chapters.

NOTES

1. Because this chapter summarizes the findings of a book, references are so numerous that the reader is referred to the relevant section of Gladys D. Ganley and Oswald H. Ganley, *Global Political Fallout. The VCR's First Decade, 1976-1985*, Ablex Publishing Corporation, Norwood, NJ, 1987, for original sources. Only references not included in that book will be cited.
2. Douglas A. Boyd, Joseph D. Straubhaar, and John A. Lent, *Videocassette Recorders in the Third World*, Longman, New York, 1989, p. 36.
3. Videos, when transmitted electronically, are very vulnerable to interception, as ABC discovered during the Chinese student uprising in June 1989, when its footage, never aired, appeared on Chinese television. For this and other interceptions of mass media videotaped footage, see: Jay Peterzell, "Betraying the Source. How the U.S. Press Helps Finger Protestors Abroad," *Columbia Journalism Review*, March/April 1990, pp. 6, 8.

4.   "Centennial Journal: 100 Years in Business. Let's Go to the Videotape, 1956," *The Wall Street Journal*, August 8, 1989, p. B-1.

5.   Many sources, including: Oswald H. Ganley and Gladys D. Ganley, *To Inform Or To Control? The New Communications Networks*, Second Edition, Ablex Publishing Corporation, Norwood, NJ, 1989, pp. 58-61. The first program on videotape, "Douglas Edwards and the News," was broadcast by CBS on November 30, 1956. (Douglas A. Boyd et al., *Videocassette Recorders in the Third World*, p. 32.)

6.   The global spread of VCRs and videocassettes is extensively discussed in the first six chapters of *Global Political Fallout*.

7.   Mark Silverman, "Mainland China Tries Regulating Vid Distribution," *Variety*, March 5, 1986, p. 104. (Article begins p. 1.)

8.   Douglas A. Boyd, "Home Video Diffusion and Utilization in Arabian Gulf States," *American Behavioral Scientist*, Volume 30, No. 5, May-June 1987, pp. 544-555. See also: Douglas A. Boyd et al., *Videocassette Recorders in the Third World*, Longman, New York, 1989, pp. 45-93.

9.   Richard Zoglin and Edward W. Desmond, "Subversion by Cassette. The VCR Boom Spells Trouble for Authoritarian Regimes," *Time*, September 11, 1989, p. 80.

10.   See Chapter 7 of *Global Political Fallout* for "What People are Watching and Where They are Watching It" (pp. 64-79). See also Chapter 5 (pp. 44-55) for the role of migrants.

11.   Douglas Boyd, "Home Video Diffusion and Utilization in Arabian Gulf States," *American Behavioral Scientist*, Volume 30, No. 5, May-June 1987, pp. 544-555.

12.   Richard Zoglin and Edward W. Desmond, "Subversion by Cassette," *Time*, September 11, 1989, p. 80; Susan Chira, "Video Madness in Taiwan: Little Rooms and Big Screens," *The New York Times*, July 22, 1988, p. A-2. Douglas A. Boyd et al.'s *Videocassette Recorders in the Third World* also makes many references to video parlors and video showings in cafes in various countries of the Third World. See pp. 19, 50, 104, 108, and 111 for comments on video parlors and cafes in Oman, the Maldives, India, Nepal, and Nigeria.

13.   "A Cup of Tea with 'The Terminator.' In the Video Cafe," *The Economist*, October 14, 1989, p. 106.

14.   "Dateline: Beijing," *The Xinhua General Overseas News Service*, December 14, 1985 (NEXIS).

15.   For the various political uses of videocassettes, see Chapter 9, *Global Political Fallout* (pp. 94-119).

16.   Robert Trumbull, "Videotapes of Slaying Smuggled Into Manila," *The New York Times*, September 13, 1983, p. A-9, and Douglas A. Boyd et al., *Videocassette Recorders in the Third World*, p. 12. In exile in Hiwaii, Marcos also availed himself of video to show he was still fit to rule, sending his Manila backers a cassette of himself lifting weights, jogging, shadow boxing, and denouncing President Corazon Aquino. ("Marcos Enters Hospital For Medical Examination," *Reuters*, February 4, 1987 (NEXIS) and "Marcos-Exercise," *United Press International*, January 29, 1989 (NEXIS). Marcos died in exile of various illnesses in 1989.)

17.   Among others, see: Judith Michaelson, "Hate on the Air: A Question of Access," *The Los Angeles Times*, August 10, 1988, Pt. VI, p. 9; David A. Kaplan, "Is the Klan Entitled to Public Access," *The New York Times*, July 31, 1988, p. H-25; Michelle P. Fulcher, "Video Soapbox Airs Material Most TV Outlets Won't Touch," *The Denver Post*, October 18, 1987, p. B-5; "Public Access Doesn't Mean the Same to All," *Chicago Tribune*, June 19, 1988, Sec. 18, p. 3; Steve Daley, "Race-Baiting Show Tests Public Access," *Chicago Tribune*, March 17, 1988, Sec. 5, p. 7; William Robbins, "Klan Group Pushes Access to TV in Missouri," *The New York Times*, May 29, 1988, p. L-23; "Neo-Nazi Use of Public Access

TV Worries Cincinnati," *Variety*, October 28, 1987, p. 9-B, and Janet Bush, "KKK Cable Controversy Hits Kansas City," *Financial Times*, August 18, 1988, Sec. I, p. 4.

18. For details on the "Death of a Princess" incident, including the spread of cassettes, see: Thomas White and Gladys Ganley, *The Death of a Princess Controversy*, Program on Information Resources Policy, Harvard University, Cambridge, MA, September 1983.

19. This plot was foiled, and Zia later died in a plane crash.

20. Thomas B. Rosenstiel, "TV, VCRs Fan Fire of Revolution," *Los Angeles Times*, January 18, 1990, p. A-14. (Article begins p. A-1.)

21. Barbara Crossette, "India Video News to Crack Government Hold," *The New York Times*, November 3, 1988, p. A-5. Richard Zoglin and Edward W. Desmond, "Subversion by Cassette," *Time*, September 11, 1989, p. 80. Newstrack did run into problems in July 1989, when some investigative reporting roused the ire of the Chief Minister of Kashmir. Following this incident, India's Film Censor Board began delaying *Newstrack's* publication, insisting on certain deletions, and (according to *Newstrack*) exceeding its authority by questioning copyright matters. (Barbara Crossette, "Indian News Program Struggles With Censors," *The New York Times*, October 22, 1990, p. A-11.)

22. Richard Zoglin and Edward W. Desmond, "Subversion by Cassette," *Time*, September 11, 1989, p. 80.

23. Douglas A. Boyd et al., *Videocassette Recorders in the Third World*, pp. 209-224. For Brazil, see pp. 20-22, 174, 185, 196-198, 200-201.

24. Ibid., p. 179.

25. Hernan Millas, "Video-cassettes Register Chile's Censored History. One of the World's Best Networks is Underground," *Mainichi Daily News*, Tokyo, March 6, 1987, p. 3.

26. "Clandestine Tape Scorns Gorbachev's Wife," *The Associated Press*, April 2, 1987, (NEXIS). Philip Taubman, "Raisa Gorbachev is the Target of a Clandestine Soviet Video," *The New York Times*, April 2, 1988, p. A-1. "In the Limelight—Again," *Newsweek*, April 27, 1987, p. 6. Nancy Cooper, "Kremlinologists Play a Video Game," *Newsweek*, April 13, 1987, p. 35.

27. Richard Zoglin with Edward W. Desmond, "Subversion by Cassette," *Time*, September 11, 1989, p. 80.

28. Paul Quinn-Judge, "Ferment Brews in Soviet Baltics," *The Christian Science Monitor*, September 21, 1988, pp. 1, 8; Bill Keller, "A Once-Docile Azerbaijani City Bridles Under the Kremlin's Grip," *The New York Times*, February 18, 1990, p. A-18. (Article begins p. A-1.)

29. Nadine Epstein, "Video Guerrillas. Salvadorean Rebels Videotape Their Cause, Then Smuggle Cassettes to US," *The Christian Science Monitor*, August 6, 1987, p. 3. Douglas A. Boyd et al., *Videocassette Recorders in the Third World*, pp. 21, 185, 198, 200, 219-220. James Brooke, "Salvadorans Use Video in the Propaganda War," *The New York Times*, August 27, 1984, p. C-17.

30. Richard Zoglin and Edward W. Desmond, "Subversion by Cassette," *Time*, September 11, 1989, p. 80.

31. Eric Selinger, "Ollieana. Sneak Review?" *The Boston Phoenix*, July 24-30, 1987, p. 2; and "That North Video," *The New York Times*, August 26, 1987, p. A-14.

32. *Global Political Fallout*, pp. 120-129.

33. Dozens of publications and TV programs reported on this happening. See, for example: Eleanor Randolph, "Plagiarism Suggestion Angers Biden's Aides. British Politician Given Credit, Senator Says," *The Washington Post*, September 13, 1987, p. A-6; E. J. Dionne, Jr., "Biden Withdraws Bid for President in Wake of Furor," *The New York Times*, September 24, 1987, p. 1.

34. Daniel Sheridan, "The Trouble With Harry. High Technology Can Now Alter a *Moving*

Video Image," *Columbia Journalism Review*, January/February 1990, pp. 4, 6. J. D. Lasica, "Photographs That Lie. The Ethical Dilemma of Digital Retouching," *Washington Journalism Review*, June 1989, pp. 22-25. Fred Ritchin, *In Our Own Image: The Coming Revolution in Photography*. Aperture, New York, 1990, p. 30. Andy Grundberg, "Ask It No Questions: The Camera Can Lie," *The New York Times*, August 12, 1990, p. H-1.

35. See, for example: Douglas C. McGill, "Camcorders Spread Video's Power," *The New York Times*, June 26, 1989, pp. D-1, D-7, and H.D.S. Greenway, "TV's Fake-Film Threat," *The Boston Globe*, October 13, 1989, p. 17.

chapter 4

PERSONAL MEDIA IN THE SOVIET UNION AND EASTERN EUROPE IN THE EARLY 1980s*1

During the last years of the 1980s, and especially in 1989, almost unbelievable shifts in political behavior took place in the Soviet Union and the communist countries of Eastern Europe. Unanticipated changes which have overtaken this book include the breakaway of several Soviet republics with independence for some, and an attempted Soviet coup in 1991. Many of the changes taking place have to do with a desperate economic need for modern resources involving communications and information.

These political changes began in Poland in 1980, when Solidarity came to the fore, and after being outlawed for some years, reemerged to assume Polish leadership in August 1989. In 1985, Mikhail Gorbachev came to power in the USSR and introduced *Glasnost* (openness) and *Perestroika* (restructuring), which have made the climate somewhat more forthcoming in that country. But most incredibly of all, in the four months between August 1989 and that year's end, Hungary disbanded its Communist party, the East Germans dismantled the Berlin Wall, Bulgaria deposed its longtime leader, Czechoslovakia eliminated the head of its Communist party, and the Romanians overthrew and executed their dictator, Nicolae Ceausescu. And in the Fall of 1990, the two Germanys reunited. This most important series of events since World War II, certainly, and in some ways of the 20th century, must have been at least in part brought about by new means of mass and personal communications. For they have provided

---

* Much of the material in this chapter has been taken from Gladys D. Ganley and Oswald H. Ganley, *Global Political Fallout. The VCRs First Decade, 1976-1975*, Ablex Publishing Corporation, Norwood, NJ, 1987, a work originally published in 1986 by the Program on Information Resources Policy, Harvard University.

means of access to information which are not controllable by central governments. These events were also pushed by a burning desire of the people for consumer products, which this new access to information had taught them ought to be attainable.

The extent of the role played by new personal or mass media in these unprecedented events is still unknown, and will no doubt be the target of years of investigation. But the development of unstoppable underground audiocassette and videocassette cultures in all these countries has been continuously reported throughout the 1980s, as previously documented by this author.[2] Pickup of cross-border television, aided by individual satellite dishes, and reception of foreign shortwave radio broadcasts, have also been both ubiquitous and uncontrollable.

The early and persistent development of such cassette cultures here took place with little if any lag time behind similar events in other nations, despite the fact that these countries have been famed far and wide for information suppression. The availability and use of pirated cassettes, the establishment of (underground) rental outlets, and the advent of video parlors, though on a more modest scale, all paralleled what was happening elsewhere. The pace and extent with which this happened in such strictly controlled societies may seem implausible. But, in fact, the heavy economic dependence on black markets and political conditions forcing information underground proved a perfect setting for the spread of these new media, just as they have in many Third World countries. These conditions also encouraged personal electronic media use in concert with equally forbidden access to foreign mass media.

There is a certain logical progression indicating that the role played by audiocassettes and videocassettes as electronic hacksaws to freedom has been considerable. With recorders and cassettes, it became possible to supplement *samizdat* (self-publishing in print) so long and so laboriously produced by typewriter, with *magnitizdat* (electronic self-publishing). Of more importance was the increasing ability of individuals to find various ways of accessing outside information independently. More important still was the new ability of individuals to successfully perform covert acts of civil disobedience by acquiring, watching, listening to, sharing, creating, and distributing information illegally. In addition to the actual knowledge acquired and spread, these new capabilities could be expected to give new confidence to formerly information-deprived people. Meanwhile, a growing awareness of the powerlessness of central governments to stop such information flows must have tended to lessen fear of authorities. It is therefore not surprising that such acts would eventually progress to what became the overt rebellions of the late 1980s.

That the stage was set for the use of these media in revolution is shown by events at the end of the decade. In July 1989, a speech by Communist Party First Secretary Jakes, meant only for the ears of Czech party officials, was secretly taped and provided to Western radio stations, who broadcast it back to the Czech public.[3] A videotaped interview with the Reverend Laszlo Tokes of Timisoara, Romania, filmed by Canadians and played on Hungarian television in mid-1989, was seen across the Romanian border and is considered by some to have sparked that country's December 1989 revolution.[4] When disturbances that led to independence efforts began erupting in various Soviet republics—the Baltics and Azerbijian—those promoting such political objectives backed their efforts with extensive taped-on-the-spot video libraries.[5] A videocassette, "The History of Islam," being circulated among the Muslims of Soviet Central Asia, could have encouraged Glasnost's first significant ethnic unrest, in December 1986 at Alma-Ata.[6] And there is little doubt that barrages of underground information, produced and distributed both electronically and conventionally for years by the outlawed Solidarity, aided its 1989 reemergence in triumph.

AUDIOCASSETTES IN THE USSR

Despite the fact that the government of the Soviet Union had long controlled all means of information production, audiocassette recorders and tapes apparently escaped that restriction. This is odd, since from the beginning the USSR has kept photocopying machines locked up and shut down, and later limited its international direct-dialing phone service after dissidents began using it.[7] But for whatever reasons, some recorders and tapes have been available to individuals in the USSR almost from their advent. The USSR itself began producing about half a million audio recorders a year in 1965, increased this to a million in 1970, to 2 million in 1975, and to 3 million a year by the 1980s.[8]

While these recorders were mainly employed for entertainment and neutral types of communications, they were also used to record foreign broadcasts and to gather, store, and disseminate protest songs, poems, and underground oral literature. By the early 1980s, audio recorders were being regularly taken on picnics where they were used to play banned songs and tape foreign shortwave broadcasts beyond the range of jammers. Radio Liberty's 700 hours of broadcasts of the full *The Gulag Archipelago*, for example, were taped for underground collections, as were foreign news accounts of the September 1983 downing of Korean Airline Flight 007 by the Soviets.[9] From the early 1980s, cassettes with forbidden religious content were being spread in large numbers across the USSR from Estonia.[10] When the Reverend Billy Graham visited the USSR in 1984, his sermons were surreptitiously taped and distributed.[11] In July 1990, hordes of Soviet citizens commemorated the 10th anniversary of the death of Vladimir Vysotsky, a poet, singer, and actor who had become "the troubadour of the Soviet soul," and whose works and appearances had been severely limited by the Soviet government. Thousands and thousands visited his grave, reciting his works, and playing audiocassettes of his voice on portable recorders. These outpourings, says *The New York Times*:[12]

> were a tribute to how the singer's repertoire was essentially bootlegged around the nation via amateur recordings.

Soviet-produced shortwave radios, which by 1975 numbered 60 million, were deliberately designed not to operate on high frequency bands, so they could not pick up foreign broadcasts. But at least by the early 1980s, the parts needed to convert them were available at electrical hobby shops, and the necessary rewiring was not hard to manage. Smuggled Western or Japanese radio-tape recorders could be had for the equivalent of $1,500, in the Ukraine, for instance, being brought in by Soviet sailors.[13]

VCRS, VIDEOCASSETTES, AND SATELLITE DISHES IN THE SOVIET UNION

The number of VCRs in the USSR in the days prior to Gorbachev were reported at the time to be quite small, although this may well have been an underestimate. Highest numbers suggested at the beginning of the Gorbachev era were only 50,000 or 60,000.[14] These reported numbers have grown steadily, and at the end of the 1980s, the estimated Soviet VCR population stood at about 2.2 million.[15]

Although a few thousand reel-to-reel model VCRs were produced and sold in the Soviet Union in the late 1970s, their price was high, they were technically unreliable, and virtually no blank tapes or programmed videotapes were ever available.[16] During the late 1970s and early 1980s, a few privileged Soviet travelers had permission to buy and bring back a VCR. Soviet diplomats posted to the U.S. or the U.N. also brought in some, and Soviet officials received some gift VCRs from foreign businessmen. However, most VCRs came into the country via bribes and Customs payoffs and the various routes employed for smuggling.[17] While the largest numbers—tens of thousands—of VCRs are in Moscow, VCRs have especially collected in border cities and ports like Odessa, Vladivostok, and Leningrad. Higher living standards and availability of cross-border TV broadcasts encourages VCR acquisition, and these conditions are present in Armenia, Georgia, Azerbaijan, Soviet Central Asia, and Estonia.[18] In Latvia, VCRs have concentrated in Riga, Ventspils, and Liepaja,[19] and in Lithuania, in the city of Vilnius.[20] These machines have thus been available for political expression to the most explosive of the USSR's diverse ethnic populations as they have begun pushing their widely varying political agendas and demands for independence.

From the first, VCRs in the USSR, on the black market or in second-hand stores, have been very expensive, often costing the equivalent of $5,000.[21] But because the government subsidizes basic needs like housing, and a lot of money has been available from black market sources, and also since there are few consumer goods to buy, many Soviets have had a great deal of discretionary income. This same situation exists, and has existed for at least a decade, not only in the USSR, but throughout Eastern Europe.[22]

Just as was the case in virtually every other country in the world, individuals in the Soviet Union rapidly gained access to a wide variety of pirated, smuggled, black market videocassettes. The content of these tapes ranged from pornography, to both newly released and older Western movies, to taped-off-the-air Western television entertainment, news programs, and political discussions. Soviets have also long been regular borrowers of videocassettes from resident foreigners such as diplomats, businessmen, and news correspondents. Early on, underground video libraries developed in the USSR, providing uncensored films on a rental basis. At least until the mid 1980s, black market videocassettes were very expensive, blank ones selling for the equivalent of $60 to $70, and Western movies from $250 to $320.[23] Legally available blank tape, always in short supply, has also been very costly, partly because it must be purchased with hard currency from foreign sources.[24]

Because of its clandestine nature, most videocassette viewing in the USSR has always taken place secretly, and due to scarcity and because the VCR is a status symbol, viewings are often communal. Shared home viewings were supplemented early on by underground "video parlors," where the owner of the VCR and videocassettes exacted entry charges. In private Soviet apartments, Western movies and pornography were and are often shown by invitation to people who pay a fee of 5 or 6 rubles. From the early 1980s, videos have been shown for steep fees in night clubs in Soviet resort towns, and, after closing hours, in Soviet cafes around the country.[25]

Wherever outside television signals can be picked up in the Soviet Union, programs have been taped off the air directly, and this has been the basis of some underground videocassette industries. All manner of

Western programming has been regularly taped from Finnish television by Estonians and sold around the USSR.[26] In Kaliningrad Oblast in the Russian Soviet Federated Socialist Republic, Western films shown on the liberalized Polish TV have also been picked up and distributed surreptitiously.[27] Interception of satellite signals using illegal dishes has provided further individual access to foreign programming. By 1990, some 15,000 private dishes, which were usually made at home, using purloined state electronic materials or such materials smuggled from the West, were estimated to be in place on Soviet rooftops.[28] The dish itself may be fashioned from bowl-shaped children's sled seats and various kinds of scrap materials. Parts of the Soviet Union are spillover areas for Western European TV, for USIA's Worldnet, for Turner's TBS, and perhaps for Japanese programming. Tapings from individual dishes not only provide their owners with information but are also the source of videocassettes for distribution, and hence, of additional black market income.[29]

Rumors exist in the Soviet Union that astrophysicists are selling Western programming which they "pick up and record" with the assistance of "the powerful antennas at their observatories."[30] Other rumors make similar allegations concerning "military personnel from powerful radar installations," or the "employees of Gosteleradio" or "the staff of 'Orbita' receiving stations."[31] While these stories have been classed by Radio Liberty Research as "folklore," that source does say that "people with official access to Western television broadcasting must occasionally find themselves tempted," and observes that "a home-made converter could easily be attached to a 'state' parabolic antenna" to deal with differences in broadcast standards.[32]

Standards and Language Barriers

Varying broadcast standards do present a major problem for Soviet individuals, both in viewing smuggled foreign videocassettes and in receiving foreign broadcasts and making off-the-air tapings. The Soviet Union employs a version of the SECAM television standard used in France, as do the Eastern European countries with the exception of Romania. Western European countries other than France, along with Romania and Yugoslavia, use the PAL standard, where conversion to the Soviet standard is more difficult than from SECAM. Until it has been converted to one of the European standards, the NTSC system used in the U.S., Canada, and Japan is very hard for Soviets to handle. Some U.S. programming, such as TBS and the USIA's Worldnet, ease the problem by being broadcast in PAL or SECAM.[33]

Foreign programming also presents language barriers, and various methods are used by individual Soviets to get around them. Sometimes a translator simply talks as the videocassette runs, and sometimes the translation is taped on an audiocassette and played along with the videocassette. In 1985, it cost about 30 rubles ($37) to have a film "dubbed" into Russian this way.[34] More films began to have Russian language soundtracks dubbed by professionals (sometimes seeking access to free movies) after the middle of the decade.[35] Less dubbing is probably found in regional languages. For instance, popular song clips are reported to be the only available Latvian language videos.[36]

While the majority of videocassettes in the Soviet Union have from the first been watched simply for diversion, even these have been feared by Soviet authorities, since they no doubt fed a desire for consumer products and Western lifestyles. Films such as "Dr. Zhivago," or the works of Alexander Solzhenitsyn, have been considered anti-Soviet. Others, like "Rambo," have overt political themes. News, documentaries, and discussion programs taped from Western TV have been considered especially worrisome. Along with adults, by the early 1980s, the "Golden Youth," or children of privileged Soviets, were actively watching underground videos,[37] as were doubtlessly many less privileged children. These young people, who are in any case the best educated and most technologically sophisticated that country has ever known, have now come of age in Gorbachev's Soviet Union.

Reactions of the Soviet government to VCRs and videocassettes have gone through several stages. In an attempt to curb the growing supplies of VCRs in the Soviet Union in the early 1980s, the KGB vigorously prosecuted Soviet officials who accepted VCRs as gifts. In 1983, then Soviet leader Yuri Andropov launched an anticorruption campaign that continued for a couple of years and included the development of a network of informants with VCRs and videocassettes as their target.[38] In 1984, an attempt was made to co-opt this video viewing by producing some home-grown videocassette recorders. Since they were not designed to operate on Western standards and lacked the capability to tape programs, these recorders could theoretically be used to control content choices. A limited number of such VCRs began to be made at the Elektronika factory at Voronezh and priced advantageously over Western/Japanese VCRs. But despite the fact that the Soviet underground quickly learned to convert these machines to handle Western movies, they did not attract Soviet buyers or catch on as Soviet bloc exports.[39] The reasons cited for this apathy were that the machines were technically unreliable, there were few repair outlets, not enough machines were being produced, and the waiting lists were too long, quotas always being behind schedule.[40] Also, unlike foreign-made VCRs, these home-grown products were not sufficiently attractive as status symbols. Despite continuing attempts at local production, 90% of all VCRs in the USSR are said to still be of Western/Japanese origin.[41]

Along with attempting to make their own VCRs, the Soviets also set up legal videocassette rental stores, the initial one opening in Voronezh in May 1985. Called a "Videoteka," this store and others that followed stocked Soviet and Eastern Bloc-made movies, with an occasional one from India.[42] This effort has been equally unsuccessful. By 1988, the official rental stores had about 600 titles available, while, just in Leningrad, there were 10,000 circulating black market titles.[43]

PERSONAL MEDIA IN POLAND

Poland's dissidents have been the most vigorous and successful users of personal electronic media for strictly political purposes in all Eastern Europe. The Solidarity movement, after being outlawed in 1981, came back in 1989 to take Polish leadership, winning 160 of the 161 seats permitted to be contested in the lower house, and 99 of the 100 seats in the Senate.[44] While making a direct correlation between access to information resources and Solidarity's political victory would probably be difficult to do, there seems little doubt that a strong role was played here by personal electronic media.

As in the USSR, audiocassettes and recorders were available in Poland from the early days, but were used for much more direct political purposes. When the Pope visited Poland in 1979, his sermons, broadcast by Radio Free Europe, were recorded and widely distributed, because the Polish people felt cheated by skimpy official Polish broadcasts. Audiocassettes were also used to support the early Solidarity movement. As the government tried to end the August 1980 strike at the Gdansk shipyard—which had launched Solidarity into prominence—delegates from the various factories to the Interfactory Strike Committee meetings taped the discussions, using multitudes of individual recorders. Each day, taped highlights were brought back and played over the factory public address system. With some slight tinkering, an American-made FM radio can be used to pick up the Polish police band. During these 1980 Solidarity demonstrations, cab drivers taped conversations taking place in police vans and passed the tapes to the shipyard strikers who, again, played them over the factory communications systems. Such tapes served to show the impotence of authorities to exert control and to boost the morale of the striking workers. At the height of these early 1980s activities, Solidarity used so many blank cassettes that they created a shortage. The Polish government, attempting to stem these political uses, temporarily withheld new cassette supplies from the public.[45]

Audiocassettes also played an active role in the major underground effort to keep alternative information flowing after Solidarity was declared illegal and martial law instituted in December 1981. That effort included lectures in churches by leading figures, clandestine performances of political cabarets in apartments, university classes at constantly shifting locations, and massive production and distribution of both printed and electronic underground literature. Political lectures and songs were duplicated on audiocassettes and widely distributed.[46] When the Polish government succeeded in establishing rather effective control over clandestine broadcasting, the Solidarity underground responded by increasing its audiocassette uses. In 1984, audiocassettes in underground circulation included, among other things:[47]

> anti-government songs recorded in underground cabarets, internment camps, and prisons; recordings of historical events from the time when Solidarity existed legally; and interviews with leaders of the Underground.

In that year, "Bratkowski's Gazette"—taped comments on current events by Stefan Bratkowski, President of the banned Polish Journalists' Association, and his readings of various other politically oriented materials— was a big underground hit.[48]

Solidarity used videocassettes as well as audiocassettes, both during its original heydey and especially in the course of pursuing post crackdown activities. The VCR has been credited with playing a major role in actually sustaining the underground Solidarity movement. Says the *Los Angeles Times*:[49]

> Solidarity kept itself alive from 1981 to 1988, among other means, by making video documentaries...and screening them in secret in church basements and community centers.

During the period of Solidarity suppression, interviews with leaders like the former head of Solidarity's Warsaw Branch, Zbigniew Bujak, who had gone underground, were videotaped.[50] By mid-decade, quite extensive use was being made of videocassettes for underground publishing, especially by the publishing house called NOWa.[51] Videos of funerals of fallen heros like Father Popieluszko and Grzegorz Przemyk, television coverage of Danuta Walesa accepting her husband's Nobel Peace Prize, British films on Solidarity, and a documentary of a polish Bishop visiting an exhibition called "The Apocalypse—A Light in Darkness" at Holy Cross Church in Warsaw, as well as a number of western films, were made available.[52] At least 20 documentary videos were also made by an emigre group in Paris "expressly for the Polish opposition market."[53] Besides underground publishing and circulating black market videocassettes, individual Poles were also able to exploit loopholes in the 1951 law used until 1987 for videocassette control, to legally set up shops vending unlicensed, uncensored videocassettes.[54] To demonstrate the heavy political uses made of videocassettes in Poland, "escapism" as a motive for watching is attributed to only 70% of circulating videocassettes.[55]

Especially during the period of Solidarity suppression, many underground audio and videocassettes were smuggled to the West, and via the Western press and global broadcasts, kept pro-Solidarity public opinion alive both abroad and in Poland. The attention of political leaders around the world was thus kept focused on the Polish situation, and support for Solidarity by Western governments and organizations fostered.

As in the rest of Eastern Europe, foreign-made VCRs quickly poured into Poland, but a few were also available legally or quasilegally. Although not buyable with zlotys, VCRs could be had at Polish hard currency stores for amounts competitive with Western prices. The more affluent Poles have had access to a great deal of expendible zlotys for many years and, on the black market, zlotys are fairly easy to turn into dollars. A government scrip called bons can also be bought with zlotys at black market rates, and the bons used to buy goods in hard currency stores.[56]

The Polish government has long made other concessions to encourage hard currency inflows. Individuals can legally possess dollars, since money from relatives living in the U.S. serves as a vital hard currency source. Poles who return to Poland with U.S. pensions have been allowed to bring in VCRs and other consumer items. A significant amount of Polish migrant labor has also been sent to work in other countries and, in compensation for hardships, have been allowed to bring in VCRs and other luxuries. One way or the other, by the mid-1980s, Poland was said to have more VCRs than any other Eastern European country—from 70,000 to 150,000. This figure had grown to 700,000 by 1987, and by the end of the decade, had reached 1.1 million.[57]

Poland, where about two dozen channels from six Western satellites can be picked up with an individual antenna,[58] has a satellite dish count of 18,000, more than many of the other Eastern European countries.[59] By 1987, homemade dishes had proliferated to such an extent that the Polish government bowed to the inevitable and made Poland the first communist country allowing individuals to legally buy and install dishes and permitting cooperatives to make them.[60]

PERSONAL MEDIA IN BULGARIA

By 1984, smuggled VCRs and videocassettes were flooding into Bulgaria at a rate that posed a real challenge to government censorship. At that time it was reported that "the number of private video sets is growing alarmingly."[61] Good sources of smuggled VCRs in Bulgaria have been international truckers who regularly traversed the country, and migrant workers, especially those from Turkey, who drive back and forth to jobs in Western Europe. For years, Bulgarian families have been turning their living rooms into video parlors, and arrests for profiting from such showings have been prevalent. "Semiofficial video cinemas" are also popular in Bulgaria, where a VCR and tapes are leased to "a coffee shop, bar, or restaurant" in return for "tax-free remuneration" to the VCR/cassette owner.[62]

Bulgaria was among the earliest of the Eastern European nations to take official action against smuggled VCRs and videocassettes, and its struggle and failure to gain control has been quite typical of all Eastern Europe. By 1981, in an attempt to co-opt the situation, Bulgaria began to officially sponsor video clubs, which, by 1987, had grown to several hundred.[63] In 1982, it set up a state enterprise called Videofilm and charged it with meeting "educational, propagandistic, ideological, advertising, official, and private demands" for videocassettes. This organization was meant to get control over largely underground marketing but was apparently ineffective, and thus in 1984, the Bulgarian Video Association was established, chaired by a highly experienced party official with a master's degree in ideological propaganda.[64] This creation of a "cultural Tzar" did not work very well either, and in 1985 Bulgaria produced legislation—the first in Eastern Europe—aimed at regulating the "import, export, registration, and distribution of video equipment and video products by private persons and legal entities."[65] The law required all imported VCRs to be registered, and allowed videocassettes to be held several days by Customs officials to be sure their contents did not "contradict the socialist social order" or were not "offensive to socialist morals."[66] Penalties listed were fairly light, but prosecution under other laws for various violations was stipulated. This included hiding VCRs and cassettes from Customs, which could bring a 6-year prison term plus fines; selling or giving a VCR or cassette as a present, which, as an act of "illegal trade," could warrant a three-year term; or "'showing pornographic films or films that foment agitation against the state," for which "an even graver penalty" could be exacted.[67] In short, at least in theory, all bases were covered. But by 1987, the regime admitted it was still "disconcerted" at not being able to gain control over what was being watched on videocassette recorders.[68] In that year, there were an estimated 50,000 VCRs in Bulgaria,[69] while by 1990, one source estimated that there were 550,000 VCRs in that country.[70]

CZECHOSLOVAKIA, HUNGARY, AND THE GERMAN DEMOCRATIC REPUBLIC

Similar developments of videocassette cultures have been reported regarding Czechoslovakia, Hungary, and the German Democratic Republic. Video parlors and "road shows"—where individual videocassettes are substituted for approved programming at state-run clubs—are common in Hungary.[71] By the mid-1980s, official video clubs and "videotheques" featuring music videos for young people to dance to had been established in Czechoslovakia in an attempt to divert youth from watching smuggled programming.[72] In 1984, both Czechoslovakia and Hungary began cooperating with companies from other countries to produce some VCRs. Hungary lowered its customs duties on VCRs fairly early and has continued to ease VCR import restrictions.[73] But by the mid- to late 1980s, 80% of circulating videocassettes in Hungary were still being smuggled and pirated. Although Hungary had been among the first to open official video rental shops, by that date it still has only limited official titles available. This is not just due to ideology but also because Western movie companies are reluctant to sign contracts for rights and, when they do, want to be paid in hard currency.[74]

As in Poland, where emigre groups sent video documentaries into the country, Czech exiles were sending politically oriented videocassettes into Czechoslovakia by the mid-1980s. Partly these cassettes contained banned films, but one emigre also produced a series of video magazines on videocassettes. These were issued bimonthly, were about 2 hours long, and contained "officially-banned cultural and political information."[75] *The Washington Post* reported in 1988 that these videocassette magazines "have been circulating around the country" and were being "copied and recopied by students and intellectuals."[76]

It is likely that the flow of politically oriented videocassettes smuggled in by emigres located in Western countries and smuggled out to the West by dissidents in Eastern Europe and the Soviet Union played an important role in the late-1980s political changes.

By the end of the 1980s, Czechoslovakia, which can pick up TV programs from West Germany and Austria, had the highest number of satellite dishes in Eastern Europe—30,000—and about 800,000 VCRs. By then, Hungary had accumulated an estimated 860,000 VCRs and 15,000 dishes.[77]

The East Germans were unique among the Eastern Europeans in being able to receive radio broadcasts in their own language. Coming from West Germany, they could be heard throughout the country. Much of East Germany—from 80 to 85%—has always been able to pick up at least some West German TV channels. In addition, satellite antennas proliferated early on. " 'The enemy of the people stands on the roof,'" East German leader Walter Ulbricht is quoted as saying. This writer says that:[78]

> At the height of the Cold War....Fighting brigades of the Communist Free German Youth (FDJ) climbed the roofs and cut down the antennas....

This proved to be a futile effort, he says, because "there were just too many" of the antennas.

The new options of videocassettes and cross-border television pickup have for several years allowed the Eastern Europeans to bring pressure against their governments for more diverse entertainment. By 1984, the East German government gave up trying to keep its residents from picking up West German television. In a bid to stem internal migration from areas near Dresden and Greifswald, which could not receive TV from the West,the government actually began sending programming from West German channels to these parts of the country by cable. To try to win back viewers to state-run TV, the German Democratic Republic introduced a number of full length films, at least a third of Western origin, into its weekly programming. These films proved to be so popular that West Germans, and especially West Berliners, began joining the East Europeans in watching them.[79]

In the case of controlled cinema, too, the people eventually forced the hand of governments. In much of Eastern Europe, the people simply refused to go to see the films that the regime considered suitable for them. In Czechoslovakia, for example, distributors of entertainment materials— "publishers, movie houses, theaters and record stores"—were required to fill quotas and to make profits before they could collect bonuses. When profits dropped, they began to bring in popular material from the West to regain their audiences and make up their deficits.[80]

PERSONAL MEDIA IN ROMANIA AND IN ITS REVOLUTION

Perhaps because the Ceaucescu government exerted such overwhelming control over the lives of Romanians, that government "neither encouraged nor restricted video equipment."[81] All the VCRs in Romania have come from foreign sources. According to a 1987 Radio Free Europe Background Report:[82]

The private importation of such equipment is not specifically banned, and foreign citizens (students) living in Romania and Romanians returning from abroad often bring video recorders and cassettes with them. Romanian citizens also receive such equipment from relatives living abroad.

Romanians, this source said, even had mail-in services for VCRs and videocassettes by foreign companies located in the U.S. and Germany. However, like the rest of Eastern Europe, most of the available videocassettes were smuggled. Although prices have been high, many Romanians, like other Eastern Europeans and the Soviets, have a lot of expendable income, so that in time VCRs became available "to an increasing number of ordinary Romanians."[83] And like the Soviets, Poles, Czechs, Hungarians, and Bulgarians, the Romanians also made money with these machines, giving clandestine shows for 5 to 15 times the admission price of a movie.[84]

When Romania suddenly exploded in rebellion in mid-December 1989, and the Ceausescus were executed, the presence of a videocassette culture quickly became evident. Romanians reported that they had kept contact with the West via networks of underground VCRs and swapped smuggled videos.[85] The Romanians had also stayed in touch with the world through cross-border television from Bulgaria, Yugoslavia, and Hungary, as well as via the radio transmissions of Voice of America, Radio Free Europe, the BBC, and some other foreign radio stations.[86]

It may have been a videocassette played on Hungarian television that actually sparked the December 1989 Romanian revolution. In early 1989, Michel Clair, a former Parti Quebecois cabinet member in Canada, along with a Montreal journalist, Reagan Roy, taped a 40-minute interview with a Romanian clergyman, the Reverend Laszlo Tokes. Tokes, the pastor of the Reformed Church in Timisoara, a city on Romania's Hungarian border, was a member of Romania's two-million-strong Hungarian ethnic group, and an outspoken advocate, not only for the rights of that minority, but for more freedom in general. The videocassette, on which Tokes spoke about "the physical and emotional destruction of Romania"[87] under Ceausescu, was aired on Hungarian television in July 1989, and was seen across the border by countless Romanians. According to Clair, pressure by Ceausescu to throw Mr. Tokes out of his church "increased immediately after the program aired," but so did public support for Tokes.[88]

In mid-December 1989, Romanian security forces attempted to arrest Tokes, but about 200 people rallied to assist him. Crowds of thousands of Romanians then quickly grouped, with security forces firing into the crowd and reportedly killing several hundreds. Rather than being subdued, the protests grew and spread rapidly to other cities. Throughout these events, the Romanian people were able to keep track of what was going on by listening to foreign broadcasts.[89] On December 21, Ceausescu attempted to assert his authority by appearing at an officially called rally in Bucharest and by giving a televised address. The speech backfired, with Ceausescu being "shouted down by protesters." He left the platform quickly, but not before the "clear look of shock on his face" was broadcast throughout Romania on state television.[90]

Ceausescu and his wife Elena fled Bucharest but were soon captured, given a two-hour trial, and, on Christmas Day, executed. The former Romanian state television station in Bucharest became the command center of the new provisional government, and excerpts from videotapes of the trial, the execution, and the executed bodies were shown repeatedly on the renamed Free Romanian Television.[91] Besides confirming the death of the dictator and his wife, the videotapes served to demonstrate that the provisional government had the situation under control, to encourage and unify those who applauded the Ceausescus' downfall, and to discourage further resistance by security forces.

By the final months of 1989, cross-border television viewing and taping had become so strong that all over Eastern Europe, TV:[92]

> became the force behind the domino, as the Poles inspired the Hungarians, the Hungarians inspired the East Germans and the East Germans inspired the Czechoslovaks....

FUTURE CHALLENGES

Beyond tape technologies and satellite dishes, other personal electronic media like personal computers and fax machines began pouring into Eastern Europe and the Soviet Union at the end of the 1980s. There was also talk of upgrading telephone systems, extending access to Western broadcasts, and providing other individual information services that a year or so before would have been unthinkable. How newly acquired freedoms and greater access to wider varieties of electronic media will combine in a political sense will be one of the great challenges of the future.

NOTES

1. Many reports by Radio Free Europe/Radio Liberty, published as Radio Free Europe Background and Situation Reports, and in the Radio Liberty Research Bulletin, will be cited in this chapter by abbreviated designations of RAD BR and SR for Radio Free Europe, and RL for Radio Liberty Research Bulletins.
2. Gladys D. Ganley and Oswald H. Ganley, *The Political Implications of the Global*

Spread of Videocassette Recorders and Videocassette Programming, Program on Information Resources Policy, Harvard University, Cambridge, MA, 1986. Published in 1987 as *Global Political Fallout. The VCR's First Decade, 1976-1985,* by Ablex Publishing Corporation, Norwood, NJ.

3. William H. Luers, "Czechoslovakia: Road to Revolution," *Foreign Affairs,* Spring 1990, pp. 93-94. (Article begins p. 77.)

4. Theresa Boyle, "Former PQ Minister Ponders Role," *Globe and Mail,* December 26, 1989.

5. Paul Quinn-Judge, "Ferment Brews in Soviet Baltics," *The Christian Science Monitor,* September 21, 1988, pp. 1, 8; Bill Keller, "A Once-Docile Azerbaijani City Bridles Under the Kremlin's Grip," *The New York Times,* February 18, 1990, p. A-18. (Article begins p. A-1.) By 1987, at least one collaborative videocassette by Estonian/Latvian dissidents had already reached Western sources. (Toomis Ilves, "Estonia," in "The Video Revolution in Eastern Europe," RAD BR/242, December 17, 1987, p. 11.)

6. Victor Yasmann, "Green Light for the Video Revolution in the USSR?" RL 441/88, September 26, 1988, p. 1.

7. Viktor Yasmann, "Photocopiers in the Era of Glasnost'," RL 371/87, September 21, 1987. The USSR's 1980 installation of international direct dialing, its cut-off 2 years later, and its selective reinstallation are described by Donald Shanor in *Behind the Lines. The Private War Against Soviet Censorship,* St. Martin's Press, New York, 1985, pp. 162-164. See also: Wilson P. Dizard and S. Blake Swensrud, *Gorbachev's Information Revolution. Controlling Glasnost in a New Electronic Era,* Volume IX, Number 8, The Center for Strategic and International Studies, Washington, DC, and Westview Press, Boulder, CO, 1987, p. 30.

8. Donald R. Shanor, *Behind the Lines. The Private War Against Soviet Censorship,* St. Martin's Press, New York, 1985, p. 159.

9. Donald R. Shanor, *Behind the Lines,* pp. 159-160, pp. 6-7, for the KAL 007 incident.

10. "Customs Chief in Trouble with Religious Literature," *Newsletter From Behind the Iron Curtain. Reports on Communist Activities in Eastern Europe,* Volume 37, Number 517/518, Stockholm, July-October 1983, p. 20.

11. Richard N. Ostling, "Billy Graham's Mission Improbable," *Time,* September 24, 1984, p. 48.

12. Francis X. Clines, "For a Loved Poet, a Moscow Eulogy. At the Minstrel's Graveside, Songs the Kremlin Hated Ring Out Again," *The New York Times,* July 26, 1990, p. A-8.

13. Donald R. Shanor, *Behind the Lines,* pp. 161-162.

14. John Miller, "The Latest Threat to Soviet Society," *The Boston Globe,* November 8, 1982, p. 1; "VCRs Go on Fast Forward: Proliferating Player and Tapes Spread Western Fare Worldwide," *Time,* December 13, 1982, p. 78; and James Melanson, "Soviets Crack A Window for U.S. Homevideo, But Floods of Rubles Unlikely," *Variety,* January 22, 1986, p. 16. See also: G.S., "Bulgaria Goes Into the Video Business," SR/13 Bulgaria, October 10, 1984, pp. 1-5, and Gladys D. Ganley and Oswald H. Ganley, *Global Political Fallout,* p. 24.

15. *Eastern Europe: Please Stand By,* Report of the Task Force on Telecommunications and Broadcasting in Eastern Europe, Advisory Committee on International Communications and Information Policy, U.S. Department of State, Spring 1990, Table, Appendix B, p. B-1.

16. Victor Yasmann, "Video in the Soviet Union: Trouble With a Capricious Stepchild," RL 129/86, March 21, 1986, p. 2.

17. Among those who discussed this situation in the Soviet Union are: Donald R. Shanor, *Behind The Lines,* p. 157, 159; Ned Temko, "Kremlin Sees Threat in Uncensored Videocassettes," *The Christian Science Monitor,* May 12, 1983, p. 2; Serge Schmemann, "Video's Forbidden Offerings Alarm Moscow," *The New York Times,* October 22, 1983, p.

A-1; Alison Smale, "Soviets Battle Black Market in Western Movie Cassettes," *Philadelphia Inquirer*, April 10, 1983, p. 1-5; and Philip Taubman, "Oh Comrade, Can I Borrow Your Rambo Cassette?" *The New York Times*, December 9, 1985, p. A-2.

18. Viktor Yasmann, "How Many Video Cassette Recorders Are There in the USSR?" RL 211/88, May 17, 1988, p. 2.

19. Dzintra Bungs, "Latvia," in "The Video Revolution in Eastern Europe," RAD BR/242, December 17, 1987, p. 19.

20. Saulius Girnius, "Lithuania," in "The Video Revolution in Eastern Europe," RAD BR/242, December 17, 1987, p. 23.

21. "VCRs That Will Spout the Party Line," *Business Week*, September 3, 1984, p. 40.

22. Richard Anderson, "Economy Gorbachev's Priority," *The Boston Globe*, March 17, 1985, p. A-21; Ian Menziers, "A Letter From Moscow. Impressions of Daily Life Tend to Push Aside Thoughts of Ideology," *The Boston Globe*, August 17, 1984, p. 2. See also: Gladys D. Ganley and Oswald H. Ganley, *Global Political Fallout*, pp. 25 and 33-40, for discussions of discretionary income in the Soviet Union, Eastern Europe, and elsewhere.

23. Philip Taubman, "Oh, Comrade, Can I Borrow Your Rambo Cassette?" *The New York Times*, December 9, 1985, p. A-2; Donald R. Shanor, *Behind the Lines*, p. 157; John Morrison, "Soviet Pornography. Dateline: Moscow," *Reuters*, August 24, 1983, (NEXIS). See also: Anna Christensen, "The Black Sea: Prostitution and Punks," *United Press International*, August 19, 1984 (NEXIS); "Out of Reach of the Curious Censors," *U.S. News & World Report*, July 23, 1984, p. 46; Serge Schmemann, "Video's Forbidden Offerings Alarm Moscow," *The New York Times*, October 22, 1983, p. A-1; "Videos, Pirates and the Underground. Soviet Union," *Index on Censorship*, March 1986, pp. 19-20.

24. Victor Yasmann, "Video in the Soviet Union: Trouble With a Capricious Stepchild," RL 129/86, March 21, 1986, p. 4. This source cited prices for blank cassettes from legal sources as being from 40 to 80 rubles.

25. John Morrison, "Soviet-Pornography. Dateline: Moscow," *Reuters*, August 24, 1983 (NEXIS); and Serge Schmemann, "Video's Forbidden Offerings Alarm Moscow," *The New York Times*, October 22, 1983, p. A-1, among others.

26. Donald R. Shanor, *Behind the Lines*, p. 154, and Toomas Ilves, "Estonia," in "The Video Revolution in Eastern Europe," RAD BR/ 242, December 17, 1987, pp. 11-12.

27. Toomas Ilves, "Estonia," in "The Video Revolution in Eastern Europe," RAD BR/242, December 17, 1987, p. 11.

28. The figure is from *Eastern Europe: Please Stand By*, Table, p. B-1.

29. Viktor Yasmann, "Direct Satellite Broadcasting in USSR: Is the Time Coming?" *Report on The USSR*, Radio Liberty, Volume 1, Number 19, May 12, 1989, pp. 5-10. For some comments on reception of cross-border TV, see Thomas B. Rosenstiel, "TV, VCRs Fan Fire of Revolution," *Los Angeles Times*, January 18, 1990, p. 1. For access by Soviet radio hobbyists to state owned electronic materials, see Viktor Yasmann, "Satellite Television in the USSR: Towards a 'New Dimension'" RL Supplement 5/87, June 29, 1987, p. 11. For uses of "flattened out borscht pots" and other home-made satellite dishes in the USSR, see Donald R. Shanor, *Behind the Lines*, p. 170.

30. Viktor Yasmann, "Satellite Television in the USSR," RL Supplement 5/87, June 29, 1987, p. 12.

31. Ibid.

32. Ibid.

33. Viktor Yasmann, "Satellite Television in the USSR: Towards a "New Dimension," RL Supplement 5/87, June 29, 1987; Viktor Yasmann, "Direct Satellite Broadcasting in USSR: Is the Time Coming?" *Report on the USSR*, May 12, 1989, pp. 5-10; Viktor Yasmann,

"Video in the Soviet Union: Trouble With a Capricious Stepchild," RL 129/86, March 21, 1986, p. 4: and Viktor Yasmann, "Are Western Video Cassettes Compatible With Soviet VCRs?" RL 212/88, May 17, 1988, pp. 1-2.

34. Philip Taubman, "Oh, Comrade, Can I Borrow Your Rambo Cassette?" *The New York Times*, December 9, 1985, p. A-2.

35. Viktor Yasmann, "Video in the Soviet Union," RL 129/86, March 21, 1986, p. 8.

36. Dzintra Bungs, "Latvia," in "The Video Revolution in Eastern Europe," RAD BR 242, December 17, 1987, p. 20.

37. For videos being watched, see: Donald R. Shanor, *Behind the Lines*, pp. 148-172; John Morrison, "Soviet-Pornography. Dateline: Moscow," *Reuters*, August 24, 1983 (NEXIS); Serge Schmemann, "Video's Forbidden Offerings Alarm Moscow," *The New York Times*, October 22, 1983, p. A-1; "Out of Reach of the Curious Censors," *U.S. News & World Report*, July 23, 1984, p. 46; Philip Taubman, "Oh, Comrade, Can I Borrow Your Rambo Cassette?" *The New York Times*, December 9, 1985, p. A-2; Philip Taubman, "Soviet Pans 'Rocky' and 'Rambo' Films," *The New York Times*, January 4, 1986, p. A-3; John Miller, "The Latest Threat to Soviet Society," *The Boston Globe*, November 8, 1982, p. 1; Alison Smale, "Soviets Battle Black Market in Western Movie Cassettes," *The Philadelphia Inquirer*, April 10, 1983, p. I-5, and Ned Temko, "Kremlin Sees Threat in Uncensored Videocassettes," *The Christian Science Monitor*, May 12, 1983, p. 2.

38. "Out of Reach of the Curious Censors," *U.S. News & World Report*, July 23, 1984, p. 46; "VCRs That Will Spout the Party Line," *Business Week*, September 3, 1984, p. 40. See also: Donald R. Shanor, *Behind the Lines*.

39. "VCRs That Will Spout the Party Line," *Business Week*, September 3, 1984, p. 40; Elisa Tinsley, "Soviet Union Sets Stage for Video Revolution," *United Press International*, September 9, 1984 (NEXIS); Elisa Tinsley, "Soviets Finally Get Tapes For Their VCRs," *USA Today*, December 6, 1985, p. A-4; and Philip Taubman, "Oh Comrade, Can I Borrow Your Rambo Cassette?" *The New York Times*, December 9, 1985, p. A-2.

40. Viktor Yasmann, "Video in the Soviet Union," RL 129/86, March 21, 1986, pp. 2-3.

41. Viktor Yasmann, "Video in the Soviet Union: Trouble With a Capricious Stepchild," RL 129/86, March 21, 1986, pp. 2-4; Viktor Yasmann, "Green Light for the Video Revolution in the USSR?" RL 441/88, September 26, 1988, p.4; "Viktor Yasmann, "How Many Video Cassette Recorders Are There in the USSR"?, RL 211/88, May 17, 1988, p. 2. John Chittock, "Russia Moves to Exploit Video," *Financial Times*, March 19, 1985; James Melanson, "Soviets Crack a Window For U.S. Home Video," *Variety*, January 22, 1986, p. 16. For other discussions of Soviet attempts to control VCRs and videocassettes see: Valerii Konovalov, "Legal Aspects of Video in the Soviet Union," RL 137/86, March 19, 1986; Viktor Yasmann, "The Collectivization of Videos?" RL 355/86, September 22, 1986; Valerii Konovalov, "Criminal Liability for Videos 'That Propagate A Cult of Violence and Brutality,'" RL 401/86, October 24, 1986; and Viktor Yasmann, "Video Versus the KGB," RL 160/88, April 11, 1988.

42. Philip Taubman, "Oh Comrade, May I Borrow Your Rambo Cassette?" *The New York Times*, December 9, 1985, p. A-2.

43. Viktor Yasmann, "How Many Video Cassette Recorders Are There in the USSR?" RL 211/88, May 17, 1988, p. 2.

44. See, for instance, Tomasz Goban-Klas, "Making Media Policy in Poland," *Journal of Communication*, Winter 1990, pp. 50-54.

45. Douglas Stanglin; Personal communications, May 1985; Timothy Garton Ash, *The Polish Revolution. Solidarity*; Vintage Books, New York, 1985, pp. 46-47; Colin McIntyre, "Dateline: Gdansk, Poland," *Reuters Ltd.*, August 29, 1980, (NEXIS).

46. John Kifner, "Cultural Revolt Budding in Poland Despite Arrests," *The New York Times*, April 3, 1984, p. 1, and Bradley Graham, "Polish Resistance Flourishes Under Eyes of Regime," *The Washington Post*, November 26, 1983, p. A-1.

47. Jack Kalabinski, "Media War in Poland: The Government vs. the Underground," *Poland Watch*, April 1984, p. 73.

48. Ibid. See also: Stefan Bratkowski, "We Cannot Surrender," *Index on Censorship*, October 1985, back cover; "In the World of Independent Culture," *Extracts From Polish Underground Publications*, Teresa Hanicka and Nika Krzeczunowicz, compilers and translators, RAD Polish Underground Extracts/8, May 21, 1985, pp. 3-9; "Fewer Setbacks, More Books: A Talk With the Independent Publishing House NOWa," *Extracts From the Polish Underground Publications*, Teresa Hanicka and Nika Krzeczunowicz, compilers and translators, RAD Polish Underground Extracts/8, pp. 3-9, 13-20; and Teresa Hanicka, "Underground Videotape Production," SR/8 Poland, May 21, 1985, p. 23.

49. Thomas B. Rosenstiel, "TV, VCRs Fan Fire of Revolution," *Los Angeles Times*, January 18, 1990, p. A-14. (Article begins p. A-1.)

50. Bradley Graham, "Polish Resistance Flourishes Under Eyes of Regime," *The Washington Post*, November 26, 1983, p. A-1.

51. Teresa Hanicka, "Underground Video Tape Production," SR/8 Poland, May 21, 1985, p. 23; "In the World of Independent Culture," "Fewer Setbacks, More Books: A Talk With the Independent Publishing House NOWa," and "NOWa-Video," all in *Extracts From Polish Underground Publications*, Teresa Hanicka and Nika Krzeczunowicz, compilers and translators, RAD Polish Underground Extracts/8, May 21, 1985, pp. 3-9, 13-20, and 29 respectively.

52. "In the World of Independent Culture," *Extracts From Polish Underground Publications*, Teresa Hanicka and Nika Krzeczunowicz, compilers and translators, RAD Polish Underground Extracts/8, May 21, 1985, pp. 3-9. For recent easing of suppression of Polish underground publications, see Tomasz Goban-Klas, "Making Media Policy in Poland," *Journal of Communication*, Winter 1990, pp. 50-54.

53. Anna Pomian, "Poland," in "The Video Revolution in Eastern Europe," RAD BR/242, December 17, 1987, p. 28.

54. Ibid., p. 27 and also, Ganley and Ganley, *Global Political Fallout*, p. 54.

55. Anna Pomian, "Poland," p. 29.

56. Arthur Jones, "The Jaruzelski Index," *Forbes*, February 13, 1984, pp. 45-46. For these and other black market details, see: Ganley and Ganley, *Global Political Fallout*, pp. 33-43. See RAD BR/242, p. 28, for the purchase of VCRs in Polish hard currency stores.

57. Teresa Hanicka, "Underground Video Tape Production," SR 8/ Poland, May 21, 1985, p. 23; "Early Warning, Miscellany," *World Press Review*, January 1986, p. 7; Anna Pomian, "Poland," in "The Video Revolution in Eastern Europe," RAD BR/242, December 17, 1987, p. 27; "Appendix B: Eastern European Media Estimates," Table, in *Eastern Europe: Please Stand By*. Report of the Task Force on Telecommunications and Broadcasting in Eastern Europe, Advisory Committee on International Communications and Information Policy, U.S. Department of State, Spring 1990, p. B-1.

58. Viktor Yasmann, "Direct Satellite Broadcasting in the USSR: Is the Time Coming?" *Report on the USSR*, Volume 1, No. 19, May 12, 1989, p. 7; Viktor Yasmann, "Direct Broadcasting Satellites: The Search for A New Approach in the USSR," RL 228/88, June 6, 1988, pp. 1-2; and John Tagliabue, "Warsaw Bids a Big Benvenuto to Italian TV," *The New York Times*, April 3, 1988, p. 6.

59. Poland, with a population of 38 million, has an estimated 18,000 dishes; Czechoslovakia, with 15.6 million, 30,000; Hungary, with 10.5 million has 15,000; Bulgaria, with 8.9 million, 1,000 dishes, and Romania, with 23 million people, "less than 100" dishes. (Dish figures (1990) are from *Eastern Europe: Please Stand By*, Table, p. B-1; population figures (1989) are from *The World Fact Book 1989*, Superintendent of Documents, Government Printing Office, Washington, DC, 1989.)

60. Viktor Yasmann, "Direct Satellite Broadcasting in USSR," p. 7. See also: Colin McIntyre,

"Eastern Bloc Joins Satellite Explosion," *The Hong Kong Standard*, May 16, 1989, p. 15, and *Eastern Europe: Please Stand By*, p. 22, for satellite dishes in Poland and other Eastern European countries. For other discussions of the uses of personal electronic media in Poland, see: Neil Hickey, "The Message for Poland's Rulers. Beware of Fresh Ideas—Your Control of TV is Slipping," *TV Guide*, August 29, 1987, pp. 17-23, and "Poland's Flourishing Independent Culture. How Videos, Audios and the Printing-Presses are Used," *Index on Censorship*, June 1986, pp. 24-26.

61. G. S., "Bulgaria Goes Into the Video Business," SR/13 Bulgaria, October 10, 1984, p. 3.
62. G. S., "Video Wave Hits Bulgaria," SR/3 Bulgaria, February 1984, p. 5.
63. "Bulgaria," in "The Video Revolution in Eastern Europe," RAD BR/242, December 17, 1987, p. 5.
64. "Bulgaria Goes Into the Video Business," SR Bulgaria/13, October 10, 1984, p. 4. See also SR/8 Bulgaria, June 29, 1985, item 6.
65. "Bulgaria," in "The Video Revolution in Eastern Europe," RAD BR/242, December 17, 1987, p. 5.
66. Ibid.
67. Ibid., pp. 5-6.
68. Ibid., p. 6.
69. "Bulgaria," in "The Video Revolution in Eastern Europe," RAD BR/242, December 17, 1987, p. 6. See also Viktor Yasmann, "Green Light for the Video Revolution in the USSR?" RL 441/88, September 26, 1988, pp. 3-4.
70. *Eastern Europe: Please Stand By*, Table, p. B-1.
71. George Jahn, "Video Cassette Black Market Flourishes in Hungary," *The Associated Press*, April 26, 1985 (NEXIS). See also Steven Koppany, "Unprepared Regime Scrambles to Meet Challenges of the Video Era," SR/10 Hungary, *Radio Free Europe Research*, September 4, 1985, p. 17, for another report of Hungarian black market video dealers.
72. F. P., "Czechoslovakia," in "The Video Revolution in Eastern Europe," RAD BR/242, December 17, 1987, p. 8.
73. V.S., "On the Verge of the Video Revolution," SR/9, Czechoslovakia, June 3, 1985, p. 31; Steven Koppany, "Unprepared Regime Scrambles to Meet Challenges of the Video Era," SR/10, Hungary, September 4, 1985, p. 21; Karoly Okolicsanyi, "Hungary," in "The Video Revolution in Eastern Europe," RAD BR/242, December 17, 1987, p. 16.
74. Steven Koppany, "Unprepared Regime Scrambles to Meet Challenges of the Video Era," SR/10 Hungary, September 4, 1985, p. 20; F. P., "Czechoslovakia," in "The Video Revolution in Eastern Europe," RAD BR/242, December 17, 1989, p. 15.
75. "Videos, Pirates and the Underground. Central and Eastern Europe," *Index on Censorship*, March 1986, p. 19. (Article begins p. 18.)
76. Jackson Diehl, "VCRs on Fast Forward In Eastern Europe. Booming Video Market Erodes State Control of Information," *The Washington Post*, April 17, 1988, p. A-26. (Article begins p. A-1.)
77. *Eastern Europe: Please Stand By*, Table, p. B-1.
78. Dieter Buhl, *Window To The West. How Television From the Federal Republic Influenced Events in East Germany*. Discussion Paper D-5, The Joan Shorenstein Barone Center on the Press, Politics and Public Policy, Harvard University, 1990. All quotes on p. 2.
79. Ibid., and also Hazel Guild, "East German Nets Spice Up Offerings with Western Pics," *Variety*, January 23, 1985, p. 53; Hazel Guild, "Allow Cable Hookup of Western TV in East German Burg," *Variety*, November 13, 1985, p. 1; and Barbara Donovan, "German Democratic Republic," in "The Video Revolution in Eastern Europe," RAD BR/242, p. 13.

80. B. Jicinski, "The East Bloc's Market for Media Imports," *The Wall Street Journal*, September 19, 1984, p. 33.
81. Carmen Pompey, "Romania," in "The Video Revolution in Eastern Europe," RAD BR/242, December 17, 1987, p. 32.
82. Ibid., p. 31.
83. Ibid.
84. Ibid., p. 32.
85. Curtis Wilkie, "Romanians Ponder Past Suffering and Future Uncertainty," *The Boston Globe*, January 1, 1990, p. 12.
86. John Kifner, "Rumanian Revolt, Live and Uncensored," *The New York Times*, December 28, 1989, p. A-1; R. C. Longworth, "In Eastern Europe, TV Was The Tool of Revolution," *Chicago Tribune*, January 7, 1990, p. 1, and Rudolph Chelminski, "The Minister Who Sparked a Revolution," *Reader's Digest*, July 1990, pp. 84-89.
87. Theresa Boyle, "Former PQ Minister Ponders Role of Video in Uprising," *Globe and Mail*, Toronto, December 26, 1989.
88. Ibid. See also: Rudolph Chelminski, "The Minister Who Sparked a Revolution," *Reader's Digest*, July 1990, pp. 86-87.
89. Vladimir Socor, "Pastor Toekes and the Outbreak of the Revolution in Timisoara," *Report on Eastern Europe*, Volume 1, Number 5, February 2, 1990, p. 25. (Article begins p. 19.)
90. Peeter Kopvillem et al., "Romania Unchained," *Maclean's*, January 8, 1990, p. 21.
91. Among many articles, see: Curtis Wilkie, "Television Galvanized an Old World Revolution," *The Boston Globe*, December 28, 1989, p. 57.
92. Thomas B. Rosenstiel, "TV, VCRs Fan Fire of Revolution," *Los Angeles Times*, January 18, 1990, p. A-10.

chapter 5

POLITICAL USES OF PERSONAL COMPUTERS

Just how easy it has become to be a personal computer political activist was demonstrated when, in early 1989, an eighth-grade boy—still several years too young to vote—logged his personal computer onto a nationwide network and asked computer users from coast to coast for help in a political protest. By capitalizing on the wide publicity surrounding President George Bush's 1988 campaign slogan, "Read My Lips. No New Taxes," the 13-year-old Pennsylvanian instituted a campaign he hoped would help head off a 50% raise the U.S. Congress was proposing to give itself. Posting his message on electronic bulletin boards around the country, he asked other computer users to promote and pass on notice of his "Read Our Lights. No Pay Raise" effort—an appeal to motorists to protest the congressional raise by driving with their headlights on. The boy is quoted as saying "I thought this would be a good way of getting my word around the nation."[1] The efforts of this young activist typify the results of a decade of broad spread of personal computers, rapidly developing computer networks, and vastly widened computer literacy.

Not all political uses of computers are that flamboyant, and in any case, personal computers (PCs) have been integrated into daily life in many countries so quickly and so thoroughly that the miraculous things they can do often seem almost pedestrian. In less than three decades, much of the world has come to depend on computers socially, economically, financially, and militarily. The computer is such a versatile technology that its uses, including political uses, take off in dozens of directions. Together with other electronic office equipment—the phone, dry copier, fax machine, and various types of printers—PCs have brought whole new activities, such as direct mailing, telemarketing, and desktop publishing, into being. Growing dependence on computers by everything from local groceries to international financial institutions has extended computer literacy and access from just a few people to untold millions. Many PC capabilities originally designed to carry out office functions have been adapted to and adopted for a wide range of political expression. The computer has thus put an enormous amount of power, including political power, in the hands of multitudes of individuals.

THE ADVENT OF THE PERSONAL COMPUTER

Personal computers, which first emerged in the mid-1970s and began to be generally available in the early 1980s, now have the power to produce, pull together, sort out, store, manipulate, and transmit information to anywhere in the world that has the equipment to receive it. As a result, they are taking on much of the work that previously required mainframes or minicomputers. Hard on the heels of desktop PCs have come laptops, which can often do more than could early desktops and are ideal for travel. As late as 1984, a "portable" computer still weighed 25 pounds and needed a wall plug, but by 1988, some laptops were weighing only four and a half pounds, using IBM PC-compatible software, and offering both battery and plug-in power. They also came equipped with modems for telephone transmission and small hard disks for extra memory. Such machines are still getting smaller, ranging down to as little as a pound— some even just ounces.[2]

More powerful computer chips and software introduced in the late 1980s are also erasing the differences between the capabilities of work stations—formerly reserved for more complex tasks—and ordinary desktop PCs. This new versatility is expected to lead to even more access, and hence, to even more computer power for individuals. PCs are also now capable of doing several things at a time, and new software for this is becoming available. For instance, there are programs that can be put to work, say, screening databank materials and collecting items to create individualized databanks, while the PC's operator goes on working. Or such programs can be instructed to roam through research networks, picking up information on specifically requested items.[3] This capability for farming out tasks and pulling in information while continuing to do other things gives one individual the power of many people. One person can thus multiply the amounts of information, including political information gathered, and reduce the time it takes to reassemble and distribute it.

Computer capabilities can now also be bought by individuals and groups from companies specializing in such services. The Citizens Against the Gun Initiative in California in 1982 were able to defeat Proposition 15 on that year's ballot in part by organizing the activities of

30,000 volunteers using such services.[4] Political candidates, their advisors, lobbying groups, and multitudes of others also make use of the rapidly growing numbers of these services. The February 1990 issue of *Campaigns & Elections* consists of a guide to various information services and other "Political Products and Services."

COMPUTER-TO-COMPUTER COMMUNICATIONS

These more complex activities are only possible because computers can communicate with each other, which has in turn been made possible by the advent of various new technologies. By the mid-1960s, modems that could convert digital information to analog for transmission over voice telephone lines had become available, so that computer users could send information to mainframes over phone lines from remote terminals. Various telecommunications technologies for computer-to-computer communications continued to be developed, and by the 1970s, value-added networks (VANs), private branch exchanges (PBXs), and other types of customer premises equipment (CPE) began to offer the capability, via phone lines, for handling just about any kind of task between computers.[5] Meanwhile, changes in standards and regulations had also occurred that legally permitted these linkages.[6] This abundance of computer types and telecommunications technologies has resulted in networking between distantly located as well as nearby computers, and the establishment of vast electronic mail, bulletin board, and voice mail systems.

DISTANT LOCATIONS

Courtesy of PCs and other electronics, it has become possible to work at locations far from established offices or the primary source of information. Amnesty International's U.S. urgent action headquarters, which alerts volunteers and governments all over the world to acts of torture, could thus be located in a small Colorado village and be run every hour of every day from the home of one couple.[7] By providing jobs at distant locations—for instance, telemarketing jobs in tiny farming towns in Nebraska, North Dakota and Iowa[8]—computers are changing the places where people can make a living. Such changes could eventually lead to changes in political dynamics. Computers, VCRs, and satellite dishes are permitting U.S. students of all ages, with varied time schedules and in remote locations, to obtain advanced degrees through electronically distributed university programs.[9] Computer networks link thousands of researchers around the world, and hundreds of thousands of students in a host of universities.[10] Business branches, banks, financial institutions, and the military are all connected by computers across many countries, continents, and oceans. This not only changes the way the world's people live, but also connects groups and individuals globally, providing political interchange along with ordinary business. As will be seen in the next chapter, a PC also allowed a hacker to instantly cross the Atlantic from Europe in order to roam about in and purloin information from computers on a U.S. national computer network, and another in the U.S. to plant an alien "worm" program that disrupted some 6,000 computers on the same network.

COMPUTERIZED ACCESS TO THE PRINT MEDIA

Well before the PC revolution really got underway, in the four weeks prior to the 1982 U.S. election, some candidates and causes sent the American public 60 million political mailers.[11] But as PCs proliferate and permit development of computerized mailing lists and PC-generated desktop publishing, multitudes of political candidates, as well as thousands of special interest groups and millions of individuals, have gained access to the power of the direct mailer. The ability to produce flyers, newsletters, and other direct mail items has thus given a print medium voice to a broad spectrum of individuals and small organizations, as well as to a growing horde of lobbyists and lobbying firms.[12]

Beyond this, the PC's growing capability has given ordinary people entry into real publishing. By the late 1980s, "for the equivalent of a car loan—somewhere between $10,000 and $30,000,"[13] an individual could own the necessary technology to publish a small newspaper. Just five years earlier, before these machines emerged and their prices came down, such a set-up would have required nearly half a million dollars. Capabilities in this regard are steadily growing. In 1989, software permitting digital typesetting and independent creation of typefaces, previously limited to only certain PCs and to expensive laser printers, became available for most PCs and for use with inexpensive printers.[14] This new technology will also vastly extend the flexibility of computer uses far beyond the realm of desktop publishing.

Although PCs are still scarce in the Soviet Union, and still mostly controlled centrally, as early as 1988 at least one, and a printer, was being used for *samizdat* production. Traditionally typewritten/carbon copied publications expanded its scope in the Soviet Union during the last years of the 1980s to address various reforms.[15] If political opportunities continue, this expansion will no doubt be aided by the personal computer.

COMPUTER BULLETIN BOARDS

Like the one mentioned at the beginning of this chapter, computer bulletin boards were made possible in the early 1980s when PCs and other computers began to be strung together in private, commercial, and specialized networks. In the U.S. alone, at least a million computer users now regularly share interests with each other by contacting one of the several thousand informal bulletin boards that come and go,[16] or by using telecommunications services provided by several online information service companies.[17]

These bulletin board networks proved themselves a ready made political platform when, in the fall of 1987, the Federal Communications Commission (FCC) proposed to increase phone rates for computer communications, which enraged individual computer users. The FCC and the U.S. Congress were flooded with thousands of protest letters when computer users not only sent letters themselves, but employed the bulletin board networks to recruit other letter writers. Thus, says *The Wall Street Journal*:[18]

> The protest highlights how the nation's vast computer-communications network can be used for political organizing on behalf of numerous causes....

In the same manner, in 1984, Thomas Tcimpidis of Los Angeles rallied the myriad home computer users of CompuServe to his defense after police confiscated his bulletin board equipment because someone had posted unauthorized telephone credit card numbers on it. Tcimpidis left messages about his plight on a number of computer bulletin boards, and readers passed the message along to yet other computer bulletin boards. "The word quickly spread through the nation," commented *The New York Times*, "in a modern-day version of the Paul Revere story."[19]

Bulletin boards have been used for many lobbying purposes, being employed, for instance, to arrange antiwar protests by linking several hundred peace groups; by the National Association of Manufacturers to inform members of relevant issues before the Congress; by a Colorado Springs man to aid his campaign for city council; and by some 1988 presidential candidates.[20] They are also being used by many people just to discuss political issues. Says *The Washington Post*:[21]

> Call a BBS [bulletin board system] today and you will find furious arguments on abortion, *glasnost*, George Bush the hero, George Bush the wimp.

Senior citizens have been brought "online" by a nonprofit system called SeniorNet, which provides bulletin board access to older individuals who have been trained to use computers at senior centers, nursing homes, and doctors' offices. Older people can now relieve isolation and loneliness by "talking" to each other via computer in the middle of the night and making electronic pen pals, but they can also use the computer to become political activists. " 'Hot' issues like catastrophic health insurance" have been debated on SeniorNet, and lobbying efforts organized in some cases.[22] Thus, political activity by PC is being practiced almost from the cradle to the grave—by the oldest seniors and by increasingly younger children.

Computer bulletin boards have also become a source of solace in times of crisis. After the San Francisco earthquake in October 1989, Californians sought company by computer for reassurance. Hundreds reportedly "checked in with each other" on these boards.[23]

Among less benign uses, computer bulletin boards are serving the interests of extremist groups who want to perpetuate white supremacist ideas and antisemitism. The Antidefamation League claims that adults attempt to attract young, would-be computer hackers into the extremist sphere by the very use of this new technology. Extremists have also used computers to circulate coded messages among their different groups and to send "hate literature" across the U.S. border into Canada. Canada ordinarily embargoes such material at Customs, but if it comes in by computer, it either goes undiscovered or does not neatly fall under the laws covering printed materials, for in Canada as elsewhere, computer capabilities have outrun legal and other institutions.[24]

In Chapter 12, it will be seen what a handy political tool these bulletin boards make in times of crisis. In that chapter, these boards will be discussed in the context of the 1989 pro-democracy movement in China.

COMPUTER GAMES

Uses of the computer by racial and religious extremist groups are not confined to the United States. In West Germany, tired old political themes have been spiffed up for a new generation by giving them a "cool" new means of expression. Here, computer game disks with extremist content are being traded by kids in school yards, and distributed electronically through bulletin boards. The games, with names "like 'Aryan Test,' and 'Concentration Camp Manager,'" are said to give points for such things as "killing Jews, Turks, homosexuals and environmentalists," while a game called "Anti-Turks Test" includes the voice of Joseph Goebbels, Hitler's propaganda minister. At least 20 such games are alleged to be in circulation. While all are illegal, it is almost impossible to catch and stop them.[25] This new source of extremist material directed at children gains added importance as new freedoms in Eastern Europe and USSR have been accompanied by the reemergence of pre-World War II types of extremism.

Politically oriented computer games are not confined to racist themes. Inspired by the Intifada uprising beginning in late 1987, a game called "Intifada" has been circulated in the Israeli Occupied Territories. Produced by the Palestinians and distributed by computer amateurs, it is said to be very popular with Palestinian children. The game pits Israelis against Palestinians, with the Israelis losing—"either by firebombs or world opinion."[26] The growing presence of such games shows that the computer can be easily adapted for the creation and dissemination of political materials to suit any occasion, and in forms that appeal to different age groups.

Politically significant in a very different way, a computer game called Tetris has come to the West from the Soviet Union. Although it contains no political message, Tetris was produced and disseminated in a very political setting. It was designed by a 30-year-old Soviet computer hacker "on an aging Soviet copy of an obsolete American computer," and adapted to PCs by a 16-year-old Soviet. Copied on computer disks, the game was then spread across Eastern Europe. Discovered in Hungary by a British software agent, it was later marketed in California.[27] According to *Newsweek*, a number of "programming cooperatives" are appearing on the side streets in Moscow, which are devising a variety of computer games, many of them with political messages. In a game called The Wall, the object is to "break through a Kremlin wall" and on the other side, "be greeted by a host of Statues of Liberty." In a game called Perestroika, "bureaucrats battle one another to death."[28] The very fact that these games can be turned out in the USSR and disseminated widely reflects the swift political changes occurring all over the USSR and Eastern Europe.

Video games American youth play are hardly devoid of political content. *The Christian Science Monitor*, for instance, describes arcade games such as "Freedom Force," where the player takes on hijackers, and "F-15 Strike Eagle," which features opponents like Libyans, Syrians, and Iranians.[29]

INCREASING COMPUTERIZED CONTACTS BETWEEN THE U.S. AND THE SOVIET UNION

The changing political attitudes of the superpowers toward each other have brought increased U.S.-USSR contacts, and these include contacts by computer. A U.S. computer bulletin board has become the electronic meeting place for American, European, and Soviet scientists. Through the auspices of the European Space Agency (ESA), scientists from all over the Northern Hemisphere are allowed to "meet" via the electronic mail services of Telenet and leave messages for each other concerning the "greenhouse" or climatic warming effect.[30] A similar electronic mail system has also been set up between the U.S. and the USSR under an agreement between a telecommunications firm in San Francisco and Moscow's Institute for Automated Systems. This permits computer users in the U.S. and the USSR to communicate directly by satellite, using the network services of Globenet. Called San Francisco/Moscow Teleport, Inc. (SFMT), the organization had already existed for some years, but until this new arrangement it had routed messages via Vienna, a slow and expensive procedure. SMFT users have included businesses and scientific organizations, database operators, U.S. and Soviet schoolchildren, and the Armenian Relief Organization.[31]

In the last days of 1988, an International Computer Club was formed in Moscow. Promoted by Soviet "computer enthusiasts" and small western business firms, the Club hoped to establish "hacker-to-hacker" contacts between Eastern and Western computer users. John Draper, a celebrated U.S. computer hacker, was reportedly among the first individuals to use SFMT to establish contacts with the Soviet club members. Such contact by individuals at that time made both Western governments and Western computer users nervous, and Draper's suggestion that the Soviet Union be connected to USENET, an international computer network, prompted vigorous computerized discussions on the network.[32]

By the late 1980s, the USSR had only a limited number of PCs, and these were mainly under government control in schools, ministries, and factories.[33] However, this appeared destined to change quickly. In 1989, Siemens of West Germany contracted to supply the USSR with 300,000 PCs, 10 times the number available from all Western Europe and the United States during the previous five years. Computers have been among those items strictly limited by the 17-member Coordinating Committee for Multilateral Export Controls, COCOM, which has long overseen and controlled exports to communist countries.[34] In response to the Siemens deal, and citing the fact that equivalent PCs are available from many countries unhampered by COCOM restrictions—Taiwan, India, China, and Brazil among them—the U.S. in mid-1989 dropped many of its restrictions on exports of PCs and laptops to the Soviet Union. Further concessions were made in 1990 on other computers and telecommunications equipment.[35]

Elsewhere in the swiftly changing communist world, in Poland, the spread of personal computers is said to be booming. "More than 400 private computer firms have sprung up, mostly in the last three years," says the *Boston Globe*, which quotes the *Warsaw Voice* as saying "In Poland it is easier to buy a computer than a tin of black shoe polish."[36] Polish election returns, in which Solidarity won control of a large part of the government, were monitored by PC-armed Solidarity members.[37]

USE OF COMPUTERS BY REVOLUTIONARY GROUPS

Like audio and videocassettes, personal computers have found uses among revolutionary groups. In 1988, almost a hundred encrypted computer disks containing the internal records of the Communist New People's Army in the Philippines were captured when the Philippine military raided a safehouse. Information contained on the disks included descriptions of how deeply the group had infiltrated the church, press, and local government, the complexities of the group's global financial structure, and its difficulties in obtaining weapons. Lapses in discipline among the group's units, and laments about the decline in the support of the middle class and students, had also been electronically recorded.[38] Islamic fundamentalists, opposing the government in Tunisia, also used computers to keep track of their underground activities. They have reportedly recorded information on such things as funds collected, robberies committed to support their cause, and the propaganda that has been distributed.[39]

THE PERSONAL COMPUTER AND GERRYMANDERING IN THE U.S.

Computers have become the new tool of "gerrymandering," that is, for carving up voting districts into weird shapes (sometimes resembling salamanders) to serve the needs of politicians or special interests. After every census, districts must be reapportioned by state legislatures to accommodate shifting demographics, with the results of such reapportionments determining a state's number of seats in the House of Representatives. Political bosses and special interest groups have traditionally used this opportunity to gain some local advantages. Although gerrymandering has always proceeded apace without the benefits of high technology, it is thought that computerization of the 1990 census will further aggravate the problem. For the first time, in 1990, the Census Bureau's Redistricting Data Office constructed computer maps showing, street by street, the entire U.S. population. Called TIGER, for Topologically Integrated Geographic Encoding and Referencing System, the maps were available to the public in various computer formats. New computer programs were also developed by vendors and consultants to make this information usable to the various political interests.[40] Since computer technology, and especially PC technology, has become vastly more sophisticated since the 1980 census was taken, experts predicted:[41]

> that a slew of political bosses and public-interest groups will be drawing up their own election maps on personal computers and flooding the state legislatures with hundreds of alternative plans to consider.

Thus, individuals and small groups with widely diverse interests now have the power to make political demands, thereby adding new players and altering the power structure of those who have traditionally controlled redistricting.

The examples of actual computer uses presented here give only a flavor of the vast new capabilities computers have recently provided. Computer capabilities are still growing rapidly, and the diversity and importance of related political activities can be expected to grow with them. The next chapter will discuss the threats that individuals can now pose to economic and security systems by abusing their new access to this powerful medium, and later chapters will take up other political uses of computers.

NOTES

1. "Names and Faces. Read My Lights," *The Boston Globe*, January 29, 1989, p. 17. See also: "Teen-Ager to Congress: Read Our Lights," *The Associated Press*, January 28, 1989 (NEXIS). The effort was also inspired by a "Read My Tea Bag" campaign urged by radio talk show hosts, in which listeners bombarded Washington with teabags in a "Boston Teaparty" effort against the pay raise. (Roy Fox, "A Tea Bag Says No to Congressional Raise," Letter to the Editor, *The New York Times*, February 1, 1989, p. A-24; Eleanor Clift, "The Tea-Bag Revolution. A Backlash Over the Congressional Pay Raise," *Newsweek*, February 6, 1989, p. 18.)

2. "Computers Start to Get Personal, 1977. Centennial Journal: 100 Years in Business," *The Wall Street Journal*, November 2, 1989, p. B-1; John Markoff, "Atari Weighs In With a One-Pound PC," *The New York Times*, April 12, 1989, p. D-7; Susan M. Gelfond, "The Laptop Market 'Is Busting Out of Its Diapers,'" *Business Week*, November 14, 1988, pp. 121-122; Maria Shao, "Beyond the Laptop: The Incredible Shrinking Computer," *Business Week*, May 15, 1989, pp. 134, 136; and Geoff Lewis, "Picking a Laptop You'll Love to Lug," *Business Week*, August 8, 1988, pp. 78-79.

3. John Markoff, "For PC's, a New Class of Software," *The New York Times*, March 8, 1989, p. D-6; John Markoff, "Powerful New Chip Ready to Be Introduced," *The New York Times*, February 27, 1989, p. D-1; John Markoff, "In An Age When Tiny Is All, Big Computers are Hurting," *The New York Times*, April 4, 1989, p. A-1, and Brenton R. Schlender, "Battle for the Desktop," *The Wall Street Journal*, March 31, 1989, p. B-1.

4. Dennis Jensen, "Computers, Control and Communication: How 30,000 Volunteers Beat the California Gun Initiative," *Campaigns & Elections*, Fall 1983, pp. 58-72.

5. *U.S. Telecommunications and Trade Policies. The Need For an Effective Information Age Model*, presented by Digital Equipment Company at Airlie House, October 1988, pp. 7-9.

6. For instance, although the technology had long been available, until the various communications services in the U.S. adopted uniform standards in 1989, Electronic Mail, or E-mail, was confined within specific networking systems. Jeffrey Rothfeder with John J. Keller and Susan Gelfond, "Neither Rain, Nor Sleet, Nor Computer Glitches...Electronic Mail is Finally Poised to Deliver," *Business Week*, May 8, 1989, pp. 135-139; Simson L. Garfinkel, "E-Mail Zaps Without a ZIP," *The Christian Science Monitor*, January 11, 1989, p. 13. For general changes in international telecommunications systems, see: Oswald H. Ganley and Gladys D. Ganley, *To Inform Or To Control? The New Communications Networks*, Second Edition, Ablex Publishing Corporation, Norwood, NJ, 1989, pp. 211-219.

7. Tad Bartimus, "With Sophisticated Electronics, They can Mobilize U.S. Protests Against Violators Around World. 2 Peace Activists in Colorado are Key Link in Human Rights Network," *Los Angeles Times*, April 24, 1988, Pt. I, p. 22.

8. Bill Richards, "Telemarketers Take Root in the Country. Computers Lead to Opportunity in Rural Areas," *The Wall Street Journal*, February 2, 1989, p. B-1.

9. Mark Ivey, "Long-Distance Learning Gets an 'A' at Last," *Business Week*, May 9, 1988, pp. 108-110. See also: Norman E. Seal, "Going Back to L'ecole at 48," *Business Week*, May 9, 1988, p. 109, and Darlene Bell-Craig, "Juggling Kids, Career—and Algebra," *Business Week*, May 9, 1988, p. 110.

10. See, for instance: John W. McCredie and William P. Timlake, "Evolving Computer Networks in American Higher Education," in *Toward a Law of Global Communications Networks*, Anne W. Branscomb Ed., Longman, New York, 1986, pp. 175-183.

11. Ralph Whitehead, Jr., "Direct Mail: The Underground Press of the '80s. More then Money, What the Senders Want is to Mold Your Thinking," *Columbia Journalism Review*, January/February 1983, p. 44. (Article pp. 44-46.)

12. Mark Lawrence, "Computers Generate the On-Line Lobbyist," *The Washington Post*, June 26, 1987, p. A-23.

13. Doug Underwood, "The Desktop Challenge. Now the Little Guy Can Own a Paper. Should the Big Guys Worry?" *Columbia Journalism Review*, May/June, 1989, p. 43. (Article pp. 43-45.)

14. Andrew Pollack, "Typesetting Gets a Digital Facelift," *The New York Times*, August 2, 1989, pp. D-1, D-7.

15. Bill Keller, "For Soviet Alternative Press, Used Computer Is New Tool," *The New York Times*, January 12, 1988, p. A-1.

16. A *Smithsonian* article describes the comings and goings of independently organized bulletin boards, which, in the 5 years between 1983 and 1988, may have numbered from 50,000 to 100,000. Thomas B. Allen, "Bulletin Boards of the 21st Century are Coming of Age," *Smithsonian*, Volume 19, Number 6, September 1988, p. 88. (Article pp. 83-93.) For one catalog of bulletin boards by area code and special interest, see: *1989 BBS Bible*, Bubeck Publishing, Collegeville, PA, 1989, cited in I. R. Shannon, "Computers in the Corridors of Power," *The New York Times*, April 11, 1989, p. C-9.

17. CompuServe, whose subscribers rose from 50,000 in 1984 to more than 460,000 in 1988, claims to be the largest of the online service vendors. (Tom Netsel, "A Guided Tour of Major Online Services," *Compute!'s Gazette*, January 1989, pp. 19-23.) Beginning "as an information and idea repository for late-night computer hackers," CompuServe permits users, among other things, to chat by computer using a citizen band "simulator," receive

electronic mail by terminal, answer back and make suggestions, post notices, access databases, and participate in dozens of special interest computer clubs. (Owen Davies and Michael Edelhart, *Omni Online Database Directory 1985*, Collier Books, Mac-Millan Publishing Co., New York, 1984, p. 279.) See also: Lawrence J. Magid, "Computer File. On-Line Services Leaping Forward," *Los Angeles Times*, July 13, 1989, Pt. IV, p. 3.

18. Bob Davis, "Hobbyists as Lobbyists: Computer Users Are Mobilized to Support Host of Causes," *The Wall Street Journal*, September 29, 1987, p. A-6.

19. Andrew Pollack, "Free-Speech Issues Surround Computer Bulletin Board Use," *The New York Times*, November 12, 1984, p. D-4. (Article begins p. A-1.)

20. Ibid. For some discussions of political uses of computer bulletin board and electronic mail systems, see: Gina M. Garramone, Allen C. Harris, and Ronald Anderson, "Uses of Political Computer Bulletin Boards," *Journal of Broadcasting & Electronic Media*, Volume 30, Number 3, Summer 1986, pp. 325-339; and Mark J. Schaefermeyer and Edward H. Sewell, Jr., "Communicating by Electronic Mail," *American Behavioral Scientist*, Volume 32, Number 2, November/December 1988, pp. 112-123.

21. T. R. Reid, "Bulletin Board Systems: Gateway to Citizenship in the Network Nation," *The Washington Post*, Washington Business, November 6, 1989, p. 28.

22. Randolph B. Smith, "The Computer Revolution Comes to the Over-55-Set," *The Wall Street Journal*, August 7, 1989, p. B-1; Marvin G. Katz, "Older Persons Find Help, New Friends By 'Turning On'—Their Computers," *American Association of Retired Persons Bulletin*, Volume 31, Number 1, January 1990, p. 1.

23. Michael W. Miller, "From the Fault Line, Electronic Tales of a Quake's Fury. Survivors Share Experiences Via Personal Computer; Triage in the Parking Lot," *The Wall Street Journal*, October 19, 1989, p. 1.

24. *Computerized Networks of Hate. An ADL Fact Finding Report*, Anti-Defamation League of B'nai B'rith, New York, January 1985, p. 2; and Andrew Pollack, "Free Speech Issues Surround Computer Bulletin Board Use," *The New York Times*, November 12, 1984, p. A-1. See also: Cheryl Sullivan, "White Supremacists: Neo-Nazi Drive to Recruit US Youth Has Some Success Among 'Skinheads,'" *The Christian Science Monitor*, August 14, 1988, p. 3.

25. "Nazi Software: The Ultimate Virus," *Newsweek*, January 23, 1989, p. 32.

26. "Video Violence," *The Nation* (of Thailand), World News Section, May 4, 1989, p. 5.

27. Michael Rogers with Carroll Bogert, "Red Hackers, Arise! A Freewheeling, Monomaniacal Computer Culture is Growing in the Kremlin's Shadows," *Newsweek*, March 20, 1989, pp. 58-59. (Quote on p. 58.)

28. Ibid.

29. Mary-Ellen McNeil, "High-Tech Toys. Video Games Children Play," *The Christian Science Monitor*, September 6, 1989, p. 12. (Article pp. 12-13.)

30. Robert C. Cowen, "World Scientists Post Climate Notes On An Electronic 'bulletin board'," *The Christian Science Monitor*, May 3, 1988, p. 19.

31. Cheryl Sullivan, "Forming Links via 'Electronic Glasnost,'" *The Christian Science Monitor*, January 25, 1989, p. 6. Elizabeth Tucker, "U.S.-Soviet Computer Link Opens Era of 'Electronic Glasnost,'" *The Washington Post*, January 4, 1989, p. D-5. "U.S.-USSR Network Opens," *Computerworld*, January 9, 1989, p. 38.

32. Evelyn Richards, "As U.S.-Soviet Computer Links Grow, So Do Connections Between Hackers," *The Washington Post*, January 4, 1989, p. D-6; Evelyn Richardson (sic), "Open Exchange of Information vs. Security Concerns; Computer Link With Soviets Sparks Mixed Feelings," *Los Angeles Times*, February 13, 1989, Pt. 4, p. 10; and John Markoff, "New Satellite Channel Opens Computer Link to the Soviets," *The New York Times*, February 19, 1989, p. A-1.

33. Estimates of the number of computers in the USSR by Western analysts vary widely. A 1987 source put their number at 30,000 mainframes and about 70,000 PCs or other small computers. Wilson P. Dizard and S. Blake Swensrud, *Gorbachev's Information Revolution. Controlling Glasnost in a New Electronic Era*, Westview Press, Boulder, CO, 1987, p. 35. A 1988 source said there were "fewer than 300,000 personal computers installed" at that time in the USSR. "Information Technology, Perestroika, and Trade," *Computer Industry Report*, Volume 24, No. 5, August 27, 1988, p. 1.

34. "East European Briefing," *Telecommunications Development Report*, Volume 4, Number 7, Pyramid Research Inc., Cambridge, MA, July 1989, p. 18.

35. Eduardo Lachica, "U.S. Adds Laptop Computers to Listing of Products That Can be Sold to Soviets," *The Wall Street Journal*, August 15, 1989, p. A-2. Philip Revzin, "U.S., Allies to Ease More Curbs on High-Tech Sales to East Europe," *The Wall Street Journal*, February 20, 1990, p. A-20.

36. Timothy Heritage, "In Poland, Steak is Rarer Than PCs," *The Boston Globe*, March 5, 1989, p. 82.

37. Michael Gartner, "Up Freedom! Faxes to the Rebels, Gunfire Via Cellular Phone," *The Wall Street Journal*, June 8, 1989, p. A-19.

38. Seth Mydans, "With Aquino Popular, the Philippine Rebels Tread Tricky Political Waters," *The New York Times*, January 15, 1989, p. 14.

39. Michel Deure, "Tunisia Accuses Iran of Plotting Revolution," *United Press International*, March 27, 1987 (NEXIS.)

40. William E. Schmidt, "New Age of Gerrymandering: Political Magic by Computer?" *The New York Times*, January 10, 1989, p. 1; Mitch Betts, "Gerrymandering Made Easy in 1990," *Computerworld*, August 28, 1989, pp. 1, 18. See also: David Shribman, "While Computers May Ease 1991 Redistricting, Politicos Will Still Say Where to Draw the Lines," *The Wall Street Journal*, February 7, 1990, p. A-20; and Fred Stokeld, "Redistricting. Battle Lines Are Drawn for 1991," *First Monday*, Fall 1989, pp. 4-7.

41. Mitch Betts, "Gerrymandering Made Easy in 1990," *Computerworld*, August 28, 1989, pp. 1, 18.

chapter 6

COMPUTER DANGERS[1]

So far, real disaster has been avoided. No killer virus has penetrated the country's electronic funds-transfer system....No stock- or commodity-exchange computer centers have crashed. No insurance-company rolls have been wiped out...."[2]

So said *Time* magazine in its September 28, 1988 issue, giving a long list of computer disasters that had been feared, but had not occurred. However, 37 days later, a computer "worm" was inserted into the Arpanet, a component of the U.S. national research computer network, Internet. By guessing passwords and exploiting security defects in the network's electronic mail system, the worm was able to get unauthorized access to the network's computers. Replicating itself swiftly, it jammed computer memories and within a few hours had disabled about 6,000 computers. Like other computer worms and viruses, this one was customized for specific computer software types, or else it might have done much more damage. Robert Morris, Jr., the son of a noted computer scientist, a 1988 Harvard graduate in computer sciences, and a graduate student at Cornell University, who could access the network from his terminal there was subsequently charged with, and convicted of, this intrusion on Internet.[3]

The worm, which spread into other networks on the Internet, disrupted computer operations at several research centers for two days. This and other incidents described in this chapter demonstrate the power that individuals can now exert against networks of computers.

The attack prompted outcries over the damage that could have been done with a more malignant program, in a more sensitive system, or by a more viciously motivated person, and demands were made for efforts to prevent a recurrence. Members of U.S. Government security agencies met, the FBI launched an investigation, government computer security precautions were stepped up, and legislation concerning "viruses" was introduced in Congress.[4] The intensity of the reactions appeared justified, since rapidly increasing global incidents of break-ins, the spread of damaging viruses, and a variety of computer crimes, had reinforced fears that a single individual, with any of many motives, using a computer anywhere in the world, could conceivably jeopardize any of the numerous computer networks that are of growing importance locally, nationally, and internationally. With millions of personal computers spread around the world, and millions of people from dozens of countries trained to use them, the security of all computer systems and of the societies that depend on them has become extremely vulnerable. For the same personal computer that has provided individuals with so much liberty has presented a like opportunity for license.

VIRUSES AND RELATED PROGRAMS[5]

The proliferation of personal computers, the widespread use of computer networks, and the ability of more and more people to produce increasingly imaginative computer programming have combined to give individuals around the world the power to intrude on, disrupt or destroy, or steal the programming and computerized property of other individuals or of institutions. A group of programs that are troublesome because they are being deliberately used to disrupt other people's computer processing includes viruses and worms, sometimes set as "time bombs." The forerunners of some of these programs may have been computer games developed by young programmers at cutting-edge research laboratories in the 1950s. The players are said to have vied to see who could concoct the most ingenious instructions to kill off each other's programs. Although potentially dangerous, the games were harmless enough at that time, since computers were still solitary and the instructions were erased after using. But similar games, called "Core Wars," became popularized in the early 1980s, when computer networking was getting into full swing and PCs had begun to become widely available.[6]

The program inserted into the Arpanet was a worm, or an independent program that is designed less to destroy data than to cause disruption by crowding out computer memory. Viruses are segments of computer code that attach themselves to normal computer programs, and by altering those programs, replicate themselves over and over, and thus become capable of infecting the software of computers with which they come into contact. Viral programs can give computers instructions, among other things, to alter or destroy information. Some viral programs are designed only to communicate some innocuous, prankish message, but serious viruses produce effects that are vicious. Some viruses cause only temporary problems, while others create destruction that is devastating. Some disruptive programs take action immediately, while others, set as time bombs, are programmed to lie quietly until something specific happens. This may be the arrival of a special date like Friday the 13th, an anniversary, or the date and name of an employee (possibly fired) is removed from a payroll. Desirable programs called Trojan Horses can be used to package and distribute such programs widely without attracting attention immediately. Damage is often so insidious that it cannot be detected, and even visible damage may go unnoticed for too long to be remedied. Alien programs that begin innocuously enough can be tampered with by other programmers, or be made virulent by alteration. Viral infections can be spread through traded software disks, software copied from computer bulletin boards, or via computer networks, by way of electronic mail systems. Viruses have become so ubiquitous in the computer community that they are now being passed on accidentally by infected demonstration disks of computer salesmen and repairmen.[7]

THE INTRUSION ON ARPANET[8]

Arpanet was a U.S. Government run system, managed by the research arm of the U.S. Defense Department, the Defense Advanced Research Projects Agency (DARPA). Arpanet was started by DARPA in 1969 as an experiment in linking computers together, in the same way the government linked the country with interstate highways. As the network grew and evolved, Arpanet was retained as a research arm, with a military arm, Milnet, being split away from Arpanet. An extension of the original Arpanet idea, in 1988 Internet included more than 500 national, regional, and local networks, some of which are sponsored by the National Science Foundation and others by the National Aeronautics and Space Administration (NASA) and the Departments of Energy and Health and Human Services. The actual number of Internet users is unknown, but is thought to be well over half a million. Internet's function is to promote more effective research by allowing computerized information exchanges between military, industrial, and university scientists and defense contractors. Research is also speeded up by allowing such scientists to share, not only information, but also scarce resources like databanks and supercomputers. Most of these Internet communications are carried out via an electronic mail system.[9]

Despite the fact that it was capable of shutting down a good portion of the Internet, the so-called Internet worm was characterized by some as relatively nonmalevolent, because it did not appear to be designed to destroy data, but to see how deeply the network could be invaded.[10] The network paralysis was claimed to be accidental, and due to a programming error which caused the worm to replicate many times faster than intended. Malevolent or not, some damage estimates ran into many millions of dollars.[11] Given the research nature of the network, it was almost impossible to put a dollar value on the shut-down, and that was not, in any case, the disturbing part of the incident. The disturbing part was that had Morris, or another person with similar training, intended to cause more damage, little appeared to hinder him.

The "Cornell" program took advantage of several Internet weaknesses, most notably defects in the electronic mail system, to get around the network's security.[12] Similar deliberate defects, useful for legitimate correction of software and program problems, are said to be common. They are often widely known to be present but left uncorrected, because elimination severely restricts flexibility for users. The Cornell program employed a list of simple English words and names of known computer users to guess the passwords of given computers. Once inside a computer, the program could move on to any other computer accessible by that password owner. Because personal computer users are notoriously careless in password choice and security, guessing dictionary words or purloining passwords is commonly used by hackers and criminals to gain unauthorized computer entry.[13]

OTHER COMPUTER ATTACKS AND INTRUSIONS

The Internet worm incident varied only in the scope of the chaos it created—and the publicity it engendered—from other attacks and intrusions in a recently escalating global series. Many thousands of "viral" incidents are said to have occurred all over the world since the mid-1980s. Four widely publicized ones are the "Christmas" virus, the "Brain" virus, the "Scores" virus and the "Peace" virus, which originated, as do other viruses, in various countries.[14] The "Christmas" virus, inserted into a European academic research network, infected software on a 350,000-terminal IBM global computer network at Christmas 1987. Operators who followed instructions appearing on their screens typed the word *Christmas*, and thus activated the viral program, which instantly infected all programs on their electronic mailing lists. Within days, the alien program had replicated sufficiently to clog the network. The "Brain" virus, which has spread globally, is said to be the brainchild of two Pakistani brothers, self-taught computer programmers. By mid-1988, Brain had infected at least 50,000 U.S. PCs and, among other damage, had destroyed data and infected about 100 floppy disks at the Providence, Rhode Island *Journal Bulletin*. This virus was attached to cut-rate computer programs sold to tourists at the brothers' store in Lahore, Pakistan, supposedly to punish people, especially Americans, for buying such pirated software. The "Scores" and "Peace" viruses both attacked Macintosh computers. "Scores" was spread through traded software.

Moving quickly through networks of PCs, it entered computers and destroyed information at several government agencies and infected half of the 400 Macintosh computers in NASA's Washington, DC area offices. "Scores" is said to have been created by an unhappy Apple Computer employee and originally directed only toward that computer company. The "Peace" virus, which carried a "peace" message, was timed to go off March 2nd, the first birthday of the Mac II computer. Within two months, it had infected 350,000 Macintoshes globally. This virus is said to have been the creature of the publisher of a Canadian computer magazine and his co-worker, and designed to demonstrate how pervasively software is pirated.

There are many other such global viral stories. But as will now be shown, an individual does not need a viral program to pose a threat to far-flung computers.

THE HANNOVER HACKER

At the time of the Internet worm intrusion, another disturbing break-in involving Internet was in the process of being revealed. This intrusion required a more complex route to gain access to Internet than was necessary for the Internet worm, being conducted intercontinentally. It also had more direct significance for both network and national and international security. For, while possibly not originally designed as an espionage project, the intruder and two other West Germans were convicted of eventually selling various types of information gained on and about the network to the Soviets.[15]

In 1986, a computer programmer in Hannover, West Germany, later identified as Markus Hess, began to use his home computer and a modem connected to a phone line to access West German computer networks that could allow him to cross the Atlantic and gain access to the Internet.[16] From his home, Hess could gain entry to computers at the University of Bremen, Germany, and both via them and directly, he was able to enter the West German Datex-P Network. From this network, Hess was able to connect to a satellite telephone link or a transatlantic cable line, which let him enter the U.S. via the Tymnet International gateway. Via Tymnet, he was then able to gain access to a computer at one of Mitre Corporation's defense contractor operations located in McLean, Virginia. Using Mitre's accounts with Tymnet, the intruder could then traverse the U.S. to a computer system at Lawrence Berkeley Laboratory in Berkeley, California. The Berkeley system put him directly into Internet's civilian research network, the Arpanet, and gave easy access to its military research network, the Milnet. For months, he followed this transoceanic, transcontinental route over and over again and, using various means of acquiring unauthorized access, attempted to gain entry to about 450 computers and actually succeeded in breaking into 40 or 50. Along with some military computers, among computers he was able to break into were some belonging to corporations that design, make, and test military and space computers of the highest levels of security. These various computers were located all over the United States, some also being at U.S. military installations in Japan and some even back in the hacker's own West Germany. Once inside the computers, this intruder not only studied the routes of entry, but also read the files and copied whatever interested him.

Unknown to the intruder, he was being tracked by one of the rightful computer users at Lawrence Berkeley Laboratories, Clifford Stoll, who was alerting himself to the hacker's intrusions by a beeper, and recording Hess's keystrokes. Hess was eventually traced through phone lines back to Hannover. He and two other West Germans were eventually indicted and convicted of selling information gathered from, or concerning, these computer networks to the Soviets. One of the others convicted was said to have also hacked through the networks.[17]

THE CHAOS CLUB

The activities of another group of West German "hackers" also has political implications. In September 1985, members of the Chaos Computer Club in Hamburg, West Germany, claimed to have been able to enter 135 computers worldwide, and to have lifted "a wealth of sensitive information about the space shuttle, Star Wars and other topics."[18] One of the victims, NASA, claimed the Club had only broken into a "worldwide library" called SPAN (Space Physics Analysis Network) that provides about 4,000 researchers with space-related information and serves as an electronic forum for scientific discussions. While making these incursions, the Club planted a "Trojan Horse" program that copied itself through the system, making later intrusions easier. NASA defused the Trojan Horse, but break-in instructions for SPAN were soon posted on a New York computer bulletin board.[19]

The Chaos Club has claimed to have about 300 hackers as members, whose purported goal is to get around bureaucratic restrictions. During the period of public crisis following the 1986 Chernobyl nuclear accident in the USSR, when, in the Club's judgment, officials falsely reassured the public, "hidden data" was purloined and fed to reporters.[20] Thus the club, via the media, was in a position to influence and possibly change West Germany's domestic and foreign policy during this crisis period.

Four years after the Chaos Club attack on SPAN, by exploiting some still-existing security flaws, an intruder inserted a virus into the SPAN network. A scheduled launch of the space shuttle Atlantis had been under heavy protest by those opposed to part of its payload—a nuclear-powered satellite it was carrying to launch into orbit. *The New York Times* reported that "security experts speculated that the program was written by someone who opposed...[the] launch."[21] This program, which infected at least 60 computers, simulated data destruction without actually doing harm and sent "vulgar messages" to SPAN users. While no damage was apparently done, SPAN was temporarily disconnected from several other networks. The scheduled launch was delayed, but the delay was blamed on the weather.[22]

COMPUTER CRIMES

By far the major percentage of computer crime between 1983 and 1986 was committed, not for political reasons, but for money.[23] Thousands of computer crimes have been documented in the U.S. alone and, since most businesses consider revelation detrimental and hide such attacks, this is thought to be only a fraction of the actual crimes committed.[24] It is claimed that falsification or theft by computer costs U.S. businesses a billion dollars a year at minimum.[25] But such computer crimes can also endanger vital parts of the economy that are necessary for defense and security. The telephone company has long been the target of computer hackers and of various rip-off schemes, and during the last decade the now several phone companies have become even more vulnerable. For, just as PCs were coming into use, much of the electromechanical equipment for routing calls was being replaced by computer-controlled switches. For instance, Pacific Bell serves 79% of its customers using computerized switching systems. Individuals can use their PCs to access the phone network, and, since electronic switches are really just big computers, they can be ordered around by instructions from these personal computers. Thus individuals, using PCs, can listen in on conversations, falsely charge bills, steal faxes, keep lines busy, or destroy data.[26] Much more important than any of these crimes is that an individual or, say, a terrorist or an organized crime group, could use a computer to interfere with the switches to disable whole communications systems.

THE COMPUTER HACKER ETHIC[27]

Attacks on computers began in the experimental days, when only a handful of people had access to computers, and some engaged in various "pranks" (like breaking into the phone company's communications system) to test the limits of the then rudimentary computer programs. The Internet worm episode split public opinion about "hackers" into camps of those who think a certain amount of such experimentation is still valid, and those who say these actions no longer have a place in a world which has become dependent on computers.

Ten types of encroachment on the computers of others that hackers in his study engaged in have been identified by one investigator. These include acquiring passwords, unauthorized use of accounts, and "browsing" through, copying, and modifying computer files. Deliberate sabotage of programs, "crashing" computer systems, and stealing or damaging computer hardware were also included.[28] But those who still follow the "hacker ethic" developed in the early days often feel that breaches are harmless and justified exploration. It was contended by one of Morris's peers that:[29]

> the United States holds a global lead in software precisely because of its hackers, people who are by nature restless, compulsive code breakers.

And some computer security experts have argued that the Internet worm implantation made a useful contribution to computer security by demonstrating and focusing attention on the vulnerability of computer networks.[30]

An ingenious "hack" is said to be a good route to a top-paying job. A computer scientist at Argonne Labs, is quoted as saying of Robert Morris, Jr., "He's somebody we would hire."[31] A *Boston Globe* columnist, after Morris's indictment, indicated that his hand should be slapped and then he should be given an assistant professorship.[32] Richard Stallman, one of the early MIT hackers who develops and gives away computer software, called the fuss over the Arpanet incident "computer-hacker hysteria."[33]

But computer managers across the U.S. are said to have generally been enraged about the Internet worm attack. "The Hackers who break into a computer system should be punished," says a letter from a computer security manager to the editor of *The Boston Globe*. Its writer, pointing out that "most college computer science departments are less than a decade old," urged that students be trained in the history of the data processing industry, and taught the importance of that industry to the economy, with the need for ethical standards being stressed.[34] One programmer from the early days of computers is quoted as saying that "a hacker [is] an anachronism in our place and time," and that "you don't find the pilot of the space shuttle trying to fly under the Brooklyn Bridge with it."[35] The subject of whether or not hacking is a crime was, appropriately enough, argued out on the Well, a Sausalito, California computer bulletin board, in early 1990. Twenty of the "nation's best hackers" from all over the country gave their opinions, and reacted to the opinions of others, during an 11-day electronic forum moderated by the editors of *Harper's*.[36] The computer community was once again of divided opinion when no prison time was included in Morris' sentence.[37]

WHY THE ATTACKS HAVE BEEN TOLERATED[38]

These various attacks on computers have been tolerated until now for a number of reasons. One is that the "hacker" mentality is still partially in place, and no new ethical or social standards have been developed to keep pace with new computer capabilities and new needs of societies. A second is that the rather abrupt onset of major computer incursions has caught corporations and governments by surprise, and that they are just getting around to taking them seriously. Third, the price of closing security gaps has been considered just too high to pay, since imposing too much security can destroy flexibility and hence many of the recently achieved advantages. Fourth, it is very hard to catch perpetrators. They are difficult to identify, and evidence is almost always circumstantial. Fifth, even if caught, what constitutes computer crime is ill defined. This last is especially true for computer incursions like those made by hackers and virus planters.[39]

THE PRICE OF CORRECTING DEFECTS IN COMPUTER NETWORK SECURITY

Some of the vulnerabilities of the Internet, for instance, were known as far back as 1984 and could have been, and sometimes were, corrected. However, the lack of security features is what permitted this vast number of researchers to communicate easily, and what makes computers in general so effective. While some security holes can be plugged, others will emerge, say experts, and tight security—isolating the computer site, encryption, severe restriction on numbers of computer users, or cessation of software exchanges—will simply make computer communications less effective and computers harder to use and less compatible. It is also feared by some that sabotage may be invited by drawing attention to flaws in an effort to get them corrected.[40]

Various security defenses have been developed or proposed, ranging from "antiviral vaccines" for specific viruses, to closer employee supervision, to better password security, to retinal scanners for legitimate computer operator identification, to data encryption.[41] But computer security is always a tradeoff between the desirable and the practical. Jack

L. Hancock, vice president of Pacific Bell, told the *Los Angeles Times* that "the fast pace of technological change virtually guarantees creation of temporary security loopholes." Hancock said, "We close what loopholes we can find," but added that an effort to provide "total security," by encryption, for example, would make the cost of phone service prohibitively expensive.[42] The *Times* quotes Hancock as saying, "Everything we do is a balance between cost, time and utility."[43]

As in most other areas where new electronic means have transformed the way things are being done, ethical standards, social conduct, security precautions, and the law all trail technology. While progress in all of these areas may bring some relief, there is no foolproof protection against a well-trained, determined individual armed with a personal computer—not even theoretically. In practice, in Spring 1990, more than a year after the Internet worm incident and more than two after the Hannover Hacker was tracked down, an intruder, entering the network by an unknown path, was busily accessing computers on Internet.[44]

The vulnerability of computer networks is symbolic of the fragility of all these new electronic technologies and of the even greater fragility of the new social, economic, and political structures they are building. Old structures that lent the world stability are rapidly being replaced by these new ones. Should they falter, there is no guarantee that there will be any stable structure to go back to.

NOTES

1. For an in-depth view of various aspects of the problems discussed in this chapter, the following books and other comprehensive publications should be referred to: Harold Joseph Highland, *Computers and Security. Computer Virus Handbook*, Elsevier Advanced Technology, Oxford, 1990; Daniel J. Knauf, *The Family Jewels: Corporate Policy on the Protection of Information Resources*, Program on Information Resources Policy, Harvard University, Cambridge, MA, January 1990; *Computer Security: Virus Highlights Need for Improved Internet Management*, General Accounting Office, GAO/IMTEC-89-57, 1989; Anne W. Branscomb, *Rogue Computer Programs—Viruses, Worms, Trojan Horses, and Time Bombs: Prank, Prowess, Protection or Prosecution?*, Program on Information Resources Policy, Harvard University, Cambridge, MA, September 1989; "The Worm Story," Special Section, *Communications of the ACM*, Volume 32, No. 6, June 1989, pp. 677-710; Steven Levy, *Hackers. Heroes of the Computer Revolution*, Anchor Press/Doubleday, Garden City, NY, 1984; Clifford Stoll, *The Cuckoo's Egg. Tracking a Spy Through the Maze of Computer Espionage*, Doubleday, New York, 1989.

2. Philip Elmer-DeWitt with Scott Brown and Thomas McCarroll, "Invasion of the Data Snatchers! A 'Virus' Epidemic Strikes Terror in the Computer World," *Time*, September 26, 1988, p. 63. (Article, pp. 62-67.)

3. Among others, see: Michael Alexander, "Morris Indicted in Internet Virus Affair," *ComputerWorld*, July 31, 1989, p. 8; John Markoff, "From Hacker to Symbol. U.S. Officials Hope One Man's Punishment Will Say That Computer Jokes Are Crimes," *The New York Times*, January 24, 1990, p. A-19; William Kates, "Student, 24, Convicted in

Computer 'Worm' Case," *The Boston Globe*, January 23, 1990, p. 1; John Burgess, "No Jail Time Imposed in Hacker Case. Creator of 'Virus' Gets Probation, Fine," *The Washington Post*, May 5, 1990, p. A-1.

4. For some reactions to the incident, see: Eliot Marshall, "Worm Invades Computer Networks," *Science*, November 11, 1988, p. 855; Phillip E. Gardner, "The Internet Worm: What Was Said and When," *Computers & Security*, Volume 8, No. 4, June 1989, pp. 283-290; John Markoff, "Computer Experts Say Virus Carried No Hidden Dangers," *The New York Times*, November 9, 1988, p. A-18; "Computer Virus Data Seized," *The New York Times*, November 18, 1988, p. B-6; "Pentagon Will Name a Team to Counter Computer Viruses," *The New York Times*, December 8, 1988, p. A-23; Michael Wines, "F.B.I. Begins Investigation of Computer 'Virus' Case," *The New York Times*, November 8, 1988, p. A-16; Alison B. Bass, "Computer Virus Halts Research," *The Boston Globe*, November 4, 1988, p. 1; Jay Peterzell, "Spying and Sabotage by Computer," *Time*, March 20, 1989, p. 25; Bruce D. Nordwall and Breck W. Henderson, "Rapid Spread of Virus Confirms Fears About Danger to Computers," *Aviation Week and Space Technology*, November 14, 1988, p. 44; and Peter J. Denning, "The Science of Computing. The Internet Worm," *American Scientist*, Volume 77, March-April 1989, pp. 126-128.

5. For discussions of viruses and worms, see: Anne W. Branscomb, *Rogue Computer Programs—Viruses, Worms, Trojan Horses, and Time Bombs: Prank, Prowess, Protection or Prosecution?*, Program on Information Resources Policy, Harvard University, Cambridge, MA, September 1989. See also: Clifford Stoll, *The Cuckoo's Egg*, Doubleday, New York, 1989, pp. 310-315; Peter J. Denning, "The Science of Computing. The Internet Worm," *American Scientist*, March-April 1989, pp. 126-128; Robin Johnston, "Combating Computer 'Worms' Has a Price. Trade-off Seen Between Open Access for Users, Security of Stored Data," *The Christian Science Monitor*, November 22, 1988, p. 4. (Article begins p. 3.); David L. Chandler, "No System Immune from 'Virus' Attack," *The Boston Globe*, December 4, 1988, pp. 1, 26; Philip Elmer-DeWitt et al., "Invasion of the Data Snatchers," *Time*, September 26, 1988, pp. 62-67; and "Computer 'Virus' Hits R.I. Paper," *The Boston Globe*, May 16, 1988, p. 25.

6. Philip Elmer-DeWitt et al., "Invasion of the Data Snatchers! A 'Virus'Epidemic Strikes Terror in the Computer World," *Time*, September 26, 1988, pp. 62-67; A. K. Dewdney, "Computer Recreations. In the Game Called Core War Hostile Programs Engage in a Battle of Bits," *Scientific American*, May 1984, pp. 14-22; A. K. Dewdney, "A Core War Bestiary of Viruses, Worms and Other Threats to Computer Memories," *Scientific American*, March 1985, pp. 14-20. See also: A. K. Dewdney, "A Program Called MICE Nibbles Its Way to Victory at the First Core War Tournament," *Scientific American*, January 1987, pp. 14-20.

7. David L. Chandler, "Despite Safeguards, Viruses Are Spreading," *The Boston Globe*, October 30, 1989, p. 32. (Article begins p. 29.) (For last comment only.)

8. Scores of articles appeared after the worm attack on Arpanet. For this section see: Eliot Marshall, "Worm Invades Computer Networks," *Science*, November 11, 1988, p. 855; "The Worm Story," Special Section, *Communications of the ACM*, June 1989, Volume 32, No. 6, pp. 677-710; Michael Wines, "A Family's Passion for Computers, Gone Sour," *The New York Times*, November 11, 1988, pp. A-1, A-28; Richard Saltus, "Computer Specialists Fear Backlash. Caution Against Security Measures That Might Affect Data Sharing," *The Boston Globe*, November 8, 1988, p. 38; Aaron Harber, "For Robert T. Morris Jr., Hacker, There's No Excuse," *The Boston Globe*, December 13, 1988, p. 50; Alison Bass, "Computer Virus Halts Research," *The Boston Globe*, November 4, 1988, p. 1; Bruce D. Nordwall and Breck W. Henderson, "Rapid Spread of Virus Confirms Fears About Danger to Computers," *Aviation Week & Space Technology*, November 14, 1988, p. 44; and John Markoff, "'Virus' in Military Computers Disrupts Systems Nationwide," *The New York Times*, November 4, 1988, p. A-1.

9. The analogy of Arpanet to national highway systems was made by Clifford Stoll (p. 60 of *The Cuckoo's Egg*). The Internet description is from Testimony of Jack L. Brock, Jr., Director, Government Information and Financial Management Issues, Information Management and Technical Division, U.S. General Accounting Office, before the Subcommittee on Telecommunications and Finance, Committee on Energy and Commerce, U.S. House of Representatives, July 20, 1989. Internet, and threats to it, are described in: *Computer Security: Virus Highlights Need for Improved Internet Management*, General Accounting Office/IMTEC-89-57, 1989. See also: John Markoff, "Making Industrial Policy at the Pentagon," *The New York Times*, November 19, 1989, p. E-4. Markoff describes DARPA as "a de facto venture capitalist for the American computer industry."

10. See, for instance, Peter Denning, "The Science of Computing. The Internet Worm," *American Scientist*, Volume 77, March-April 1989, p. 126 (Box). Peter Denning is the Director of the Research Institute for Advanced Computer Science at the NASA Ames Research Center.

11. Aaron Harber, "For Robert T. Morris Jr., Hacker, There's No Excuse," *The Boston Globe*, December 13, 1988, p. 50. The Artificial Intelligence Laboratory at MIT alone reported that it expected a three-day loss of its $50,000-a-day operations. (Alison B. Bass, "Computer Virus Halts Research," *The Boston Globe*, November 4, 1988, p. 1.)

12. Clifford Stoll says the worm "attacked computers through four pathways: Bugs in the Unix *Sendmail* and Finger programs, guessing passwords, and by exploiting paths of trust between computers." (Clifford Stoll, *The Cuckoo's Egg*, Doubleday, 1989, p. 320.) See also: Bruce D. Nordwall and Breck W. Henderson, "Rapid Spread of Virus Confirms Fears About Dangers to Computers," *Aviation Week and Space Technology*, November 14, 1988, p. 44; John Markoff, "The Computer Jam: How It Came About," *The New York Times*, November 9, 1988, p. D-10; Peter Denning, "The Science of Computing. The Internet Worm," *American Scientist*, Volume 77, March-April 1989, p. 126.

13. Peter Denning, "The Science of Computing," *American Scientist*, Volume 77, March-April, 1989, p. 127.

14. Articles referred to in this section are: "Vengeance by 'Virus,'" *U.S. News & World Report*, October 3, 1988, p. 10; Edward J. Joyce, "Software Viruses: PC-Health Enemy Number One," *Datamation*, October 15, 1988, pp. 27, 30; David L. Chandler, "Computer Viruses Growing Menace. Damage Potential Enormous; 'Vaccines' Fall Short," *The Boston Globe*, May 30, 1988, pp. 33-35; "Newspaper Computer is Infected With a 'Virus,'" *The New York Times*, May 25, 1988, p. D-18; "Computer 'Virus' Hits R.I. Paper," *The Boston Globe*, May 16, 1988, p. 25; "Sabotage Aimed at Computer Company Destroys Government Data," *The New York Times*, July 4, 1988, p. 8; Robin Shatz, "New, Not Deadly, 'Virus' Hits Macintoshes," *The Boston Globe*, April 26, 1988, p. 35, and Mark Trumbull, "Computer 'Viruses' Infiltrate Government," *The Christian Science Monitor*, July 14, 1988, pp. 3-4. See also: Anne W. Branscomb, *Rogue Computer Programs— Viruses, Worms, Trojan Horses, and Time Bombs: Prank, Prowess, Protection or Prosecution?* Program on Information Resources Policy, Harvard University, Cambridge, MA, 1989, pp. 1-10, for a discussion of numerous viral and other malevolent programs, and a list of references for various aspects of alien programming.

15. "2 W. Germans Get Suspended Terms as Computer Spies," *Los Angeles Times*, February 16, 1990, p. A-14; "3 Spy Hackers Avoid Prison in West Germany," *International Herald Tribune*, February 16, 1990, p. 3; "Hackers Indicted on Suspected Espionage," *Financial Times*, August 17, 1989, p. 2, and "W. German Computer Hackers Accused of Spying for Soviets," *The Boston Globe*, August 17, 1989, p. 21.

16. This fascinating story is told by the "hacker tracker" himself: Clifford Stoll, *The Cuckoo's Egg. Tracking a Spy Through The Maze of Computer Espionage*, Doubleday, New York, 1989. The electronic pathway the hacker followed is diagrammed on the

inside covers of Stoll's book. See also: David L. Chandler, "The Spy Who Stayed Too Long. Caught 'Rifling' U.S. Military Computers," *The Boston Globe*, November 14, 1988, pp. 29, 31; David L. Chandler, "Hacker Case: It Took One to Find Them," *The Boston Globe*, March 4, 1989, p. 2; Philip Elmer-DeWitt with Rhea Schoenthal and Dennis Wyss, "A Bold Raid on Computer Security. The Hannover Hacker is Tracked Down by a Berkeley Whiz," *Time*, May 2, 1988, p. 58; Jay Peterzell, "Spying and Sabotage by Computer," *Time*, March 20, 1989, p. 25; John Markoff, "For PC's, a New Class of Software," *The New York Times*, March 8, 1989, p. D-6; and Timothy Aeppel, "Computer and Spy: Worrisome Mix. West German Espionage Case Reminds West That Reliance on Computers Poses New Risks," *The Christian Science Monitor*, March 7, 1989, p. 4.

17. "W. German Computer Hackers Accused of Spying for Soviets," *The Boston Globe*, August 17, 1989, p. 21; "Hackers Indicted on Suspected Espionage," *Financial Times*, August 17, 1989, p. 2. "2 W. Germans Get Suspended Terms as Computer Spies," *Los Angeles Times*, February 16, 1989, p. A-14; "3 Spy Hackers Avoid Prison in West Germany," *International Herald Tribune*, February 16, 1990, p. 3.

18. William D. Marbach with Andrew Nagorski and Richard Sandza, "Hacking Through NASA. A Threat—Or Only An Embarrassment?" *Newsweek*, September 28, 1987, p. 38.

19. Ibid.

20. Gail Schares, "A German Hackers' Club That Promotes Creative Chaos," *Business Week*, August 1, 1988, p. 71. In 1984, this article says, the Club found a security defect in the electronic mailbox system used for its customers by the German phone authority, the Bundespost. When the Bundespost ignored its warnings, the Club chose one customer, a savings bank, and programmed its computers to place "thousands" of calls to the Club's headquarters, resulting in a phone bill of $75,000.

21. John Markoff, "Computer Network at NASA Attacked by Rogue Program," *The New York Times*, October 18, 1989, p. A-22.

22. Ibid.

23. Ronald Rosenberg, "System Sabotage: A Matter of Time. Major Disasters Averted—So Far," *The Boston Globe*, December 6, 1988, pp. 1, 24. This was based on a National Center for Computer Crime Data Census. See also: Katherine M. Hafner with Geoff Lewis, Kevin Kelly, Maria Shao, Chuck Hawkins, and Paul Angiolillo, "Is Your Computer Secure? Hackers, High-tech Bandits and Disasters Cost Business Billions," *Business Week*, August 1, 1988, pp. 64-72.

24. Richard C. Hollinger, "Computer Hackers Follow a Guttman-Like Progression," *Sociology and Social Research*, Volume 72, No. 3, April 1988, p. 199. Professor Hollinger of the University of Florida at Gainesville cites a number of book-length works and articles by Donn B. Parker on the subject of computer crime.

25. Davis Bushnell, "Programmed for Crime. Firms Can Cut Losses by Preparing for Possible Theft by Computer," *The Boston Globe*, December 12, 1988, p. 10. A *Business Week* article gives a figure of $3 to $5 billion. (Katherine M. Hafner et al., "Is Your Computer Secure?" *Business Week*, August 1, 1988, p. 65. Article begins p. 64.)

26. John Markoff with Andrew Pollack, "Computer 'Hackers' Viewed as a Threat to Phone Security," *The New York Times*, July 22, 1988, pp. A-1, D-5.

27. For the story of the original hackers at MIT, see: Steven Levy, *Hackers. Heroes of the Computer Revolution*, Anchor Press/Doubleday, Garden City, NY, 1984.

28. Richard C. Hollinger, "Computer Hackers Follow a Guttman-Like Progression," *Sociology and Social Research*, Volume 72, No. 3, April 1988, p. 199.

29. John Markoff, "Learning to Love the Computer Whiz," *The New York Times*, November 8, 1988, p. A-16.

30. John Markoff, "How a Need for Challenge Seduced Computer Expert," *The New York Times*, November 6, 1988, pp. A-1, A-30.

31. "Spreading a Virus. How Computer Science Was Caught Off Guard by One Young

Hacker," *The Wall Street Journal*, November 7, 1988, p. A-6. (Article begins p. A-1.) Rick Stevens is being quoted.

32. David Nyhan, "A Hacker Worth Hiring," *The Boston Globe*, August 3, 1989, p. 13.

33. John Markoff, "How a Need for Challenge Seduced Computer Expert," *The New York Times*, November 6, 1988, p. A-30. (Article begins p. A-1.) See also: John Markoff, "One Man's Fight for Free Software," *The New York Times*, January 11, 1989, p. D-1, and Richard Stallman, "The Computer-hacker Hysteria," *The Boston Globe*, December 29, 1988, p. 15.

34. Martin Snow, Manager, Computer Security, Wolf & Co. of Massachusetts, Sharon MA, Letter to the Editor, *The Boston Globe*, December 12, 1988, p. 13.

35. Tom Ashbrook, "Mavericks of the Megabyte. Do Hackers Hurt or Help?" *The Boston Globe*, November 22, 1988, p. 65, quoting Ed Fredkin. See also: Alison Bass, "Some See Computers as Fair Game," *The Boston Globe*, November 8, 1988, p. 38.

36. The results were published as "Forum. Is Computer Hacking a Crime?" *Harper's*, March 1990, pp. 45-57.

37. John Burgess, "No Jail Time Imposed in Hacker Case. Creator of 'Virus' Gets Probation, Fine," *The Washington Post*, May 5, 1990, p. A-1; John Markoff, "Computer Intruder Is Put on Probation and Fined $10,000," *The New York Times*, May 5, 1990, p. 1.

38. Articles referred to in this section are: Philip Elmer-Dewitt et al., "Invasion of the Data Snatchers. A Virus Epidemic Strikes Terror in the Computer World," *Time*, September 26, 1988, pp. 62-67; Jeff Gerth, "Intruders Into Computer Systems Still Hard to Prosecute," *The New York Times*, November 5, 1988, p. 7; Fred Kaplan, "FBI 'Virus' Probe Moves to Cornell," *The Boston Globe*, November 9, 1988, p. 14; Richard C. Hollinger, "Computer Hackers Follow a Guttman-Like Progression," *Sociology and Social Research*, Volume 72, No. 3, April 1988, p. 199; and Spencer S. Hsu, "'Virus' Inquiry Hears Vital Harvard Testimony," *Harvard Crimson*, December 3, 1988, p. 3.

39. For discussions of the laws and legal considerations regarding computer crimes, see: Anne W. Branscomb, *Rogue Computer Programs—Viruses, Worms, Trojan Horses, and Time Bombs: Prank, Prowess, Protection or Prosecution?* Program on Information Resources Policy, Harvard University, Cambridge, MA, September 1989, pp. 20-42; Robert P. Bigelow, "Computer Security Crime and Privacy," *The Computer Lawyer*, Volume 6, No. 2, February 1989, pp. 10-19; and Robert P. Bigelow, *Computer Contracts*, 3.06, Matthew Bender & Company.

40. See, among others: Robin Johnston, "Combating Computer 'Worms' Has a Price. Trade-off Seen Between Open Access for Users, Security of Stored Data," *The Christian Science Monitor*, November 22, 1988, pp. 3-4; David L. Chandler, "No System Immune From 'Virus' Attack," *The Boston Globe*, December 4, 1988, p. 1; and John Markoff, "Dilemma for Designers: Protection of Computers," *The New York Times*, December 3, 1988, p. A-8.

41. Mark Clayton, "As Computer Viruses Multiply, So Do Software Remedies," *The Christian Science Monitor*, December 12, 1988, p. 16; Davis Bushnell, "Programmed For Crime. Firms Can Cut Losses by Preparing for Possible Theft By Computer," *The Boston Globe*, December 12, 1988, p. 10; Ronald Rosenberg, "For a Chicago Agency Suspicious of its Staff, the Eyes Have It," *The Boston Globe*, November 14, 1988, p. 3; and Peter Denning, "The Science of Computing. The Internet Worm," *American Scientist*, Volume 77, March-April 1989, pp. 126-128.

42. Bruce Keppel, "Telecommunications Experts Warn of Hackers' Growing Sophistication," *Los Angeles Times*, July 24, 1988, Pt. IV, p. 2.

43. Ibid.

44. John Markoff, "Computer System Intruder Plucks Passwords and Avoids Detection," *The New York Times*, March 19, 1990, p. A-12.

chapter 7

HONESTY AND DISHONESTY IN VOTING—A TALE OF TWO COUNTRIES

Choosing the leaders who will represent you is one of the most precious privileges of mankind and one of the most difficult to attain and to hold onto. Computers and other personal media have recently become deeply involved in this choosing process. Their role in gerrymandering in the U.S. has been described, and their uses in U.S. national elections in 1988 will be discussed in Chapter 11. The introduction of these new tools, which can be used in such a variety of ways and which change the way things can be done on so many levels, could lead to shifts in the status quo in either democratic or nondemocratic countries. Many countries are presently introducing or reinstating democratic elections, or changing their voting processes, making it all the more imperative to look at the roles the new personal media have already played and could play here.

Two examples where personal media have, or could be, used to alter the voting process in important ways are therefore examined. In one instance, democratic processes were obtained, in the other, they might be threatened. The first is the case of the Chile plebiscite of 1988, in which democratic elections were restored after a long period of dictatorship. This return of representative government was the result of many and complex pressures on the Pinochet government. One such pressure was the fact that the opposition was able to independently collect information on the voting results and to have compilations available—for the Pinochet government, the global media, and the world to know—at the same time as the official voting figures. Both security and speed were obtained by using networks of secretly placed fax machines and PCs in conjunction with a central computer. The second is the case of the United States, where conversion to computerized voting could be exposing this democratic process to new kinds of illegal tampering.

COMPUTERS AND FACSIMILE IN THE 1988 CHILE PLEBISCITE[1]

The Chilean Constitution, prepared under the direction of General Augusto Pinochet, who had ruled Chile since the overthrow of Salvador Allende in 1973, was approved by Chilean voters in a questionably honest plebiscite in 1980. The Constitution provided for another plebiscite, to take place sometime in 1988 or 1989, to decide on Pinochet's continued rule. If the vote in this second plebiscite was "yes," then free elections for a president were to be delayed until 1997. If it was "no," then presidential elections were mandated within about a 12-month period.

More than a year before the plebiscite date of October 5, 1988 was announced, the 16 feuding anti-Pinochet parties of Chile, highly motivated to defeat the dictator, decided to settle their differences and began to organize themselves to actively campaign against the "Yes" effort. With strong pressure on Pinochet from many outside sources[2] and with the blessings of the foreign media and much of world public opinion, these opposition parties formed themselves into one group as the "Command for the No." The "No" then set up an organizational structure to prepare for the plebiscite, putting tens of thousands of volunteers to work to get out a heavy vote of all citizens rather than just those encouraged by Pinochet to vote. After serving throughout the campaign in a variety of ways, on the day of the vote, these volunteers watched the polls to detect fraud, manned the phones, and served as messengers to get information on the vote to Santiago.

Because fraudulent election reporting by the Government was feared to be a virtual certainty, elaborate plans were deemed necessary to obtain independent information on voting results. The Command for the "No" therefore set up two parallel communications networks, one composed of multiple facsimile machines, and a second of personal computers, located at secret places all over Chile. On the day of the plebiscite vote, these networks were to be used to send voting results from the 22,000 individual polling places around the country to a central "No" computer in Santiago where they would be compiled and counted. Two systems were felt to be necessary as a safeguard against government interference, so that, if information should be disrupted on one, or accidentally fail to get through, it could still get through on the other.

Following the terms of the plebiscite, the opposition was allowed to have observers at each of the polling places, and the "No" arranged to have at least two observers at each site on the day of voting. These observers were to watch for and report any evidence of fraud and, when the polls closed, get the voting results immediately off to Santiago.[3] Messenger service was arranged for part of the information during the final leg of its journey to the Command's central computer, and for all of the Santiago votes—about 40% of the total.[4] Through this carefully constructed information chain, the opposition assured itself of having the same results, with the same speed, to report to the voters as did the Pinochet Government.

A second organization, the Committee for Free Elections—whose members were anti-Pinochet, but which took no partisan role during the campaign—also set up a central computer in Santiago for the occasion. This Committee, too, placed volunteer observers at each polling place and obtained independent information on the vote count. Unlike the "No," the Committee had its voting results phoned in to its central computer, coding the messages to protect against interception. This system provided yet another check on both the "Yes" and the "No" figures.

It had been arranged that the official registration, voting, and counting systems would be run by the quasi-independent Electoral Service, directed by Juan Ignacio Garcia, who had helped run earlier, democratic elections. Under various pressures, the Electoral Service had instituted several measures against vote fraud, such as special ballots and voting boxes, poll observers, and computerized vote counting. The Electoral Service also provided waterproof ink to mark each voter to prevent duplicate voting. With the electorate also being pressed by the "No" to vote, the Electoral Service succeeded in registering 90% of all those eligible.[5] To be sure the registration methods were fair, the "No" also set up computers to "track the reliability of the government's voter registration records."[6]

The Chilean Ministry of the Interior compiled voting results, too, which were theoretically as unofficial as those of the opposition.[7] But it was well recognized that, unless every loophole was closed, the election results could, in fact, be determined by that Ministry.

Prior to the voting, several nongovernment opinion polls indicated a lead for the "No" of about 55%, with about 45% projected for the "Yes" vote. Some Chilean government polls saw Pinochet ahead but only by a close margin. Only one poll, conducted by a University of Chile team of economists, predicted a substantial "Yes" victory.[8]

There was great fear by the "No" that the Pinochet Government would find ways to disrupt its independent efforts. Anxiety on this count was heightened when, on the weekend prior to the vote, explosives planted at high-voltage electric towers caused electrical outages in half the country and resulted in widespread blackouts.

But all proceded as planned, and shortly after the polls closed, the Committee for Free Elections released computer projections showing a 12% lead for the "No." A French opinion poll gave the "No" a 20% lead, based on exit interviews. And when 40% of the vote was in, the Command for the "No" itself reported that it was leading by 18%.[9]

However, when less than 4% of the vote had been counted—giving the "Yes" a lead of almost 8%—the Government stopped giving results on television.[10] This led again to great fear that the Government would be able to sabotage the opposition effort, regardless of the numbers that were showing. But at 2 a.m. the Interior Ministry reported that its unofficial count also showed that the "Yes" had lost by about 12%. And at about 2:30 a.m., the Interior Minister appeared on TV to say that "the government stood by 'its unbreakable decision to comply with the Constitution and the law and see that it is complied with.'"[11]

The fairy tale ending to the story is that Fall 1989 saw Chile almost routinely proceeding toward a December presidential election. *The New York Times* reported that:[12]

> Political headquarters are stacked with posters and banners, while the candidates worry about newspaper space and air time and finding the money to pay…for the likes of computers and cellular telephones.

On December 14th, Patricio Aylwin, the Christian Democrat who had headed the largest group in the "No" effort, won more than 55% of the vote for the Chilean presidency.[13]

Timely independently derived voting information could be very important in settling arguments where voting results are contested. In the disputed Mexican election of July 1988, for instance, the opposition claimed that the government used the excuse of a computer breakdown to obscure voting figures. In past Mexican elections, which leading Institutional Revolutionary Party (PRI) candidates had won since 1929, long delays had routinely occurred before returns were released, which regularly sparked "cooking the books" charges. In 1988, the opposition in Mexico was assured that no such delays could possibly occur, since the vote would be tracked by the Government's central computer and the results released almost immediately.[14] However, with the polls closed, and the main opposition candidate, Cuauhtemoc Cardenas, making a strong showing, the Mexican Government pleaded a central computer breakdown and stopped reporting voting figures. Six days then passed before any official count was released, during which this candidate and his supporters could do little but fume, demonstrate, and complain about a "technical equivalent of a coup d'etat,"[15] because, unlike the Chilean "No," it had no hard-and-fast independent voting information to fall back on.

The PRI eventually claimed that 50% of eligible voters voted, and that it received 70% of these votes. But Alejandro Gil-Recasens, who headed a Mexican consulting and polling firm, Comunicacion Politica, said that he estimated the turnout at about 35%, and saw the vote as closely divided.[16]

POSSIBLE HAZARDS OF COMPUTERIZING THE U. S. POLLS

Even as the success story in Chile was playing itself out, it was being suggested that possible threats by individuals to the U.S. system of voting could be looming. That is, the question was raised of whether, with the gradual introduction of the computerized ballot in the U.S. since 1964, the door may not have been opened to let U.S. elections be thrown or even a presidency be stolen.

Old methods of voting in the U.S.—paper ballots and voting machines—are known to be prone to tampering and mistakes, and when votes are counted too slowly, fraud is often suspected. New computerized methods make everybody happier by whizzing through the counting and allaying suspicions. But just prior to the 1988 presidential election, the author of a *New Yorker* article asked such questions as whether such systems "count accurately," whether "they are vulnerable to fraud," and whether too many votes were not being lost accidentally.[17] He then answered by saying that, no, computerized systems don't always count accurately; yes, they are *extremely* vulnerable to fraud; and yes, large numbers of votes are lost through accidents due to flaws in the system. Further, he said, such losses could just as easily be caused deliberately. David Beiler, senior partner of a Washington, DC political research firm, has expressed similar concerns. Writing in *Campaigns & Elections*, Beiler said that, while "to date, a court has yet to rule that an election was 'stolen' by a computer," concerns were nevertheless growing, especially in the case of close elections.[18] Similar concerns have also been addressed in a series of 1989 *Los Angeles Times* articles.[19] All these authors cite opinions by experts that range from a strong probability that significant computerized voting fraud will never happen to the virtual certainty that it will occur.

Computerized voting comes in three basic forms—punch cards counted by computer, a *mark-sense* system where the ballot is written but the results are counted by a computerized scanner, and a *direct-recording electronic* system (DRE), where everything is done electronically. Altogether, the computerized systems are now used by nearly two-thirds of all U. S. voters, and this is expected to be about 100% by the mid-1990s.[20] Punch cards are favored by some, because they can be hand counted if the results are questionable. However, the punched out pieces of card stock produce "hanging chad" which frequently produces an inaccurate count and "makes it all but impossible to get the same result twice." Although the DRE is efficient and eliminates the paper and printing costs that make elections so expensive, it leaves no independent "audit trail" to be checked if the results are challenged.[21] According to Beiler, "Each system has its particular advantages, but they share certain vulnerabilities."[22] He quotes Robert Naegele, a consultant to the Federal Election Commission and to New York and California, as saying:[23]

> They all use programs, and programs are open to tinkering—particularly anything that can run on a personal computer.

The *New Yorker* article described a wide variety of ways by which a single person could shift votes electronically. As one example, Michael Shamos, Pennsylvania's voting systems examiner was cited as having given that state's Bureau of Elections a scenario in which a person could easily commit computerized voting fraud. That individual could take a concealed punch card into the voting booth which, when electronically read, would cause the tabulating computer to reset its counters to the desired values. The card, Shamos said, could be put into the envelope meant for the secret ballot, dropped into the ballot box, and delivered to the computer without arousing the suspicions of election officials. The computer would then simply follow the card's instructions to change the vote total for the desired candidate.[24] Computerized fraud could also be conducted from a remote time and place by inserting a programmed time bomb.[25]

Howard Strauss, associate director of Princeton University's Computer Center, was asked by the *New Yorker* what types of people might tamper with computerized voting, and Strauss pointed to:[26]

> election-system venders and their programmers and consultants, election-system operators, the Federal Election Commission, technical mavens of all kinds, and election officials and workers.

He added that any of these people might be induced to fix computers for others, such as political candidates, various special interests, or agents of foreign governments.

In a close race, not too many figures would need to be shifted to alter the results of an entire election. For instance, in the 1988 presidential election, George Bush got 426 electoral votes while Michael Dukakis got only 112. But in nine states, the count was so close that "as few as 552,000

votes switched from Bush to Dukakis could have reversed the outcome."[27]
Said one writer of Dukakis:[28]

> He lost five big chunks by just 2 percent of the vote in each state. Switch just
> one voter in 50, and 117 electoral votes shift from Bush to Dukakis.

Or, in the total election, "persuade one voter in 20 to go the other way—
and the outcome is reversed."[29]

Beiler pointed to strange happenings in the November 1988 Senate
election in Florida, in which Votomatic punched cards were used, and
where the Republican candidate won over the Democratic candidate by .8
percent or 33,000 votes. In four large counties where Democratic margins
were usually widest, more than 200,000 people who voted for the president
simply failed to vote for the senate. This was a much higher incidence
than had occurred in this locale in previous elections, and much higher
than that found where the same system was used elsewhere. Later
analyses by *Campaigns & Elections* and by *The Miami News*, Beiler says,
"suggests that these 'missing' votes were overwhelmingly Democratic."[30]
Whether this dropoff in votes just happened, or was accidentally caused
by poor ballot design or some other problem, or whether it was due to
tampering was in question.[31]

Ignorance by election officials at the precinct and other levels concerning computers, what can be done with them by a determined person,
and how to spot such intrusions, has been cited as one of the prime
problems. Not enough money is allocated or training given to election
officials for them to be able to understand the technology well enough to
"conduct elections correctly in the computer age," a George Washington
University professor told the *Los Angeles Times*, adding that such
problems are solvable.[32]

The concerns related to computerized voting in the U.S. are under
active examination, but such problems may just be beginning. Systems in
which voting will eventually take place by personal computer, by phone,
or by cable TV are already envisioned. These raise even greater problems
of data interception and of destruction of the secret ballot by supplying
means to identify the voter.[33] While those who handle computerized
elections can be trained to be more knowledgeable about computer
security, they may be more than matched by determined computer users
who every day become increasingly sophisticated.

These two examples of political uses of personal computers point to
the problem posed by the advent of all new personal media: They can be
extremely useful tools for enhancing freedom, but they can also open a
whole range of unanticipated dangers.

NOTES

1. The best description of PC/fax networks was Shirley Christian, "Pinochet Foes Guard Against Fraud," *The New York Times*, September 13, 1988, p. A-3, and Shirley Christian, personal communication. Other computer/fax references are: Shirley Christian, "Polls are Crowded as Chileans Decide Future of Pinochet," *The New York Times*, October 6, 1988, p. 1; James F. Smith, "Amid Tension and Rumors of Violence, Chileans Vote Today on Pinochet," *Los Angeles Times*, October 5, 1988, p. 7; James F. Smith and William R. Long, "Vote Due on Pinochet's Future," *Los Angeles Times*, June 18, 1988, pt. 1, p. 1; Richard Waddington, "Opposition Struggles to Overcome Chileans Distrust at Poll," *Reuters*, September 25, 1988 (Nexis); Carla Anne Robbins, "Saying No to Pinochet Power," *U.S. News & World Report*, October 17, 1988, pp. 48-49; Barbara Gamarekian, "How U.S. Political Pros Get Out the Vote in Chile," *The New York Times*, November 18, 1988, p. B-6; *Reuters*, October 5, 1988; and Annie Burns, "Political Postcards. Chile," *Campaigns & Elections*, May/June 1989, p. 27. (Series begins p. 22.) Among the many articles concerned with the various aspects of the plebiscite were: Harry Anderson with Joseph Contreras, "The Verdict of the People," *Newsweek*, October 17, 1988, pp. 38-39; Eugene Robinson, "Pinochet Risks Rejection in Plebiscite He Designed," *The Washington Post*, October 5, 1988, p. 1, and "Pinochet Accepts His Defeat," *The Washington Post*, October 7, 1988, p. 1; Shirley Christian, "Pinochet Foes, Bolstered by Polls, Hope to Oust Him in Vote Today," *The New York Times*, October 5, 1988, p. A-1, "Chileans Vote; 2 Sides Clash on the Returns," *The New York Times*, October 6, 1988, p. A-15, "Regime of Pinochet Accepts Defeat in Chile's Plebiscite; Foes Urging Reconciliation," *The New York Times*, October 7, 1988, p. A-1, and "In Chile, Feud Mars Passage to Elections," *The New York Times*, January 30, 1989, p. A-1; Tim Frasca, "High Stakes in Chile: Return to Democratic Heritage?" *The Christian Science Monitor*, October 5, 1988, p. 1; Daniel Drosdoff, *United Press International*, Dateline Santiago, October 5, 1988, p.m. cycle (Nexis); Roger Cohen, "Early Results in Chile Suggest Opposition Win," *The Wall Street Journal*, October 6, 1988, p. A-15, and "Close Vote on Chile's President Is Seen, Raising the Specter of Increased Strife," *The Wall Street Journal*, October 5, 1988, p. A-29; and Pamela Constable, "Chile Votes; 2 Sides Claim Lead," *The Boston Globe*, October 6, 1988, p. 1.
2. Through open support, using funds mainly supplied by the congressionally mandated National Endowment for Democracy, the U.S. aided the opposition with various types of political consultants and provided financing to help buy computers, fund the Committee for Free Elections, fund poll-taking groups, and fund parts of the get-out-the-vote effort. See: *Reuters*, October 5, 1988; Shirley Christian, "Pinochet Foes, Bolstered by Polls, Hope to Oust Him in Vote Today," *The New York Times*, October 5, 1988, p. A-1; John Greenwald and Laura Lopez, "Chile, Fall of the Patriarch," *Time*, October 17, 1988, p. 37, and box, "How Much Did the U.S. Help?" p. 37; Pamela Constable, "Pinochet Loyalists Rethinking Tactics. Chilean Opposition's Upbeat TV Ads Helped Carry 'No' Vote, Analysts Say," *The Boston Globe*, October 24, 1988, p. 4; Barbara Gamarekian, "How U.S. Political Pros Get Out the Vote in Chile," *The New York Times*, November 18, 1988, p. B-6; and Peter Hakim and Peter D. Bell, "U.S. Policy Toward Chile—A Success," *The Christian Science Monitor*, November 14, 1988, p. 18.
3. On the day of the vote, several hundred foreign observers reinforced the "No" observers. (Carla Anne Robbins, "Saying No to Pinochet Power," *U.S. News & World Report*, October 17, 1988, p. 49. Article begins p. 48.)
4. Shirley Christian, "Pinochet Foes Guard Against Fraud," *The New York Times*, September 13, 1988, p. A-3; Shirley Christian, "Polls Are Crowded As Chileans Decide Future of Pinochet," *The New York Times*, October 6, 1988, p. A-1; and James F. Smith,

"Amid Tension and Rumors of Violence, Chileans Vote Today on Pinochet," *Los Angeles Times*, October 5, 1988, p. 7.

5. Shirley Christian, "Pinochet Foes Guard Against Fraud," *The New York Times*, September 13, 1988, p. A-3. See also: Eugene Robinson, "Pinochet Risks Rejection in Plebiscite He Designed," *The Washington Post*, October 5, 1988, p. 1, and Shirley Christian, "Polls Are Crowded as Chileans Decide Future of Pinochet," *The New York Times*, October 6, 1988, p. A-1.

6. Annie Burns, "Political Postcards. Chile," *Campaigns & Elections*, May/June, 1989, p. 27. (Series begins p. 22.)

7. Shirley Christian, "Pinochet Foes Guard Against Fraud," *The New York Times*, September 13, 1988, p. A-3.

8. Shirley Christian, "Pinochet Foes, Bolstered by Polls, Hope to Oust Him in Vote Today," *The New York Times*, October 5, 1988, p. 1. See also: Roger Cohen, "Close Vote on Chile's President is Seen, Raising the Specter of Increased Strife," *The Wall Street Journal*, October 5, 1988, p. A-29.

9. *Reuters*, October 5, 1988 (NEXIS); Roger Cohen, "Early Results In Chile Suggest Opposition Win," *The Wall Street Journal*, October 6, 1988, p. A-15.

10. Pamela Constable, "Chile Votes; 2 Sides Claim Lead," *The Boston Globe*, October 6, 1988, p. 1. See also: Roger Cohen, "Early Results in Chile Suggest Opposition Win," *The Wall Street Journal*, October 6, 1988, p. A-15; and Shirley Christian, "Chileans Vote; 2 Sides Clash on the Returns," *The New York Times*, October 6, 1988, p. A-1.

11. Shirley Christian, "Regime of Pinochet Accepts Defeat in Chile's Plebiscite; Foes Urging Reconciliation," *The New York Times*, October 7, 1988, p. A-1.

12. Shirley Christian, "Strangely, Chile Race Seems Normal," *The New York Times*, October 10, 1989, p. A-3.

13. See, for instance, Shirley Christian, "A Moderate Leads Chile. Patricio Aylwin," *The New York Times*, December 16, 1989, p. A-5.

14. Multiple articles regarding the Mexican election appeared in *The New York Times*, for instance, between July 6-15, 1988. And see specific references in this section.

15. Larry Rohter, "Opposition Leader Claiming Victory in Mexico. Calls For Protests," *The New York Times*, July 10, 1988, p. A-1. See also: Larry Rohter, "Relief for Salinas. Buying Time in Mexico," *The New York Times*, October 23, 1988, p. E-5.

16. Alejandro Gil-Recasens, "Political Postcards. Mexico," *Campaigns & Elections*, May/June 1989, pp. 26-27. (Series begins p. 22.)

17. Ronnie Dugger, "Annals of Democracy. Counting Votes," *The New Yorker*, November 7, 1988, p. 40. (Article pp. 40ff.) See also: "Computerized-Voting Hazards," *The Boston Globe*, Editorial, November 12, 1988, p. 22, and a reply to this editorial by Michael J. Connolly, Secretary of State for Massachusetts, "Elections Clear of Computer-voting Fraud," Letter to the Editor, *The Boston Globe*, November 27, 1988, p. A-26.

18. David Beiler, "A Short in the Electronic Ballot Box. Concern Rises Over Fraud in Computerized Voting," *Campaigns & Elections*, July/August 1989, p. 39. (Article pp. 39-42.)

19. William Trombley, "Computers: Bugs in the Ballot Box. Glitches, Security Gaps," *Los Angeles Times*, Section 1, p. 1; "Accurate Vote Tally With Computers Can be Elusive. Programming Errors Often Blamed," *Los Angeles Times*, July 3, 1989, Section 1, p. 1; "State Counts on 1% Sample to Detect Fraud," *Los Angeles Times*, July 3, 1989, Section 1, p. 3; "Electronic Elections Seen As An Invitation to Fraud. Level of Protection Debated," *Los Angeles Times*, July 4, 1989, Section 1, p. 1; and "Paper Ballots' Days May be Numbered. Rapidly Changing Technology," *Los Angeles Times*, July 4, 1989, Section 1, p. 28.

20. David Beiler, "A Short in The Ballot Box," *Campaigns & Elections*, July/August, 1989,

pp. 39; Ronnie Dugger, "Annals of Democracy," *The New Yorker*, November 7, 1988, p. 40; Calvin Sims, "Computerizing the Voting Booth," *The New York Times*, November 2, 1988, p. D-8; and "Voters Could Get Picture From Computerized Booth," *USA Today*, November 3, 1988, p. 8-B.

21. William Trombley, "Paper Ballots' Days May Be Numbered," *Los Angeles Times*, July 4, 1989, Section 1, p. 28.
22. David Beiler, "A Short In The Ballot Box," *Campaigns & Elections*, July/August 1989, p. 39.
23. Ibid., pp. 39-40.
24. Ronnie Dugger, "Annals of Democracy," *The New Yorker*, November 7, 1988, p. 59.
25. William Trombley, "Electronic Elections Seen As An Invitation to Fraud," *Los Angeles Times*, July 4, 1989, Section 1, p. 1.
26. Ronnie Dugger, "Annals of Democracy," *The New Yorker*, November 7, 1988, p. 103.
27. "Just How Close?" *The Boston Globe*, Editorial, November 14, 1988, p. 18.
28. David Nyhan, "One Voter in 20 Made the Difference for the Republican Ticket," *The Boston Globe*, November 10, 1988, p. 15.
29. Ibid.
30. David Beiler, "Shortfall in the Sunshine State. Some Point to Computer Problems in the 1988 Florida Senate Outcome," *Campaigns & Elections*, July/August 1989, p. 40. (Article pp. 40-41.) See also: William Trombley, "Accurate Vote Tally With Computers Can Be Elusive. Programming Errors Often Blamed," *Los Angeles Times*, July 3, 1989, Section 1, p. 1.
31. This incident is described, and a sample ballot shown, in William Trombley, "Accurate Vote Tally With Computers Can Be Elusive," *Los Angeles Times*, July 3, 1989, Section 1, pp. 1, 3, 22.
32. William Trombley, "Electronic Elections Seen As An Invitation to Fraud," *Los Angeles Times*, July 4, 1989, Section 1, p. 1.
33. William Trombley, "Paper Ballots' Days May Be Numbered," *Los Angeles Times*, July 4, 1989, Section 1, p. 28.

chapter 8

THE USE OF FACSIMILE BY PANAMANIAN DISSIDENTS AND IN OTHER POLITICAL SITUATIONS

As has been seen, audiocassettes, the direct-dial phone, and dry copiers helped topple the Shah of Iran in 1978-79, and smuggled videocassettes assisted Corazon Aquino in unseating the late Ferdinand Marcos in 1983-84. Audiocassettes, videocassettes, satellite dishes and cross-border TV and radio can be presumed to have played an important role in destabilizing the communist governments of the USSR and Eastern Europe. And personal computers have been put to a wide number of political uses. In the second half of the 1980s, facsimile followed in the footsteps of these earlier electronic personal media, and in 1987-88, was used as part of a concerted attempt to unseat Panama's General Manuel Antonio Noriega. When, in mid-1987, Noriega cut off Panamanian citizens' access to news, various groups of Panamanians living in exile kept them informed of what was happening by faxing large quantities of information into the country. Noriega did not succumb to this attack, remaining in power until physically removed by the U.S. Government after a December 1989 military invasion. Nevertheless, this incident confirms that another simple, quick, easy, and economically feasible way to barrage targets with politically explosive materials across national boundaries had been established two years prior to the widely publicized use of fax during the 1989 Chinese pro-democracy movement (Chapter 12). This was a brand new way to pipe large amounts of banned information into a country. Only a short time before—during the 1983-84 Philippine revolution, for example—news clips could only be mailed in, or bodily smuggled past Customs.[1]

The use of facsimile was especially practical in the particular instance of Panama, because large numbers of modern fax machines were in place to support that country's international service economy, and many of those machines were under the control of anti-Noriega sympathizers. With the rapid growth of fax use globally in the second half of the 1980s, and the increase in electronic services, machines are now available in substantial numbers in a wide variety of countries. Just a few examples beyond that of Panama will be discussed in this chapter, but they involve incidents in such diverse places as Japan, Israel, Great Britain, South Africa, Brazil, the Persian Gulf area, the United States, and the Soviet Union.

Facsimile combines an ease of use, low cost, flexibility, variety, and speed of transmission that surpasses such capabilities of most personal media. Thus far, facsimile lacks the immediacy of audio's spoken voice and video's spoken-voice-plus-moving-picture, although that, too, is in the future.[2] But fax delivers ready-to-distribute information—exact copies of still pictures, charts, drawings, text, newsletters, and anything else that is photocopyable—instantaneously, and at the cost of a prorated phone call. Fax fits perfectly with global time differences, turning those differences to an advantage. For example, faxed inquiries sent from the U.S. in the evening to Europe or Asia generate answers during what is already the working day there, and these answers are on U.S. desks the next morning. Questions from Europe or Asia are similarly addressed during the U.S. working day, with answering faxes returned that evening.

Facsimile is basically a combined phone line and copying machine, with a scanner reading the images on a page and translating them into digital data, with a modem being used for the phone transmission, as is the case with ordinary computer transmission. On receipt, the process is reversed, and the exact image of the original document is printed.

Facsimile is an old technology, in use by the mass media and some business and government offices for a long time, but until recently too cumbersome and expensive for the general user. Invented in 1842 by a Scotch clock maker, it was then very crude and its transmission limited. The Germans updated facsimile in the 1920s, and the Americans again in the 1940s, so that it could transmit newspaper pictures and weather maps for long distances. The newest, much improved, and portable fax machines are mainly Japanese. Used extensively in Japan for some time, the popularity of fax in the U.S., for instance, began only in 1986 and 1987, when prices dropped radically.[3]

As late as 1988, there were only about 1.8 million fax machines in the U.S., but by 1992, sales are expected to reach 2.7 million annually.[4] This compares to about 50 million PCs in use in the U.S. by the late 1980s, so it is obvious that the fax revolution is just beginning.[5]

DELIVERING BANNED INFORMATION INTO PANAMA[6]

During the late 1980s, Panama's opposition to the continued leadership of General Manuel Antonio Noriega was the Civic Crusade, a coalition of more than 100 civic groups. Largely an upper middle-class movement, its members were mainly businessmen and professionals. The Civic Crusade made concerted use of both the new personal electronic media and the mass media. Its members were often active lobbyists in the U.S., promoting their cause on U.S. television.[7]

After General Noriega closed down independent radio stations and newspapers in Panama in mid-Summer 1987, Centro Panameno de Noticias (CPN)—the Panamanian News Center—was formed and became one of the most active groups of Panamanian exiles to transmit banned information into that country. Based in Washington, DC, and funded, housed, and staffed by the Civic Crusade, CPN was run by exiled Panamanian businessmen, lawyers and journalists, aided by other exiles and volunteer students.

The CPN effort was especially active during the late summer and fall of 1987. During this period, CPN's staff clipped relevant articles from several major U.S. newspapers daily, then used Apple computers to translate them into Spanish and to lay them out again electronically. With added logos and appropriate credits to honor copyrights, the uncensored clippings, along with some original articles, were then faxed to multiple fax machines in businesses and corporations, mainly in Panama City. Copies were then sent on to cities around the country through a widespread intra-Panamanian fax network. Wherever they were sent, sympathetic recipients photocopied the faxes to produce massive stacks of sheets for street corner distribution. Some radio stations in Colombia and Costa Rica also picked up CPN material and beamed it into Panama, and CPN prepared some special broadcast programs for these stations.

Besides the Panamanian News Center, other Panamanian groups in the U.S., especially in Miami, transmitted articles by exiled Panamanian journalists and small, independently produced, underground newspapers into Panama. Dr. Miguel Antonio Bernal produced a biweekly faxed edition of his underground newspaper, *Alternativa*, which enjoyed a massive circulation. Unaltered hot-off-the-press clippings from newspapers in such countries as Switzerland, Spain, Great Britain, and several Latin American countries were also faxed into Panama by dissidents at many locations.

In Fall 1987, CPN alone reputedly sent about 50 sheets of this desktop published information into Panama daily. Circulation figures are cloudy, since, for security purposes, each distribution center deliberately remained ignorant of the activity of others. But at its highest, it has been estimated that up to 30,000 sheets of fresh news directed to an audience of perhaps 50,000 were passed out daily just in the capital, Panama City. Panamanian-based fax users were also able to supply those in exile with up-to-the-minute news on the local situation. And facsimile was used during this period to send messages from the Panamanian underground to the mass media. In April 1988, for instance, the Movement for National Unity, which claimed to be made up of Panamanian officers and enlisted men, sent *Reuters* a faxed message that urged Noriega's resignation.[8]

Fax messages are susceptible to interception and tracing, but, perhaps for economic reasons, the Noriega government left this transmission alone, interrupting the activity only at the point of street distribution. Roberto Eisenmann, exiled Editor of Panama's *La Prensa* and a coordinator of the facsimile/computer effort, has said that the interests of the Panamanian government would not have been served by disrupting international communications, since this would have also disrupted the economy.[9] Simple novelty also no doubt played a role, as it has with other new personal media in other political situations. Authorities were most probably caught off guard and were thus unprepared to deal with unexpected high-tech intrusions.

Despite this information barrage, Noriega's opposition was unsuccessful in unseating him. One reason is that the effort remained strongest with the upper middle class, and unlike the Iranian or Philippine examples that have been shown, never fully engaged the support of the Panamanian people.

OTHER POLITICAL USES OF FACSIMILE

Beyond these uses of facsimile in Panama, those previously described for the Chile plebiscite, and others to be presented concerning the Chinese pro-democracy movement, a number of instances of political uses of facsimile have already surfaced:

...In May 1988, Japanese police found a fax machine in the Tokyo apartment of an alleged Red Army terrorist. The apprehended owner of the fax was said to be posing as an international trader. Records of the fax transmissions showed frequent contacts with people in Milan, Brussels, and Amsterdam, cities "where Red Army members are believed to be active." Police were reported to believe that the man traveled to make contacts with other terrorists and that he was using the fax machine, among other things, to get his orders.[10]

...The Palestinians involved in the Intifada uprising in the Israeli-occupied territories have directed their activities via numbered leaflets. But these leaflets and other instructions have also been distributed by fax to the Intifada's far-flung leadership. In early September 1989, *The Economist* reported that, in the Gaza Strip, access to fax machines might be denied to Palestinians in an attempt to keep leaflets and instructions regarding Intifada activities from being sent to Palestinian Liberation Organization leaders abroad.[11] The article commented, however, that such denial "looks pretty easy to circumvent," since earlier attempts to stop international phone calls from the Gaza Strip had resulted in calls simply being made from Israeli East Jerusalem.[12]

...During a Fall 1988 mail strike in Great Britain, *The Times* of London installed a fax machine to receive letters to the editor, and many companies resorted to fax to get mail around Europe.[13] Fax and other personal media have also served as a strike-breaking mechanism in Britain. Faxing from machines at home was used during the 1989 British rail strike, when it was often impossible to get to work, such fax machines being supplemented by a host of rented mobile phones and radio pagers.[14]

...In early 1989, upwards of 50 U.S. radio talk show hosts banded together to urge the public to defeat a proposed Congressional pay raise, using phone lines and fax machines to coordinate their activities. They also made then House of Representatives Speaker Jim Wright's fax number available to the public so his machine could be flooded with anti-pay raise messages.[15]

...After a Supreme Court decision in July 1989 threatened to undermine American women's right to have legal abortions, Pro-Choice advocates used faxed news releases, along with PCs and phones, to mobilize supporters.[16]

...In the jungles of the Amazon, Indian leaders, aided by human rights and environmental interest groups, have used fax machines, two-way radios, and home made videos in their efforts to stall Brazilian hydroelectric projects.[17]

...In early 1990, Nelson Mandela, imprisoned for 28 years for his political activities in South Africa, used a fax machine to negotiate his release from jail, as well as to assist in planning "the outlines of what could be the future of South Africa."[18] A South African political satirist was quoted by *The New York Times* as quipping at a dinner theater show, "Who would have thought...that a faceless man with a fax machine could run the country from a prison?"[19] Mandela was released from jail in Spring 1990 and became an active political force internationally.

...During the military standoff in the Persian Gulf after Iraq annexed Kuwait in August 1990, a two-page fax giving suggestions for how to behave during a chemical warfare attack appeared anonymously at embassies and businesses in countries of the Gulf area. The *Financial Times*, calling the fax "a bizarre form of psychological warfare," said it was not known whether it represented "Iraqi intimidation" or "Saudi-American propaganda," or was "just some do-gooder trying to save lives."[20] And by September 1990, AT&T was arranging a fax transmission service to connect families back in the U.S. with American service men and women in the Saudi Arabian desert.[21]

...As *The New York Times* has pointed out, "The famous 'hotline' between the White House and the Kremlin" is not a phone but a fax machine.[22] In March 1989, Alpha Graphics Printshops of the Future set up a reproduction center in Moscow. This included facilities for commercial U.S./Soviet fax transmissions, which are replacing the up to four weeks mail delivery. Alpha Graphics's owner remarked that, aside from the lack of phone lines, there was no delay in sending documents, "since there is no censorship or customs delays of electronic messages."[23] Virtually all of the business of Americans in countries of Eastern Europe is being conducted via fax machine.[24]

JUNK FAX AND THE FIRST AMENDMENT

Because fax machines are kept on all the time to receive desired communications, they also attract the unwanted—junk fax. Ads that used to be mailed at the sender's expense now arrive by phone/fax, using the recipient's expensive fax paper and tying up the sending and receiving lines. By 1989, several states had moved to restrict junk fax, and others and the U.S. Congress were making noises about doing so.[25] Elliot Segal, vice president for marketing of Mr. Fax, the pioneering company for faxed ads for fax paper, is said to have "faxed himself in the foot" when he organized the National Fax Users Committee to urge Connecticut's governor to veto that state's anti-junk-fax legislation. The governor became convinced that an anti-junk-fax law was important when the group flooded his fax machine with veto requests and held up the line while he was waiting for a real flood disaster report.[26]

While some have hailed anti-junk-fax legislation as progress, others have attacked such restrictions as a violation of free speech protected by the First Amendment and as a reactionary move by the establishment against new personal media freedoms. This objection may be met by New York's legislation, which limits unsolicited faxes to evening hour transmission and a length of five pages, rather than simply banning them.[27]

LEGAL USES AND PRIVACY QUESTIONS

Because fax, like other new technologies, has created possibilities that never existed before, a new set of legal problems is also appearing. A judge in New York's civil court ruled in November 1988 that fax could be used to serve legal papers "such as court orders," although not summonses. Previously only the U.S. mail or "in-person delivery" has been acceptable for such service. The ruling caused controversy in legal circles, with some attorneys questioning facsimile's reliability.[28]

Fax transmission may endanger individual privacy rights, because fax messages, especially when sent to wrong numbers, can be read by many, and sometimes inappropriate, people. Ontario, Canada's Information and Privacy Commission is among those responding to this problem, in June 1989 issuing a set of "Guidelines on Facsimile Transmission Security."[29]

NEW USES OF FACSIMILE FOR INFORMATION DISTRIBUTION

The Wall Street Journal, which publishes several editions in various places in the U.S. and other countries, has been transmitting its mocked up pages by facsimile and satellite to remote printing sites for several years.[30] The *Financial Times,* which has been faxing its paper from London for printing in Frankfurt since 1979, has also combined sophisticated Pagefax with satellite transmission for printings in West Germany, France, the U.S., and Japan.[31] The same sort of thing is going on with other newspapers. But with the rapid spread of upgraded and downsized fax machines, alternatives to the regular press are also springing into being. News releases by fax are easy, quick, and inexpensive compared to mailings. Via a PC and fax board, Digital Publications of Norcross, Georgia, for example, sends news releases to some 5,000 "newspapers, broadcast stations, trade magazines and writers,"[32] keeping these releases timely by chopping the several days required for mail delivery. The computer waits until after 11 p.m., when transmission can be had for very little.[33]

In a first of its kind, the *Hartford Courant,* a Times Mirror Company newspaper, began publishing *Faxpaper* in April 1989. This single-paged newsletter released the next morning's news at 5 p.m. the day before, thus making it competitive with television. MCI Communications Corporation, which provides "broadcast" delivery of multiple faxes for many customers, sends *Faxpaper* to about 2,000 subscribers.[34] Most companies that subscribe are said to make photocopies for their executives, many of whom can't get home in time for the evening TV news. Within a couple of months after *Faxpaper* was launched, the Gannett Company had also begun experimenting with a similar fax-delivered paper which would provide day-before summaries of *USA Today* stories.[35] In January 1990, *The New York Times* began sending a 6- to 8-page faxed synopsis of the next day's news to corporate subscribers and travelers in Tokyo. Faxed from New York at 10 p.m., the news is immediately available in Tokyo, where, with a 13-hour time difference, it is already the next day, mid-morning.[36]

Fax has lent itself to even more specialized information services. For instance, early every weekday morning, Telescope Networks, Inc. of New York faxes its subscribers a publication called *Tele-Scope Fax Alert*. This newsletter contains short summaries of articles dealing with telecommunications issues from several news sources. Full transcripts can then be ordered by fax, using a faxed form. Transcripts are also sent by fax, usually with same day service.[37]

FAX MACHINES AND THE BREAKDOWN OF ORGANIZATIONAL COHERENCE

Like the phone and the personal computer, the fax machine is becoming so ubiquitous that it is destroying the previous glue of organizations. In governmental organizations and the private sector alike, the traditional centralized control over communications that institutions have used to maintain consistent policy lines is being eliminated by fax machines.[38] Faxed copies are entering organizations from so many sources through so many recipients that questions are being raised of how to tell genuine documents from faked ones. The United Nations, for instance, is studying such questions as "How do organizations…control or document the use of fax?" and "How do they distinguish between what's official communication and what's not?"[39] The erosion that can result from such lack of communications control could eventually lead to the formation of very different types of organizations. These are the same types of forces being exerted by the many new media that are removing information controls from the hands of whole governments and turning them over to individuals.

NOTES

1. Gladys D. Ganley and Oswald H. Ganley, *Global Political Fallout. The VCR's First Decade*, Ablex Publishing Corporation, Norwood NJ, 1987, p. 95. Corazon Aquino's husband, Benigno, was assassinated in August 1983, and Corazon Aquino became

President of the Philippines in February 1986. For other uses of information technologies in the Philippines during this revolutionary period, see the above reference, pp. 94-98, 114-115, 131.

2. "New Fax Machines Utilize TV Signals," *The Japan Times*, May 30, 1989, p. 12.

3. Some machines can send multipaged documents and, via memory chips, can store phone numbers and do automatic and delayed dialing. With some machines, copies can be "broadcast" to multiple fax addresses at a single sitting. Truly streamlined fax models send pages in 3 seconds and reproduce art work with great clarity, but require high-speed digital networks for transmission. While the most popular fax machines so far are stand alone models, fax can also be sent in conjunction with a PC, using a fax board. Faxes can be used with mobile phones from cars, and are expected to soon be generally on airplanes. Ready to come onstage are hybrid computer/fax machines, which will permit editing on pressure sensitive screens while the sender and receiver stay online. Models are also expected that will include audiovisuals and transmit by TV signals rather than over phone lines. Upgraded, downsized, and less expensive faxes have recently become available in public places the world over—in hotels, airports, hospitals, and copying centers—and in large and small businesses and home offices. (Daniel B. Wood, "Is There a Phone Fax in Your Future?" *The Christian Science Monitor*, January 20, 1989, p. 13; Donald J. Ryan, "How Facsimile Works," (box), *Data Communications*, April 1987, p. 112; Les Honig, "Know the Fax," *USAir*, February 1989, pp. 88-92; Calvin Sims, "Coast to Coast in 20 Seconds: Fax Machines Alter Business," *The New York Times*, May 6, 1988, p. A-1; Susan M. Gelfond, "It's a Fax, Fax, Fax, Fax World," *Business Week*, March 21, 1988, p. 136; "Starsignal's Color Fax," *The New York Times*, February 2, 1989, p. D-13; Peter H. Lewis, "If You Really Want a Fax Board, Ask About...," *The New York Times*, February 28, 1989, p. C-5; Malcolm Brown, "Always at the End of a Phone," *The Times* (of London), March 22, 1988, p. 20; "Phones and Faxes on Planes by 1991," *The Boston Globe*, June 11, 1989, p. A-8; George F. Will, "The Basin Runneth Over," *Newsweek*, January 30, 1989, p. 80; Christopher O'Malley, "Where PC-Fax Pays Off," *Personal Computing*, June 1989, pp. 91-98; James P. Miller, "Device Shows Changes As They are Made in Fax," *The Wall Street Journal*, June 5, 1989, p. B-1; "New Fax Machines Utilize TV Signals," *The Japan Times*, May 30, 1989, p. 12; Georgia Dullea, "For That Special Valentine, It May be Love at First Fax," *The New York Times*, February 14, 1989, p. 1; Beth Ann Krier, "Fax Fever; From Business Tool to Homework Aid to Monkey Business, the Machine's Taken Over," *Los Angeles Times*, January 25, 1989, Section 5, p. 1; Keita Fukuyama, "Innovations Give Fax Machines Wider Roles," *Nikkei*, January 21, 1989, p. 24; Ronald Rosenberg, "Fax: Faster Than a Speeding Fed Ex Truck," *The Boston Globe*, June 12, 1988, p. A-1; David Blum, "Fax Mania. Read It and Weep," *New York*, November 21, 1988, pp. 38-44 and cover.)

4. "Office Machine Association Expects 50% Jump in US Fax Sales," *AdAge*, September 14, 1989, p. S14. (From *Tele/Scope Fax Alert*, September 15, 1989, p. 2.)

5. Fax use is quickly pushing ahead of Telex and cutting into Federal Express delivery. In some cases, it is also gaining on voice phone calls. For instance, 53% of all calls between Hong Kong and the U.S. in 1986 were faxes. Between 1986 and 1989, fax machines in Hong Kong quadrupled, reaching 70,000. The upsurge of U.S. trade with countries of the Pacific during the last few years, with its communications barriers of time zones, languages, and alphabets, accounts for much of this popularity. See: Michael Westlake, "Facsimile. Quiet Revolution That Makes Sense," *Far Eastern Economic Review*, February 19, 1987, p. 57; Dean Foust with Resa W. King, "Why Federal Express Has Overnight Anxiety," *Business Week*, November 9, 1987, pp. 62, 66; Dori Jones Yang, "A Fast Ride on Hong Kong's High-Tech Wave," *Business Week*, May 22, 1989, p. 111; and Jolie Solomon, "Business Communication in the Fax Age. Machines Foster Speed, Clarity—And Impatience," *The Wall Street Journal*, October 27, 1988, p. B-1.

6. Reports on activities of the Panamanian News Center and others faxing into Panama are by Susan Benesch, "Getting the Fax Into Panama," *Columbia Journalism Review*, January/February 1988, pp. 6, 8; Linda Feldmann, "Noriega Opposition-in-exile Becomes Lobbying Force in the U.S.," *The Christian Science Monitor*, March 7, 1988, pp. 3-4; "Panamanians Use Technology to Balk Censor," *The New York Times*, February 14, 1988, p. 13; Don Steinberg, "Fax Network Keeps Panama Informed Despite Censorship: Connectivity," *Information Access Company*, Ziff-Davis Publishing Co., August 25, 1987, Volume 4, p. C-1, (NEXIS); and "How An Underground Paper Surfaced," Elizabeth Brannan Jaen, Letter to the Editor, *The New York Times*, November 20, 1990, p. A-20.

7. Douglas Tweedale, "Noriega Faced With High-Tech Opposition," *United Press International*, March 3, 1988 (NEXIS). The elevated positions that provided Noriega's opposition with access to communications riches also drew criticism. Because opposition members enjoyed a high lifestyle, Noriega himself charged them with being simply a group of unhappy elites. The U.S. press at times described Panama's well-to-do derisively. *The Washington Post* portrayed them as showing solidarity with the resistance by waving white hankies from air conditioned cars and yacht decks, and by having their maids prepare tape recordings of clanging pots and pans (a symbol of lower-class protest) to be played on expensive stereo speakers from upper-class balconies. (William Branigin, "Panama Portesters Take Work Break; Leaders Skip Rally for Trade Fair," *The Washington Post*, March 13, 1988, p. A-29. See also: Marjorie Williams, "The Panama File. A D.C. Attorney's 'Revolution By Litigation,'" *The Washington Post*, March 22, 1988 p. D-1.)

8. Angus MacSwan, Dateline: Panama City. *Reuters*, April 21, 1988. (NEXIS).

9. Don Steinberg, "Fax Network Keeps Panama Informed Despite Censorship; Connectivity," *Information Access Company*, Ziff-Davis Publishing Co., August 25, 1987, Volume 4, p. C-1 (NEXIS). For discussions of Panama's service economy, see, for instance, James LeMoyne, "Consensus Emerges in Panama: Noriega Has Won," *The New York Times*, May 23, 1988, p. A-3.

10. "Terrorists May Have Used Fax to Communicate," *Mainichi Daily News*, Tokyo, May 16, 1988, p. B-12.

11. "Israel and the Palestinians. Exhaustion," *The Economist*, September 2, 1989, p. 40.

12. Ibid.

13. Craig R. Whitney, "In a Flash, Britons Outwit Mail Strike," *The New York Times*, September 9, 1988, p. A-3.

14. Della Bradshaw, "How to Strike a Blow for the IT Revolution," *Financial Times*, July 11, 1989, p. 16. The mail strike had stimulated a great fax buying spree, and by 1989, about 15% of UK businesses had acquired the machines. In 1984, there were only 10,000 fax machines sold in the UK, while by 1989, this was expected to grow to more than a quarter of a million. See: Terry Dodsworth, "Facsimile Machine Market Slows After Four Boom Years," *Financial Times*, July 4, 1989, p. 8.

15. E. J. Dionne, Jr., "Waves on Airwaves: Power to the People?" *The New York Times*, February 15, 1989, p. A-20. The concept of fax is familiar to talk show hosts and disk jockeys, who routinely use it to receive information and requests from listeners. (Les Honig, "Know the Fax," *USAIR*, February 1989, pp. 88ff., and Beth Ann Krier, "Fax Fever; From Business Tool To Homework Aid to Monkey Business, The Machine's Taken Over," *Los Angeles Times*, January 25, 1989, Section 5, p. 1.) Congressional fax machines are said to be increasingly "jammed up' with appeals from various lobbying groups." ("So-called 'Junk' Fax Messages Are Under Fire," *Research Recommendations*, October 23, 1989, p. 3.)

16. Scott Armstrong, "Activists Gear Up Faxes and Phones To Rally Support," *The Christian Science Monitor*, July 11, 1989, p. 1.

17. Carl Zimmer, "Tech In The Jungle. In The Amazon, Indians Have Decided That The Camcorder Is Mightier Than The War Club," *Discover*, August 1990, pp. 42-45.

18. John F. Burns, "Mandela, 'Faceless Man With a Fax,' Negotiates His and Country's Future," *The New York Times*, January 30, 1990, p. A-3. See also: "Mandela Reportedly Using Fax Machine," *The Boston Globe*, November 9, 1989, p. 40.

19. John F. Burns, "Mandela, 'Faceless Man With a Fax,'" *The New York Times*, January 30, 1990, p. A-3.

20. "News in Brief. Fax And Fiction of the Chemical Warfare Issue," *Financial Times*, August 15, 1990, p. 3.

21. "'Dear Joe...' Mail By Fax," *The New York Times*, September 14, 1990, p. A-12, and Margie G. Quimpo, "AT&T Wants Just the Faxes For Troops in Saudi Arabia," *Washington Post*, September 13, 1990, p. A-35.

22. Peter H. Lewis, "Personal Computers. The Facts on The Fax," *The New York Times*, January 10, 1989, p. C-6.

23. "First Commercial Fax Transmission From United States to Moscow Completed by AlphaGraphics," *Newstab, Tele/Scope Fax Alert*, March 22, 1989.

24. Richard Bissell, personal communications, April 1990. During a 10-day period in September 1990, this author (in the U.S.) and her husband (in Eastern Europe) tested the fax systems of three hotels, one each in East Berlin, Budapest, and Warsaw. Daily faxes sent back and forth encountered only minor transmission problems.

25. "Congress Considers Banning 'Junk Fax,'" *International Herald Tribune*, May 27-28, 1989, p. 3; John Durie, "Fax Unto Others as You Would be Faxed," *The Australian*, May 11, 1989, p. 19; Jerry Knight, "How a U.S. Technopreneur Faxed Himself in the Foot," *International Herald Tribune*, May 30, 1989, p. 5; "So-called 'Junk' Fax Messages Are Under Fire," *Research Recommendations*, Volume 40, No. 42, October 23, 1989, p. 3; Peter H. Lewis, "Personal Computers. The Etiquette of Fax Transmission," *The New York Times*, March 21, 1989, p. C-8; and Kirk Johnson, "Heading Off 'Junk Fax' at the Wire," *The New York Times*, January 20, 1989, p. B-1.

26. Jerry Knight, "How a U.S. Technopreneur Faxed Himself in the Foot," *The International Herald Tribune*, May 30, 1989, p. 5. See also: "Awash in Copies, O'Neill's Aides Denounce Fax Attacks," *The New York Times*, May 13, 1989, p. A-28.

27. "Lax Fax," *Privacy Journal*, Volume XV, No. 11, September 1989, p. 6.

28. "Fax Ruling Causes A Legal Stir," *The Wall Street Journal*, November 22, 1988, p. B-1.

29. See also: "Ontario Develops Fax Guidelines," *Transnational Data and Communications Report*, August/September, 1989, p. 29; and "Lax Fax," *Privacy Journal*, Volume XV, No. 11, September 1989, p. 6.

30. Robert Arnold Russel, "One Year That Changed the World," *Saturday Night*, April 1984, p. 24. (Article pp. 23-31.)

31. Clive Cookson, "Printing Under the Sun. On the Mechanics of Producing the Financial Times in Five Locations, Including Tokyo," *Financial Times*, June 5, 1990, p. 16. See also Note 14, Chapter 1.

32. "High-Tech Junk Mail," *The New York Times*, December 21, 1988, p. D-7. See also: Peter H. Lewis, "The Facts on the Fax," *The New York Times*, January 10, 1989, p. C-6.

33. Ibid.

34. "In Hartford, News by Fax," *The New York Times*, April 4, 1989, p. C-19.

35. Alex S. Jones, "Fast Way to Get News That's Hot Off the Fax," *The New York Times*, July 3, 1989, p. 29; Mary Lou Carnevale, "News Media's Slogan One Day May Be 'Just the Fax

Ma'am' if Trend Persists," *The Wall Street Journal*, October 6, 1989, p. B-3. See also: "Decoder Upgrades Fax For Newsletters," *Financial Times*, October 14, 1989, p. 8.

36. "Times to Begin a Fax Synopsis," *The New York Times*, November 14, 1989, p. D-21.

37. Tele/Scope Fax Alert is described as "Your Morning Bulletin of Top Telecom News." It offers summaries and transcripts of articles from sources like *The New York Times*, *The Wall Street Journal*, *United Press International*, *Financial Times* of London, and various corporate news releases.

38. Richard Bissell, personal communications, April 1990.

39. Beth Ann Krier, "Fax Fever," *Los Angeles Times*, January 25, 1989, Section 5, p. 1.

chapter 9

ELECTRONIC NEWS RELEASES AND PROGRAM LENGTH COMMERCIALS*

It is generally agreed that the modern way to "fight city hall" and get political and social views across is to gain access to the airwaves, that is, to tap into the technological powers of the mass media. But paid ads are frequently too expensive for ordinary people. Cheap and effective ways of gaining access are to stage demonstrations that will turn political messages into news and thus draw free mass media coverage, or to promote some idea that is interesting or controversial enough to prompt an invitation to appear on radio or television. Another method now open to individuals and organizations is to prepare audio or videotaped news releases with sufficiently intriguing messages that television or radio stations will air them for nothing.[1]

More professional video news releases from many sources are also gaining access to free air time. But audiences frequently reject what they recognize as overt political, social, or commercial sales pitches. To get around this, both producers and broadcasters are increasingly taking pains to obscure the original source and/or intent of many political or company video productions. As a result, commercial, lobbying, and political pieces are being confused with public service announcements and, even worse, are being passed off by news programs as objective reporting. What began as an occasional effort has greatly expanded, thanks to the rapidly increasing availability of commercial public relations and media services. Provision of such tapes pushing self-serving

---

* Some of the material in this section was originally researched for the Program on Information Resources Policy, Harvard University, and a few of the incidents have been described in Gladys D. Ganley and Oswald H. Ganley, *Global Political Fallout. The VCR's First Decade 1976-1985*, Ablex Publishing Corporation, Norwood, NJ, 1987, pp. 107-109.

messages has now turned into a flourishing industry and various alleged abuses are attracting criticism.

VIDEOTAPED NEWS RELEASES DISGUISED AS OBJECTIVE NEWS

Today's videotaped news release (VNR), or sponsored news programming,[2] as it is sometimes being called may have had its beginnings in some silent black and white clips used in the late 1950s.[3] Now rapidly escalating in use, some releases are slanted to push specific products or social, economic, or political positions. In an increasing number of cases, an effort is being made to enhance the chances of getting the releases included in news programs by disguising their messages as objective news. Television news programs are being bombarded with such videotaped productions. Early on, these releases were sometimes mailed or hand delivered and arrived sporadically, but now they are also routinely satellited and arrive on a regular basis. While the releases are also prepared with the major TV networks in mind, their main use is by local television stations, where resources tend to be limited but where news reporting is rapidly expanding.[4]

Beyond individual and small group productions, dozens of public relations firms are being paid by various interests to prepare what look like legitimate news items, but are really lobbying or sales efforts for some specific paying client. Many companies have also set up their own departments to develop such disguised promotion.[5] While a lot of this activity is commercial in intent, some of it has political implications, and all of it is blurring the line between what is objective news and what isn't.

The phenomenon of disguising promotional material is not confined to television, but has spread across the mass media. Radio is involved in similar audiotaped releases, and the print media not only use thinly disguised press releases, but are increasingly running ads that mimic news, as they attempt to cope with rising costs and the competition of broadcasting.[6]

However, videotaped releases have been cited by their critics as especially troubling. While there are those who contend that the videotaped press release is no different from the ordinary print release, which has been around for a long time and used copiously, critics say that the power of the picture, combined with deliberate tailoring to make the releases look like "real news," render these videocassettes the bearers of not only deceptive but very forceful messages. This combines with the fact that 65% of all U.S. adults purportedly depend primarily on TV for their information and mainly watch the news on local TV stations. The video news release has thus been classed by some as a worrisome ethical issue.[7] While such critics may well have axes to grind, video news releases can package and distribute deceptive messages in a new way and, as such, bear watching.

The usual electronic press release is a 90-second segment that can easily be inserted, in whole or in part, into a news program.[8] A videotape package, according to *The Wall Street Journal:*[9]

> typically includes pieces that can be run immediately as well as interviews and background shots that can be combined with a news staff's own reporting.

Various ploys that are used to make the pieces look like "news" rather than public relations, a sales talk, or a political message, have been described as: hiring TV personages with name recognition to do them; having professional journalists using pseudonyms do them; blurring the "reporter's" identity and whereabouts, or keeping the "reporter's" lines as a voice-over off camera; leaving labels off the tapes, so each station can insert its own typeface to make a video release look like its own reporting; and having a dark blonde "reporter" do the interview with back to camera. "Every station has a reporter with dark blonde hair," says one article.[10]

During the 1980s, the volume of videotaped news releases grew to huge proportions. Medialink, a major video release distributor, estimated that, in 1989, in excess of 3,200 such releases would be delivered. Some of these releases command vast audiences. For instance, over 70 million people are said to have seen at least parts of one such release concerned with a shift in Sears's pricing policies.[11] A disguised ad for a prescription heart attack drug—not permitted to be advertised to the public directly—ranked sixth in viewership of 1989's top-10 VNRs and attracted 27.2 million viewers.[12]

VIDEO NEWS RELEASE USERS AND SOURCE IDENTIFICATION

The major network news programs and larger media markets only occasionally use such video releases and, when they do, require clear labeling. For example, for lack of time and want of another source of information, in late 1988, all the networks, including Cable Network News, used parts of a promotional video—identified as such—by Drexel Burnham Lambert Inc., when a settlement of Federal securities-law violations was made concerning that company.[13]

In contrast, there appears to be virtually no limit to the use of VNRs by local television stations, a practice that is rapidly growing. In surveys in 1987, A. C. Nielsen found that up to 67% of TV stations that responded had used a whole or a part of a video news release within the previous week. Did they identify the source? Thirty-one percent of the stations surveyed said they did, 18% said only if it was "relevant to the story," and 12% said they didn't.[14] Other reports have said that the entire video is often used, combined with the voices of the station's broadcasters, and that identification at smaller stations is "'spotty and varied.'"[15] The president of one video production and distribution company is quoted as saying:[16]

> My anecdotal feel is that with any given release easily 40 percent of the stations that use it run it intact. And I would say the majority of users don't identify the source.

TV news executives are said to find VNRs "a necessary aid to their profession,"[17] and more, not less, use of these releases by local TV news programs is expected as stations rapidly increase the scope of their news coverage.

The disguised releases are often used without apology. As one news director said, "We're a small operation and can't cover things outside of the metropolitan area. Anyway, all stories are slanted to some extent."[18]

VIDEO NEWS RELEASES BY FOREIGN LOBBYISTS

Video news releases on U.S. television are not limited to those provided by U.S. nationals. In Spring 1985, Gray & Company, of Washington, DC, came under fire from the U.S. Justice Department for allegedly preparing and distributing video news releases for foreign clients without registering as a foreign agent. Prior to the meeting of President Reagan and Japanese Prime Minister Nakasone in early 1985, Gray distributed "news" reports showing U.S. produce being shipped to Japan and featured the U.S. Ambassador to Japan saying that "Japanese markets aren't as closed as we might think."[19] This "news item" was, however, paid for by the government of Japan, and was directed ultimately—via local U.S. television viewers—at the U.S. Congress. Japan was trying to keep legislation from being passed that could restrict import of Japanese goods into the U.S.

Another Gray production featured a former Washington, DC WTTG TV anchorwoman (later a Gray vice president) appearing as a "reporter" holding an "exclusive interview" in Morocco with that country's King

Hassan II, concerning a recent treaty between Morocco and Libya. At the end of the interview, the "reporter" mimicked the news by doing a "standup conclusion," saying:[20]

> The political fallout from the Treaty may not yet be over, but any harsh reaction from the West must be tempered with the acknowledgment that Morocco is strategically important to the United States.

At that time, Gray & Company had a large budget supplied by the Moroccan government to say positive things about that country.

PROGRAM LENGTH COMMERCIALS

Beyond the 90 second "news" segment, the *program length commercial*—PLC for short—has also come into considerable use. *The Columbia Journalism Review* describes a half-hour show posing as a special news report on violent crime which was actually "a slick thirty-minute commercial...to sell the Nova XR 5000 stun gun...."[21] To simulate news, this video, which the authors say "is only one among dozens" being shown on TV, employed a combination of documentary footage, dramatized crime scenes, crimes being "reported," scenes of people calling the police department, Justice Department crime statistics, narration by an actor posing as an anchor, tips on crime prevention, and even program breaks for other commercials. This article also describes a PLC called "Consumer Challenge," which purported to be investigative journalism, complete with simulated anchor and backup reporters, but which was actually a disguised pitch for JS&A's BluBlocker sunglasses. Another PLC, called "Legal Hotline," mimicked a public affairs discussion of legal rights by featuring "attorneys" but was in fact an advertisement for a legal referral service.

The Wall Street Journal has drawn attention to a Financial News Network series of six half-hour segments called "Planning Your Financial Future," which had the appearance of "other TV business shows," saying:[22]

> It is hosted by NBC-TV correspondent Bob Berkowitz, is loaded with financial planning advice and features interviews with reporters from *The New York Times*, *Forbes*, and *Money magazine*.

But, it turns out, this was just a long commercial for an insurance and financial services firm, The New England, of Boston. This company had paid for the airtime and all costs of the series and its promotion, plus $1,000 each to the participating reporters—a total of $365,000. When an uproar arose concerning this series, The New England claimed it was not an ad but rather "objective, unbiased financial planning." Critics said the sponsor should have been identified throughout the showing in clearly visible type. These critics also panned the growing practice of journalists appearing for pay in commercials.[23] FNN airs about 2 hours a day of such commercially produced material by many companies, and other cable and independent television stations also make use of such programming.

The FCC lifted the ban on similar commercials in 1984, although, except for some cable networks, PLCs must still be identified as ads. The problem, critics say, is that disclaimers are easily missed, since they appear only briefly "at the beginning or end of the programs."[24]

Like the 90-second video news releases, PLCs are tempting, because they save TV stations money. The makers of PLCs and many broadcasters defend them, but they are viewed by some as "a serious public policy question," because they defraud the public, and could ruin the credibility of legitimate reporters."[25]

USE OF VIDEO NEWS RELEASES BY CONGRESSIONAL MEMBERS AND CANDIDATES FOR ELECTION

Since the early 1980s, members of the U.S. Congress have been irritating the national news media by sending taped news to their local news stations and thus bypassing the overly suspicious, harshly questioning Washington, DC reporters in favor of kinder, less sophisticated, and less powerful locals.[26] As early as 1982, 46% of all congressional offices were said to be producing video releases from their congressman and sending them to television stations in their state and district, usually on a monthly basis.[27] Such footage has often lacked information to show that it was paid for and provided by a politician.[28] House of Representatives press secretaries, who have increased from 54 to 250 since 1970, now interview their own congressmen, and their VNRs, furnished free, have largely replaced the objective stories formerly supplied by political reporters.[29]

The use of such disguised programming also spread over into the 1988 presidential election campaign. For instance, Michael Dukakis aired two hour-long programs made to look like TV talk shows on cable television. In both shows, Dukakis answered questions posed by a moderator, but in both cases, the "moderator" was actually a Dukakis political supporter. The only identification of the program as an ad was said to be a brief notice at the beginning, announcing that "The Dukakis for President Campaign presents the program."[30]

INCREASINGLY SOPHISTICATED TRANSMISSION

In 1987, Potomac Communications, Inc. of Washington, DC began a satellite and video service called Daily Business Satellite to transmit groups of video press releases directly and simultaneously to 650 local television stations. Transmissions were made on a regular schedule every day, so that editors would get used to routinely reviewing the releases. Although it was said to have taken pains to avoid any conflict of interest, Potomac was at that time also acting as the Washington bureau for some 300 TV stations, including all of the ABC network affiliates.[31]

In Fall 1989, Transcontinental Television, a subsidiary of a joint venture that includes ABC, began sending VNRs by satellite to ABC's affiliate stations. These transmissions took place just before, and on the same channel as, two regular ABC news feeds. Critics immediately protested that the proximity of the sponsored video release feed to that of the regular news could damage the latter's integrity. The president of a large public relations firm confirmed that the move provided legitimacy to the VNRs, saying that "It does lend the imprimatur of one of the three major broadcasters to video news releases."[32] Although ABC's news division is not involved with the transmission, it has been predicted that the convenience, and the approval implied by the close relationship of the feeds, will encourage previously hesitant stations to begin using the releases.

For personal freedom, the acceptance of video news releases by the mass media is a two edged sword. While it gives individual producers a chance to have their say, it can make the information the public receives from the mass media suspect. All news outlets can be harmed if misuse of releases by some damages overall news credibility. It does not help that the use of these releases is escalating at a time when objectivity is also being corroded by docudrama, reenacted and simulated news, and the use by broadcasters of increasing amounts of amateur news footage. While only a limited number of VNRs are as yet devoted to political subjects, the growing acceptance of these releases makes them a ready vehicle for political uses. Their uses by political candidates will be discussed in Chapter 11.

NOTES

1. As an aid to this sort of endeavor, Tony Schwartz, the creator of the famous "Daisy" antinuclear ad for Lyndon Johnson's 1964 presidential campaign, has released some how-to videos called "Guerrilla Media: A Citizen's Guide to Using Electronic Media for Social Change." The videos purportedly demystify the electronic media and show amateurs how to produce spots with simple equipment and how to get radio and TV

stations to run them. The first tape was introduced by New York City's Mayor, Ed Koch, who called it "'Tony Schwartz's gift to the democratic process.'" The first of a planned "dozen" videos, released in 1988, ran 2 ½ hours and cost $299. Vended through Varied Directions, Inc. of Camden, Maine, its expected buyers were said to be "colleges and activist groups." (Tom Shales, "Tony Schwartz, On The Citizen Channel; The Political Adman And His Guerrilla Guide to Airing Grievances," *The Washington Post*, March 3, 1988, p. D-1.) See also: Douglas C. McGill, "Strategies for Social Visionaries," *The New York Times*, March 10, 1989, p. D-5.

2. Randall Rothenberg, "Video New Releases Get Network Aid," *The New York Times*, September 11, 1989, p. D-12.

3. N. R. Kleinfield, "The Video News Release: Let the Viewer Beware," *The New York Times*, January 2, 1989, p. 33.

4. Ibid., and also: Jeanne Saddler, "Public Relations Firms Offer 'News' to TV. Electronic Releases Contain Subtle Commercials for Clients," *The Wall Street Journal*, April 2, 1985, p. 6, and Paul Harris, "J.D. Calls Flack On the Carpet Over TV Feeds," *Variety*, April 3, 1985, p. 49.

5. N. R. Kleinfield, "The Video News Release: Let the Viewer Beware," *The New York Times*, January 2, 1989, p. 33.

6. Daniel Akst, "L.A. Times's Plan to Run Press Releases Stirs Debate," *The Wall Street Journal*, April 21, 1988, p. 33; John Morton, "This is Not an Advertorial," *Washington Journalism Review*, June 1988, p. 12; and Jonathan Alter, "The Era of the Big Blur. More and More Advertisers Are Giving Their Pitches a Journalistic Spin," *Newsweek*, May 22, 1989, pp. 73-76.

7. N. R. Kleinfield, "The Video News Release: Let the Viewer Beware," *The New York Times*, January 2, 1989, p. 33; Randall Rothenberg, "Video News Releases Get Network Aid," *The New York Times*, September 11, 1989, p. D-12; Paul West, "The Video Connection. Beaming It Straight to the Constituents," *Washington Journalism Review*, June 1985, pp. 48-50; and Ted Dracos, "News Directors Are Lousy Managers," *Washington Journalism Review*, September 1989, p. 39. Most of the articles referred to in this chapter cite the concerns of critics about VNRs. None of the articles appear to suggest that video releases diguised as objective news are a good idea.

8. Sandra Sugawara, "Putting Out the News on Videos. Young D. C. Firm Produces Taped Press Releases," *The Washington Post*, August 10, 1987, pp. D-1, D-9.

9. Jeanne Saddler, "Public Relations Firms Offer 'News' to TV. Electronic Releases Contain Subtle Commercials For Clients," *The Wall Street Journal*, April 2, 1985, p. 6.

10. Paul West, "The Video Connection. Beaming It Straight to the Constituents," *Washington Journalism Review*, June 1985, pp. 48-50.

11. Randall Rothenberg, "Video News Releases Get Network Aid," *The New York Times*, September 11, 1989, p. D-12.

12. Joanne Lipman, "'News' Videos That Pitch Drugs Provoke Outcry For Regulations," *The Wall Street Journal*, February 8, 1990, p. B-6.

13. N. R. Kleinfield, "The Video News Release: Let the Viewer Beware," *The New York Times*, January 2, 1989, p. 33.

14. Sandra Sugawara, "Putting Out the News on Videos. Young D. C. Firm Produces Taped Press Releases," *The Washington Post*, August 10, 1987, p. 9.

15. Randall Rothenberg, "Video News Releases Get Network Aid," *The New York Times*, September 11, 1989, p. D-12.

16. N. R. Kleinfield, "The Video News Release: Let the Viewer Beware," *The New York Times*, January 2, 1989, p. 33. Robert Kimmel, president of Audio TV Productions, is being quoted.

17. Randall Rothenberg, "Video News Releases Get Network Aid," *The New York Times*, September 11, 1989, p. D-12.

18. Jeanne Saddler, "Public Relations Firms Offer 'News' to TV. Electronic Releases Contain Subtle Commercials For Clients," *The Wall Street Journal*, April 2, 1985, p. 6. Robert Byrd, News Director of WGPR, Detroit, is quoted.

19. Ibid.

20. Mary Battiata, "Trouble Spots in Public Relations-Journalism Connections," *The Boston Globe*, March 31, 1985, p. A-96.

21. Jeffrey Chester and Kathryn Montgomery, "TV's Hidden Money Games: I. Counterfeiting the News," *Columbia Journalism Review*, May/June 1988, pp. 38-42. (Quote on p. 38.)

22. Joanne Lipman, "TV Series on Personal Finance Stirs Debate Over Separation of News and Advertising," *The Wall Street Journal*, February 10, 1988, Section 2, p. 23.

23. Critics cited by Lipman were Jack O'Dwyer, an editor of the public relations industry publication, *Newsletter*, Osborn Elliott, formerly Dean of the School of Journalism of Columbia University, and Richard Salant, former CBS News president.

24. Jeffrey Chester and Kathryn Montgomery, "TV's Hidden Money Games: I. Counterfeiting the News," *Columbia Journalism Review*, May/June 1988, p. 38.

25. Ibid., p. 40.

26. Paul West, "The Video Connection. Beaming it Straight to the Constituents," *Washington Journalism Review*, June 1985, pp. 48-50.

27. Anne Haskell, "Live From Capitol Hill Where Politicians Use High Tech to Bypass the Press," *Washington Journalism Review*, November 1982, p. 49. (Article pp. 48-50.)

28. Paul West, "The Video Connection," *Washington Journalism Review*, June 1985, pp. 48-50; Mary Collins, "News Of The Congress BY The Congress," *Washington Journalism Review*, June 1990, p. 32. (Article pp. 30-34.) For other discussions of congressional uses of the videotaped news release, see: Jeffrey B. Abramson, F. Christopher Arterton, and Gary R. Orren, *The Electronic Commonwealth. The Impact of New Media Technologies on Democratic Politics*, Basic Books, Inc., New York, 1988, pp. 52, 102. See this reference also (pp. 134, 185) for some uses of video releases by organized labor and chambers of commerce. And for some politically oriented public service videos by companies, see: Barbara Scherr Trenk, "What's New in Getting Out the Vote. Grow Your Own In-House Lobbyists," *The New York Times*, February 7, 1988, p. F-17.

29. Mary Collins, "News Of The Congress BY The Congress," *Washington Journalism Review*, June 1990, p. 30. (Article pp. 30-34.)

30. "Notebook. Dukakis' TV Ads Spur Legal Queries," *The Boston Globe*, March 4, 1988, p. 12.

31. Sandra Sugawara, "Putting Out the News on Video," *The Washington Post*, August 10, 1987, pp. 1, 9.

32. Randall Rothenberg, "Video News Releases Get Network Aid," *The New York Times*, September 11, 1989, p. D-12. Richard Edelman, president of Daniel J. Edelman, Inc., is being quoted. Transcontinental Television is said to be a separate subsidiary of Worldwide Television News, a joint venture comprised of Capital Cities/ABC, Bond Media of Australia, and Great Britain's ITN. Transcontinental Television, according to Rothenberg, was formed to operate the new distribution service called Global Link.

chapter 10

HOSTAGE TAKERS, VIDEOS, THE MASS MEDIA, AND THE CONDUCT OF FOREIGN POLICY*

The decision to put the photo on page 1 was obvious and logical....The videotape was an integral part of the story. It was what the president and the rest of the nation were reacting to.[1]

For more than half a decade, videotapes of American hostages in Lebanon have been regularly passed by their terrorist captors to the mass media. Just as regularly, they have appeared on prime time U.S. TV and on the front pages of American magazines and newspapers. With the same regularity, they have inflamed American public opinion and the Congress and caused attempts to change U.S. foreign policy.[2] For a powerful new political weapon is in place and is being implemented in the form of the following cycle:

...Terrorists in Lebanon make videotapes of the individual American hostages they are holding.

...The tapes are released to the mass media via one of the Beirut news outlets.

---

* The role of the mass media in terrorism is a subject of great complexity, as is the political situation in Lebanon, in the Middle East, and between the U.S. and Iran. This chapter attempts only to give a sense of the interplay involved between individual or small groups of terrorists, the mass media, the general public, and governments, via the mechanism of the new personal medium of videotapes. It is further limited to a discussion of *U.S.* political reaction to *U.S.* media coverage of videos released by *Iranian and Lebanese* terrorists of individual *American* hostages.

...In the name of informing the public, but also because the excitement is enormously profitable, the American mass media can be counted on to run these videos for days on TV and front pages, to write multiple stories around them, and to add interviews, videos, and photographs of hostage relatives, friends, and acquaintances.

...Hostage relatives, in their anguish, can be counted on to show emotion or make pitiful and pleading statements on camera or, also on camera, to denounce the efforts or question the motives of the U.S. government. Families have also become adept at playing their own media game, often setting up lobbying groups and calling press conferences. In hopes of getting hostages released, media attention is often welcomed.

...All this, in turn, inflames general U.S. public opinion—well primed by the 444 day Iran hostage crisis of 1979-1981.

...Experts on foreign policy, terrorism, the media, etc., flock onto TV, and various people pressure the President to "do something."

...The U.S. Congress goes up in smoke, recommending various actions and demanding action by the President.

...The President has the choice of either acting, which may imperil larger objectives, get the hostages killed, or create bigger problems—not excluding war—or standing fast and possibly making the U.S. appear indecisive and impotent to its enemies, allies, and its own people.

...The story is sometimes kept alive beyond any inherent news value, or even public indignation, because this cycle, once in motion, becomes a form of macabre (and cheap) mass entertainment.

...Any suggestion that media coverage be toned down is vehemently resisted—perhaps rightly so—by the American mass media, as a violation of the First Amendment, and of the media's right and duty to inform the public.

But freedom to create a publicity storm carries a potent price tag. For, by adroit manipulation, a small band of terrorists, or even a single individual, can parlay the new personal medium of videotape into a tool to take control of the vast technological resources of the mass media. It can use those resources, in a matter of hours, to sway the opinion of millions of Americans and the nationals of multiple countries, to dilute U.S. influence, and to complicate not only U.S. foreign policy, but also the relationship of the U.S. government with the American people.

Since the late 1960s, terroristic acts of all kinds have increased radically, paralleling faster means of travel, the growth of instantaneous communications, and a tendency toward guerrilla and low intensity warfare. Acts of terrorism are usually the weapon of the militarily weak and rely heavily on publicity to be effective. The alleged complicity of the mass media, especially television, in providing such publicity, and what is moral and not moral to report, are the subjects of continuous discussion and growing literature. It is generally agreed that the interaction between terrorists, the mass media, the public, and governments has come to play an important role in both domestic and foreign affairs in many countries. There is no such agreement on just how the mass media of free countries might report these events differently while still retaining their all-important press freedoms.[3] For individuals, a free press is the surest safeguard of a democratic system of government. The dilemma is how to maintain that freedom in the face of new technologies that have caused vast shifts in the power of both mass and personal media.

THE HEZBOLLAH, OR THE PARTY OF GOD

Information on the organization and activities of terrorist groups in Lebanon is generally vague, but it is possible to piece together the following. Although organizations with a variety of names have claimed credit for the kidnappings of Americans and other foreigners in Lebanon, they are believed to be mainly shadow groups under the Party of God, or Hezbollah, umbrella. "They just change labels," former French hostage Jean Paul Kauffmann is quoted by *Newsweek* as saying.[4] The U.S. State Department has described Hezbollah as:[5]

> Known or suspected to have been involved in numerous anti-US terrorist attacks, including the suicidal truck bombing on the US Marine barracks in Beirut in October 1983 and the US Embassy annex in September 1984. The group is responsible for the kidnaping and continuing detention of most, if not all, US and other Western hostages in Lebanon.

The Department says that Hezbollah is "dedicated to creation of Iranian-style Islamic republic in Lebanon," that it is "closely allied with and largely directed by Iran in its activities," that it "receives substantial amounts of financial, training, weapons, explosives, political, diplomatic, and organizational aid from Iran," and that "Tehran...exerts significant influence over...[Hezbollah's] kidnaping of Westerners in Lebanon ... and has approved—and in some instances may have encouraged—its seizing of some Western hostages."[6]

COUNTERMEASURES AGAINST HOSTAGE TAKERS

Taking and holding hostages for long periods of time has proved an effective weapon in the chaos of the Lebanese civil war, because finding a terrorist and his or her captive is next to impossible, and extracting the captive alive and without killing innocent bystanders is even more difficult. Sophisticated intelligence countermeasures by the U.S. are all but useless. Supposedly, the U.S. can examine specific locations in Lebanese cities, such as streetcorners or buildings, by photographing or remote sensing them from reconnaisance planes and satellites.[7] It was able, it is said, to establish that the terrorists who blew up the Beirut annex to the American Embassy with a car bomb had practiced beforehand at the Iranian Revolutionary Guard base in the Bekaa Valley. According to *U.S. News & World Report*:[8]

> Satellite photos show an obstacle course that had been set up there identical to the one in front of the barracks; the photos even show the driver's tracks in the dirt....

The U.S. also easily intercepts electronic communications.[9] But Hezbollah's terrorists work in small bands, often avoiding the use of media such as phones that can be monitored and traced electronically. They stay very mobile, moving around a lot, and keeping rooms at various locations. Their groups are composed of people who are relatives, or well know to each other, and are therefore almost impossible to infiltrate. In any case in the later 1980s, on the ground intelligence gathering in Lebanon became much more difficult.[10]

MOTIVATIONS FOR HOSTAGE TAKING

The motivations behind hostage takings and videotape releases by the Hezbollah are murky, but appear to serve several related purposes. American hostages may be used to pressure the U.S. government to urge Israel to refrain from bombing or otherwise compromising Hezbollah strongholds. Efforts to get their prisoners released has been an almost constant objective. Another motive is to punish Israel for invading Lebanon and as the overall enemy of the Muslims, again by pressuring Israel's closest ally and source of financing, America. An ultimate goal here is to weaken the U.S./Israeli alliance in any way possible. Hezbollah also continues to punish the U.S. for past sins against Iran. And finally, the fate of hostages has been kept as a live issue for ammunition against any unwanted military or political activity by the U.S. or any of its allies.[11] Overall, hostage videos have proved a very useful tool in the long-drawn-out Middle Eastern and Persian Gulf struggle.

TYPES OF HOSTAGE VIDEOS

The first hostage videotapes were prepared and released by the government-sponsored Iranian terrorists who held hostages in Teheran's American Embassy during 1979-1981, in the form of pitiful holiday specials. These videotapes were transmitted from the captured U.S. Embassy building via a microwave connection to Iran's government controlled VVIR (Voice and Vision of the Islamic Republic) national television and released to American TV networks. Before being allowed to go home, the hostages were also made to deny on video that they had been mistreated during their captivity.[12]

Although the videos of hostages passed to the mass media by terrorists in Lebanon have been amateurish productions, they have been sufficiently varied in type to maintain mass media and public interest. They have had pitiful, demanding, accusatory, confessional, and retaliatory themes, with some videos combining several of these elements. *Pitiful* videos of hostages, even when no threats or demands are made, are powerfully effective in arousing the emotions of hostage families, the American public, and the Congress. *Demanding* videos, in addition, make some specific request, with the hostage's life at stake if it is not granted. *Accusatory* videos have the hostage attack the U.S. government, appealing over its head to the American public, or attack the American public itself, so that the public will seek to shift the blame to the government. In *confessional* videos, the hostage is forced to confess to some dire sin, such as being a spy for the U.S. government. And *retaliatory* videos show pictures of real or purported dead bodies, and make true or fictional pronouncements that a hostage has been executed for some unwanted act by the U.S. or its allies. Retaliatory videos are also used to put real teeth into terrorists' threats and thus reinforce the political value of all hostage holding.[13]

All of the videos are aimed at undermining the confidence of Americans and their allies in U.S. leadership, and that leadership's confidence in its own abilities. All are dramas designed to transform the power of the terrorist to humiliate, degrade, hold helpless, and even kill a single hostage, to a similar symbolic power over the U.S. public and its government. All are concrete propaganda products aimed, in Prime Minister Margaret Thatcher's words, at gaining the "oxygen of publicity."[14]

For without publicity to fan the flames of public opinion, it is politically useless to hold or even kill a hostage.

Samples Of The Various Video Types

The variety of approaches taken in these amateur video dramas is interesting, in that they give some indication of how future videos could be developed in more professional hands. Amateurishness has its own strength, however. The very homemade quality of the video releases— dark, grainy, and patched together—effectively conveys the horror of people held prisoner in dark hidden places.

A video containing *demands* voiced by hostage Marine Lieutenant Colonel William R. Higgins was released within a few days of his February 1988 capture. On the tape, Higgins, who was in command of a multinational observer group attached to the United Nations Truce Supervisory Organization in Lebanon when captured, said that as a condition for his release, all Israeli forces would have to be withdrawn from Lebanon, all "Mujahedeen, Lebanese and Palestinians" would have to be released from the prisons "inside the Zionist regime in occupied Palestine," and the U.S. government would have to "stop sending delegations to the Middle East" and stop intervening in Lebanon.[15]

Long-time hostage Terry Anderson, former Middle East Bureau Chief for the Associated Press, and David Jacobsen, who had headed the American University hospital in Beirut, have been the subjects of several videos. In October 1986, after the Reagan Administration had cooperated with the Soviet government for the release of Nicholas Daniloff, whom the Soviets had arrested in retaliation for the U.S. arrest of one of their people, Anderson and Jacobsen appeared jointly in an *accusatory* video. In it, Anderson asked whether "the American people know why we are in captivity" or why American "Marines and others" had been killed in bombings. "All this is the result of Reagan's policy," Anderson said. Appealing to U.S. public opinion, Anderson noted that "we are not surprised" at Reagan's actions but are "surprised that the American people still listen to what Reagan says."[16] On the same video, Jacobsen added that only the U.S. government was continuing "This nonsensical situation."[17]

A *confessional* video was released in July 1987 featuring Charles Glass, a freelance reporter and former ABC News correspondent, who was later released or escaped from his captors. On the tape, Glass said:[18]

> I used the press as a cover for my main job with the C.I.A. I collect information for the benefit of the C.I.A. For that I made secret missions. They ordered me to do that.

Any link with the C.I.A. or other government agency by Glass was denied by the White House and the U.S. State Department.[19]

A *retaliatory* video showing a hanged body claimed to be that of British journalist Alec Collett was released by terrorists in Lebanon in April 1986 with a note saying that the alleged execution had been "in retaliation for Britain's complicity in the US air raids on Tripoli and Benghazi" a few days earlier.[20] The previous week, the body of American Peter Kilburn, a librarian at Beirut's American University library, along with bodies of two British teachers, had been found outside Beirut. Their purported murderers, the so called "Arab Commando Cells," left word saying that the three had been killed for the raid on Libya.[21]

Release By Terrorists Of Still Pictures

Still pictures have also been used by the terrorists, interspersed with the videos. They provide variety, often leave the status of the hostage doubtful, and are thus effective in maintaining tension.

HOSTAGE VIDEOS OF SUMMER 1989

A new round in the videotape war began on July 28, 1989, when the Israelis captured a prominent Hezbollah cleric and militant leader, Sheik Abdul Karim Obeid. On July 31, when their demands for the Sheik's release were not met, the Hezbollah group holding Marine Lieutenant Colonel William Higgins released a videotape showing a hanged body, purportedly that of the Colonel.[22]

The tape consisted of two segments, one showing a dangling body with bound bare feet hanging from a noose, "his body turning slowly."[23] The second segment showed a face close up, which was said to be identifiable as that of Colonel Higgins.[24] An accompanying note said the execution had been in retaliation for Obeid's kidnapping and because "criminal America and the Zionist enemy" had ignored the release deadline.[25]

A few hours after the release of the Higgins "execution" video and message, a still photograph of hostage Joseph Cicippio, who had been Comptroller at the American University of Beirut, was made available by a supposedly different group of terrorists. This message set a new deadline for Israel's release of the Sheik, saying that Cicippio would be killed and the execution "broadcast on all the screens in the world" (i.e., another gory videotape would be forthcoming) if the demand was not heeded.[26] This contact was swiftly followed by a videotape of Cicippio emotionally reading a dictated script pleading for the release of the Sheik, "because they are serious to hang us and the period become very soon and the hours very little," and adding that "we the American people are always the victims of Israel's politics."[27] Coming as it did just after the video of Colonel Higgins' hanged body, the impact of this video—as no doubt planned—was multiplied many times over. *Maclean's*, for one, focused on the political power of these videotape releases, saying that "the two videotaped sequences...put the leaders of three nations [the U.S., Israel, and Iran] on the spot" and at the same time endangered "the fragile peace of the Middle East."[28]

The drama was continued less than three weeks later, when the French, responding to intensified fighting in the Lebanese civil war, began sending warships to the Eastern Mediterranean. This aroused fears among the Lebanese Muslims that the French intended to aid the Christians, whose shipping the Muslims had been blockading. On August 19, Cicippio's captors, who also held Edward Tracy, a book salesman, responded by releasing a photocopy of a previously released Tracy photo and a renewed threat to the lives of both Cicippio and Tracy. This time, however, the threat was not tied to Obeid's release, but rather accused the U.S. of egging France on, and said that "foolhardiness" by the French would put the lives of the two American hostages in danger.[29]

RESPONSE OF THE MASS MEDIA TO THE HIGGINS/ CICIPPIO VIDEOS

The response of the mass media to the Higgins/Cicippio videos was typical of their response to all hostage videos. CBS, NBC, and CNN all played the Higgins tape in toto, showing the hanged body twisting and turning. The tape also appeared over and over on the local TV stations, and at least parts of the tape were shown again whenever there was a new development in the hostage situation. NBC did say it considered the Higgins tape "too graphic" to be shown during the afternoon it first appeared, but showed it on the Evening News. ABC, which claimed to have become more sensitive about hostage tapes after its former corre-spondent Charles Glass was captured and became the subject of a videotape, used "freeze-frame photos" rather than the moving video.[30]

In the case of the Cicippio video, again only ABC refused to run the tape, ABC News President Roone Arledge citing "concern that the network not be 'used as a vehicle by terrorists.'"[31] Only a small portion of the audio was used by ABC, and a 10-second clip of the video shown with the voice not of the hostage, but of anchor Peter Jennings. CBS, NBC, CNN, and many local stations ran the video in its entirety, and, again and again, showed selected segments.[32]

Stills from the Higgins tape were printed by many American newspapers. After protests were received from *The Boston Globe*'s readers concerning its two-column front-page picture of the Higgins video, the *Globe*'s "Ombudsman," Robert Kierstead, defended the action, calling the video "history" and "news," and crediting the *Globe*'s managing editor with the quote at the beginning of this chapter.[33] According to Kierstead, at least 17 major U.S. newspapers published stills from the video, 12 featuring them on their front pages.

After the release of the Cicippio video, his wife, Elham Ghandour, made a plea to his captors to free him at a televised Beirut news conference. Described as passionate, emotional, and dramatic, her videotaped statement got a lot of play in the media. Only cursory attention was paid to the statement of Colonel Higgins' wife, Marine Major Robin Higgins, when, at a televised press conference in Washington, DC, she accepted her husband's death with quiet dignity.

Like many hostage family members, Cicippio's family had tried to keep the hostage issue alive in the media. Cicippio's brother had long maintained a display on the lawn of his home in Norristown, PA, with a placard for each of the hostages. Each evening after the 11 o'clock news, he reportedly changed the numbers on each placard to update the number of days each hostage has been in captivity.[34] As they had done several times before, hordes of reporters journeyed to Norristown, took pictures of the display, and interviewed everybody. From Norristown, *Maclean's* reported that "the drama attracted reporters from across the United States and from Canada and Germany."[35] All over the United States, ex-hostages, hostage family members, friends, and acquaintances were rounded up for interviews to give the hostage situation a local angle.

RESPONSE OF THE U.S. GOVERNMENT

While the mass media have their faults, their role has been complicated by confusion of heads of state regarding how to govern in the presence of the new power of instantaneous communications. At the time of this crisis, there had also been a hiatus in the foreign policy experience of two successive U.S. presidents. Both President Carter and President Reagan had been tried in the terrorist crucible and found wanting.[36] Both were sincerely concerned for the hostages and their families, but neither was able to provide satisfactory leadership in the face of media pressure and family emotion. Perhaps most importantly, both had had to deal with the Ayatollah Khomeini.

President Bush, unlike his predecessors, had a wealth of diplomatic, foreign policy, and intelligence background to draw on and got good marks for his handling of the Summer 1989 situation.[37] Through a combination of personal and general diplomacy, third party assistance, and threats of military strikes against Iran's training ground in Lebanon, he was able to cool the rhetoric and to get the death threat against Cicippio rescinded.[38] Initially he had heightened tensions, however, by canceling a cross country trip and returning to Washington.[39] But, said *The Christian Science Monitor*, the President "may have had no choice...because the vivid and gruesome videotape was airing on the television networks."[40] Not returning could have left a sense of leadership void, said *The Monitor*, which would have instantly been jumped on by the Congress and the media.[41]

Ultimately, the greatest thing the Bush Administration had going for it was that the Ayatollah Khomeini was dead, and, in the midst of the crisis, a more moderate regime came to power in Iran, under President Hashemi Rafsanjani, creating various changes in policy.[42] Whether Rafsanjani's leadership style did not run to terroristic videotapes, or whether he put pressure on the terrorists, is as yet unknown. Whatever the cause, the terrorists backed off, and the issue died as a publicity/news producer for lack of new fuel.

The hostage video concept was soon to be enlarged, however. After his August 1990 annexation of Kuwait, Iraqi President Saddam Hussein lifted the use of this type of video to a new level. Taking thousands of foreigners captive, he interviewed groups of his victims directly on television. While President Bush massed hundreds of thousands of troops across the border in Saudi Arabia, Hussein exacted the televised political obeisance of foreign delegation after delegation who came seeking the release of family members and of countrymen and women. He thus shifted the hostage video from amateur to professional quality. From use by a band of obscure terrorists for often murky reasons, as a head of state, he used the hostage video to attain specific military and political objectives. And from a single, hand delivered piece of tape passed to whatever medium might be willing to use it, he made the hostage video into an ongoing series of shows, delivered in a structured way by his own controlled media.[43]

Although still quite experimental, the hostage video has already proved its versatility. It is now ripe for future exploitation, which can be expected to grow increasingly sophisticated.

NOTES

1. Thomas Mulvoy, Managing Editor of *The Boston Globe*, is quoted in Robert L. Kierstead, "A Grim But Newsworthy Picture," *The Boston Globe*, August 7, 1989, p. 15.
2. Several Western countries in addition to the U.S., and even the Soviet Union, have had

hostages taken in Lebanon, and all the Western countries have experienced media events, public reactions, and policy difficulties such as those described here. In August 1989, in addition to eight Americans, Great Britain, Italy, Ireland, and West Germany all still had hostages being held in Lebanon, and Belgium, Switzerland, Sweden, Norway, and France had previously had hostages held there. (*The Christian Science Monitor*, table, "Western Hostages Missing in Lebanon," August 2, 1989, p. 2.)

3. For some discussions of the controversial role of the media, especially television, during the 17-day crisis brought on by the 1985 hijacking of TWA Flight 847, see the following articles: Charles Krauthammer, "Looking Evil Dead in the Eye," *Time*, July 15, 1985, p. 80; Jonathan Alter, "The Network Circus. TV Turns Up the Emotional Volume," *Newsweek*, July 8, 1985, p. 21; Mary McGrory, "It Was a Drama Made For Television," *The Boston Globe*, July 3, 1985, p. 13; Alex S. Jones, "TV in the Hostage Crisis: Reporter or Participant?" *The New York Times*, July 2, 1985, p. A-7; Jonathan Alter with Michael A. Lerner and Theodore Stanger, "Does TV Help or Hurt? Journalists Are Accused of Giving Terror a Platform," *Newsweek*, July 1, 1985, pp. 32, 37; Edwin Diamond, "The Coverage Itself—Why It Turned Into 'Terrorvision,'" *TV Guide*, September 21, 1985, pp. 6-13; Neil Hickey, "The Impact On Negotiations—What the Experts Say," *TV Guide*, September 21, 1985, pp. 20-23; David Halberstam, "The Bottom Line: How to Do it Right the Next Time," *TV Guide*, September 21, 1985, pp. 24-25; Stephen Klaidman, "TV's Collusive Role," *The New York Times*, June 27, 1985, p. A-23; "Lessons For the Networks," *Newsweek*, July 15, 1985, p. 24; and James Kelly, with John Borrell and Lawrence Mondi, "Getting Into the Story. The Hostage Crisis Catches Journalists in the Cross Fire," *Time*, July 1, 1985, p. 48.

4. Russell Watson, with Douglas Waller, Ann McDaniel, Theodore Stanger, and Christopher Dickey, "Hostage Showdown," *Newsweek*, August 14, 1989, p. 17. (Article pp. 14-18.)

5. *Patterns of Global Terrorism*, 1988, U.S. Department of State, Publication 9705, March 1989, p. 59.

6. Ibid., pp. 59, 60, 45. For Iran's political, financial, and clerical influence, see also: Nora Boustany, "Khomeini's Death Seen as a Blow to Radical Shiites in Lebanon," *The Washington Post*, June 9, 1989, p. A-32; Brian Duffy with Steven Emerson and Richard Z. Chesnoff, "Iran's Agents of Terror," *U.S. News & World Report*, March 6, 1989, pp. 20-23; Russell Watson et al., "Hostage Showdown," *Newsweek*, August 14, 1989, p. 17; Mary Curtius, "Second Death Vowed if Israel Keeps Sheik," *The Boston Globe*, August 1, 1989, pp. 1-2; John Kifner, "Terrorist Group's Pro-Iranian Roots," *The New York Times*, August 2, 1989, p. A-11; Fouad Ajami, "Inside the Mind of a Movement," *U.S. News & World Report*, August 14, 1989, p. 28; "The Enduring Terrors of The Party of God," (Box), *U.S. News & World Report*, August 14, 1989, pp. 22-23; and A. M. Rosenthal, "On My Mind. The Death Squad," *The New York Times*, August 1, 1989, p. A-19. For background on the Hezbollah, see: Ehud Ya'Ari, "Rafsanjani May Not Be Able to Deliver," *The Wall Street Journal*, August 16, 1989, p. A-12; John Kifner, "Terrorist Group's Pro-Iranian Roots," *The New York Times*, August 2, 1989, p. A-11; Fouad Ajami, "Inside the Mind of a Movement," *U.S. News & World Report*, August 14, 1989, p. 28; Walter S. Mossberg and Barbara Rosewicz, "Hezbollah Frustrates a Gulliver-like U.S. Tiny Faction Plays Hostage Shell-Game, and Bush Can't Move," *The Wall Street Journal*, August 4, 1989, p. A-4; and "The Enduring Terrors of the Party of God," (Box), *U.S. News & World Report*, August 14, 1989, p. 22.

7. Walter S. Mossberg and Barbara Rosewicz, "Hezbollah Frustrates a Gulliver-Like U.S. Tiny Faction Plays Hostage Shell-Game, and Bush Can't Move," *The Wall Street Journal*, August 4, 1989, p. A-4, and Bernard Weinraub, "U.S. Readied Strike on Lebanon Bases; Hostage is Spared," *The New York Times*, August 4, 1989, p. 1.

8. Brian Duffy with Louise Lief, Kenneth T. Walsh, Peter Cary, Bruce B. Auster, and Richard Z. Chesnoff, "Talk Firmly and Send the Ships," *U.S. News & World Report*, August 14, 1989, p. 26. (Article pp. 22-26.)

9. Walter S. Mossberg and Barbara Rosewicz, "Hezbollah Frustrates a Gulliver-Like U.S. Tiny Faction Plays Hostage Shell-Game, and Bush Can't Move," *The Wall Street Journal*, August 4, 1989, p. A-4, and Bernard Weinraub, "U.S. Readied Strike on Lebanon Bases; Hostage is Spared," *The New York Times*, August 4, 1989, p. 1.

10. C.S. Manegold with Douglas Waller, Richard Sandza, Christopher Dickey, and Theodore Stanger, "The Failure of American Intelligence," *Newsweek*, August 14, 1989, p. 17. (Article pp. 16-17.) "CIA Can't Trace US Hostages," *The Christian Science Monitor*, August 17, 1989, p. 2.

11. Ehud Ya'Ari, "Rafsanjani May Not Be Able to Deliver," *The Wall Street Journal*, August 16, 1989, p. A-12, and *Patterns of Global Terrorism*, 1988, U.S. Department of State, Publication 9705, March 1989, p. 59.

12. Mel Laytner, "Hostages-Television," *United Press International*, December 26, 1980 (NEXIS); and Lanse Jones, "Hostages," *United Press International*, December 27, 1980 (NEXIS). See also: Oswald H. Ganley and Gladys D. Ganley, *To Inform Or To Control? The New Communications Networks*, Second Edition, Ablex Publishing Corporation, Norwood, NJ, 1989, p. 60, and Gladys D. Ganley and Oswald H. Ganley, *Global Political Fallout. The VCR's First Decade*, Ablex Publishing Corporation, Norwood, NJ, 1987, pp. 105-106. The Iranian kidnapping, with its resultant media blitz, was precipitated by President Carter when he permitted the deposed Shah to enter the United States for medical treatment. The hostage crisis served two major political purposes for Khomeini: It allowed him to punish Carter by bogging down the last year of his presidency and contributing to his loss of the 1980 presidential election, and it served to divert attention from serious dissentions within Khomeini's own newly formed Islamic government.

13. A show of terrorist power is also provided by another type of video, the "farewell" video stressing ultimate sacrifice for the cause left behind by car bomb drivers embarking on suicide missions. Various non-Hezbollah Muslim factions in Lebanon have long released such videos, but because of religious disputes regarding suicide missions, Hezbollah hesitated for quite awhile before releasing such videos. ("15 Reported Killed in Israeli Raid on Palestinian Bases in Lebanon," *The Boston Globe*, July 11, 1985, p. 9. "3rd Car Explosion in South Lebanon in A Week Kills 10," *The New York Times*, July 16, 1985, p. A-1. Ehud Ya'Ari, "Rafsanjani May Not Be Able to Deliver," *The Wall Street Journal*, August 16, 1989, p. A-12.)

14. Among many sources, Thatcher's 1985 comment to the American Bar Association meeting in London is quoted in George Bain, "The News in a Dangerous Era," *Maclean's*, August 26, 1985, p. 44.

15. "Higgins' Statement," *The Boston Globe*, February 23, 1988, p. 7.

16. The complete text of the video transcript is given in: "Statements by Anderson, Jacobsen," *The Boston Globe*, October 4, 1986, p. 7. See also: Charles P. Wallace, "Two Hostages Shown on Tape Making Plea for U.S. Help. Effort for Daniloff Cited," *The Boston Globe*, October 4, 1986, p. 1, and Ihsan A. Hijazi, "Hostages Tape a Plea For More Effort By U.S.," *The New York Times*, October 4, 1986, p. 4.

17. "Statements by Anderson, Jacobsen," *The Boston Globe*, October 4, 1986, p. 7.

18. Ihsan A. Hijazi, "A Captive Journalist Says, On a Videotape, He Spied," *The New York Times*, July 8, 1987, p. A-3. In June 1985, Glass had conducted spectacular and highly controversial interviews for ABC of hostages held by Lebanese terrorists during the TWA 847 hijacking. (Tom Shales, "Hijacking of TWA Flight 847. How ABC Scored Its Coup in Beirut," *The Boston Globe*, June 23, 1985, p. 18.)

19. White House spokesman, Marlin Fitzwater, said that such videos were usually made "with coercion and perhaps even with torture." ("U.S. Denies a C.I.A. Link," *The New York Times*, July 8, 1987, p. A-3.)

20. Farouk Nassar, "British Hostage Reported Killed," *The Boston Globe*, April 24, 1986, p. 8. (Article begins p. 1.)
21. Ibid.
22. While the FBI concluded after some days that the dead man was indeed Higgins, medical experts and intelligence sources were said to be of the opinion that Higgins had died or been tortured to death months earlier. (Russell Watson et al., "Hostage Showdown," *Newsweek*, August 14, 1989, p. 16; Jim Muir, "Lebanese Shiites Dispute Gains to Israel From Kidnapping," *The Christian Science Monitor*, August 2, 1989, p. 3; Adam Pertman and John W. Mashek, "FBI Says Higgins was Hanged Man in Tape," *The Boston Globe*, August 8, 1989, p. 10; Maureen Dowd, "White House Suggests Talks On Captives May Go Slowly," *The New York Times*, August 8, 1989, p. A-6, and John Bierman, with Eric Silver, William Lowther, Lara Marlowe, and Andrew Phillips, "Hostages to Terror," *Maclean's*, August 14, 1989, p. 23.)
23. Ihsan A. Hijazi, "Videotape Released. Act is Called Retaliation for Seizure of Cleric by Israeli Forces," *The New York Times*, August 1, 1989, p. A-6. (Article begins p. A-1.)
24. Ibid.
25. Mary Curtius, "Second Death Vowed if Israel Keeps Sheik," *The Boston Globe*, August 1, 1989, p. 1. See also: Jim Muir, "Lebanese Shiites Dispute Gains to Israel From Kidnapping," *The Christian Science Monitor*, August 2, 1989, p. 3.
26. Ihsan Hijazi, "Videotape Released. Act Is Called Retaliation for Seizure of Cleric by Israeli Forces," *The New York Times*, August 1, 1989, p. A-6.
27. Ihsan A. Hijazi, "Group Suspends Decision to Kill A U.S. Captive," *The New York Times*, August 4, 1989, pp. 1-A, 6-A (quote on 6-A).
28. John Bierman et al., "Hostages to Terror," *Maclean's*, August 14, 1989, p. 20.
29. "French Action in Beirut Could Harm Two US Hostages, Their Captors Warn," *The Boston Globe*, August 2, 1989, p. 13. See also: Ihsan A. Hijazi, "Beirut Captors Say French Move Imperils Hostages," *The New York Times*, August 21, 1989, and Hijazi, "France Says It Plans No Military Role in Lebanon," *The New York Times*, August 22, 1989, p. A-7.
30. Bill Carter, "Most Networks Show the Tape," *The New York Times*, August 1, 1989, p. A-6.
31. Bill Carter, "ABC News Refuses to Air Plea by Hostage," *The New York Times*, August 4, 1989, p. A-6.
32. Ibid.
33. Robert L. Kierstead, "A Grim But Newsworthy Picture," *The Boston Globe*, August 7, 1989, p. 15.
34. Craig S. Palosky, "Cicippio's Family Has Hope Restored," *The Boston Globe*, August 2, 1989, p. 12. Among the numerous pictures of Thomas Cicippio's placards were: Photo, *The New York Times*, August 2, 1989, p. A-11, and Photo, *The New York Times*, August 4, 1989, p. A-6.
35. Hilary Mackenzie, "One Family's Agony. The Cicippio Family Waits and Hopes," *Maclean's*, August 14, 1989, p. 24.
36. Carter's failure to resolve the Iran hostage crisis, and especially his failed attempt to rescue the hostages, probably cost him a second term as president. Reagan endured six years of helplessness at the hands of Hezbollah and tarnished his tenure with the Iran/ Contra scandal.
37. Joseph Sisco, a former diplomat and Under Secretary of State for Political Affairs in the Nixon and Ford Administrations, for instance, spoke approvingly of Bush for preventing the U.S. Government from getting bogged down on this one issue, for pursuing avenues of force and diplomacy in a complementary way, for not settling for a "quick fix," for consulting with the Congress before acting, and for ignoring threats and addressing positive possibilities for solutions. (Joseph J. Sisco, "Bush's Deft Hostage Policy," *The New York Times*, August 15, 1989, p. A-21.) *The Christian Science Monitor*

commented that "President Bush had managed an adroit mixture of action and restraint that minimized the media-fed power of the kidnappers." (Marshall Ingwerson, "Bush's Response to Kidnappers Gets High Marks. Diplomacy and Lessons From Past Presidents are Helping Him Handle Tensions, Analysts Say," *The Christian Science Monitor*, August 7, 1989, p. 1. See also: Randolph Ryan, "The Limits of Power," *The Boston Globe*, August 23, 1989, p. 19.)

38. See, for instance, Mary Curtius, "Shiite Group Suspends U.S. Hostage Execution," *The Boston Globe*, August 4, 1989, pp. 1, 2; Richard Lacayo, "Not Again," *Time*, August 14, 1989, pp. 14-23.

39. Bernard Weinraub, "President Calling Off Trip, Meets With Aides Over Crisis," *The New York Times*, August 1, 1989, p. A-1.

40. Marshall Ingwerson, "Bush's Response to Kidnappers Gets High Marks. Diplomacy and Lessons From Past Presidents are Helping Him Handle Tensions, Analysts Say," *The Christian Science Monitor*, August 7, 1989, p. 2. The person quoted was Robert Hunter, director of European studies at the Center for Strategic and International Studies, Washington, DC.

41. "I think the media would have made mincemeat of him if he hadn't come back...because of the videotape," *The Monitor* article quoted a former Carter National Security Council staff member as saying. (Ibid.)

42. On August 30, 1989, Rafsanjani won approval for all 22 members of his cabinet, which omitted the most rigid of the anti-Western hard liners. (Alan Cowell, "Iranian President Wins Approval of His Choices for Cabinet," *The New York Times*, August 30, 1989, p. A-3.)

43. For the first Hussein TV show with the hostages, see, for example, *Newsweek's* September 3, 1990 cover, and Elaine Sciolino, "Iraqi TV Shows a Smiling Leader With Grim-Faced British Captives," *The New York Times*, August 24, 1990, p. 1.

chapter 11

PERSONAL ELECTRONIC MEDIA IN THE 1988 U.S. ELECTION CAMPAIGN

Compared to other sectors in the United States, political candidates and parties were not particularly quick to adopt new technologies, but the use of new personal electronic media was in full swing by the 1988 election. The huge field of presidential candidates in the primaries of that election prompted vigorous use of any tool that could possibly stave off the competition. Many efforts begun tentatively in earlier elections also came to fruition in 1988. As *The New York Times* put it:[1]

> There were dozens of typewriters and three computers in the campaign office when Michael S. Dukakis ran for governor…in 1982. His 1988 Presidential campaign headquarters has dozens of computers and three typewriters.

The political uses of new personal media in the 1988 campaign included many like those discussed in previous chapters but some new angles were added. Among these were the extensive use of satellite transmitted TV; the computerized targeting of TV audiences; the use of cable television; the massive assembly of databases and use of political intelligence; computerized control and communications between headquarters and the field; inundation of computer selected targets by direct mail and telemarketing; the use of "attack" videos, "living room videos," instant response ads, and electronic direct mailers; computerized collection and dissemination of specialized news; and flooding of the mass media news with electronically delivered news releases and candidate interviews.

The wider implications of new personal media for the U.S. political process will be left to specialists. The state-of-the-use of these media in the '88 election campaign will be presented here as a reflection of the deep inroads these media have made in American life and society during less than a decade, of their adoption for political purposes by candidates for election, and as indicators of their probable political uses by more varied groups in the future.

SATELLITE TELEVISION AND CABLE STATIONS

Probably the most interesting use of new technologies by the 1988 candidates was their extensive employment of satellite-delivered television. Satellite delivery of videotaped news and other programming to anywhere there was a receiving dish, coupled with portable video cameras and with uplinks including the C-band truck, transformed network news gathering more than a decade ago. A combination of satellite delivery and cable TV outlets also gave religious and educational groups, businesses, and others the opportunity to tailor programming for delivery to specially targeted audiences.[2] By the 1988 election campaign, the ever increasing number of cable TV stations combined with cheaper and more convenient satellite uplinks and the steady growth of media rental services gave the candidates some really new options. The imaginative uses that were made of this combination during a campaign situation points to a powerful new area for varied types of future political exploitation.

There are about 8,000 cable systems in the United States, and more than half of all U.S. homes have cable access.[3] Cable viewers are also thought to have more interest in public affairs than average TV viewers. And, since cable stations are limited to small areas, or special interests—religion, sports, financial news, or ethnic groupings, for instance—specific audiences amenable to a given message can be easily targeted. Because cable is eager for customers, it is extremely cheap compared to most broadcast stations. On a small station, a 30-second ad could be had for only a few dollars.[4] Satellite time is relatively expensive, however, costing about $500 a minute.[5]

During the 1988 20-state Super Tuesday campaign, presidential candidate Richard Gephardt was described as renting a TV studio, buying satellite time for a TV address, and, via teleconferencing, successively answering the questions of viewers in five cities in five states: Texas, Maine, Louisiana, Georgia, and Oklahoma. For just $2,000, he addressed an audience totaling about a million, although targeting these audiences in the first place had cost quite a bit of money.[6] At one point, candidate Robert Dole placed a satellite feed to four television stations in Iowa and one in Boston. The half-hour of satellite time cost his campaign less than a half-minute ad in the Boston area. "I was all over Iowa today," said Dole.[7] Candidate Michael Dukakis was able to reach a million and a half potential viewers, targeted through 100 cablers in six states at one time. The studio, satellite transmission, and cable transmission time cost was as little as a cent and a half per household.[8] For this, Dukakis is said to have gotten a 1-hour teleconference in which he could answer questions phoned in from viewers. The effort was pronounced "an historic first in presidential campaigning" by his campaign manager, Susan Estrich.[9] Political analyst Ray Strother has called this kind of teleconferencing "completely new: the first we've seen of it," and proclaimed it "the future of American politics."[10]

KU-BAND TRUCKS

The Ku-band satellite uplink truck, introduced in 1984, is the most novel addition to the satellite uplink galaxy. Smaller, easier to handle, more mobile, and especially cheaper than the C-band truck long used by the television networks, over recent years these trucks have allowed local television stations to compete with the networks in many aspects of news gathering.[11]

Until half a decade ago, the process of getting pictures from a field videocamera converted to microwave and beamed to a satellite was too expensive and difficult for almost anyone besides the TV networks. But, as the 1988 presidential campaign approached, about 130 Ku-Band trucks, which operate as field production and transmission units, had become available. Besides their other advantages, Ku-band trucks operate on frequencies used only for satellites, while C-band shares frequencies with telephones and microwaves, and transmission thus requires more advance planning than Ku-band, as well as coordination and reservations. While the purchase price of a Ku-band truck is still from $350,000 to $750,000 each, these trucks can be rented for as little as $3,500 a day, and facilities have rapidly grown to meet the need for satellite time arrangements.[12] Falling prices and increased convenience resulted in the fact that satellite trucks attending national political party conventions grew from half a parking lot's worth in 1980 to a whole parking lot's worth in 1984 to two parking lots' worth in 1988.[13]

Election Politics has called Ku-band a candidate's "technological trump card," which "can psych out opponents while providing a devastating production and news advantage."[14]

Presidential primary candidate Paul Simon was among the Ku-band truck users. During the February 1988 caucuses in Iowa, he rented a truck and was thus "able to do a series of 'live' late-afternoon interviews with local television stations from Omaha to Chicago."[15]

WATCH PARTIES

Watch parties are said to have been pioneered by Walter Mondale in 1984, who held "more than 5,000 on one day" in conjunction with a "five-minute national TV spot."[16] Like those focused around "living room videos," this TV-oriented version of parties is used for political benefits or orientations held in houses or as smallish events in local hotels or other centers. These events may be timed to a paid TV spot, but are also sometimes used on the occasion of a debate, a general address by a candidate, or of some other special TV appearance. During the 1988 campaign, Pat Robertson gave a satellite "watch party" for about 5,000 people in Texas, aimed at 70 TV outlets, a dozen homes with satellite dishes, and a hotel ballroom in Austin.[17] Several candidates set up parties in 1988 tied to a debate on the first of December. Among them, Richard Gephardt is said to have scheduled 2,000 parties in 50 states timed to coincide with this event, and Bruce Babbitt, 185 parties.[18]

ELECTRONIC NEWS RELEASES AND OTHER QUESTS FOR "FREE MEDIA"

At the Iowa caucuses alone, more than 30 local TV stations from all over the country brought along satellite trucks. Since this increased the ease with which news could be reported live, the candidates barraged the stations with offers of live interviews.[19] But candidates also used their own satellite transmission efforts to inundate the local stations with electronic news releases. Albert Gore paid $6,000 to have a videotape of the announcement of his candidacy sent by satellite "to every local station in the country."[20] Bruce Babbitt and Pierre S. du Pont IV satellited their Iowa debate to all local stations.[21] Richard Gephardt's campaign paid $7,000 to have a crew make a videotape of his trip through the south and offered highlights via satellite to 25 television stations (12 of whom accepted).[22]

Various companies, such as One on One Service and Potomac Communications, arranged satellite interviews with the candidates by local stations, with the candidates paying for the satellite time.[23] During the build-up to Super Tuesday, *The New York Times* reported that news directors at TV stations in several states were being flooded with offers of "two-minute interviews via satellite from some remote location."[24]

This satellite blitz of local stations worried some people, because it was felt that the stations could be politically "used," especially where reporters were less sophisticated and inexperienced with handling campaign aides.[25] *The Wall Street Journal* referred to critics who "say the new technology helps candidates stage-manage the news by paying for coverage."[26]

R.D. Sahl, Boston's WNEV-TV News co-anchor, has said the fear is that satellite interviews, set up with little warning, can help candidates control the situation and evade tough questions.[27] Philip Balboni, news director at Boston's WCVB-TV, is quoted as saying "Candidates are getting perilously close to buying news coverage."[28]

AUDIOCASSETTES AND VIDEOCASSETTES

Pat Robertson was the candidate who made the most concerted use of audiocassettes, which he sent out all over the country as direct mailers. At least 300,000 audiocassettes were sent into Iowa and New Hampshire before their caucuses and primary, 200,000 into South Carolina alone before Super Tuesday, and "hundreds" more into Alaska.[29] The tapes were said to be used, among other things, to "burn the negatives," that is, to "break down people's reluctance to vote for a former religious broadcaster."[30] In January 1988, Robertson's bill for audio- and videocassette reproduction was reported to be $408,000.[31]

Videocassettes began to be used as direct mailers by any group only in 1987,[32] and the build up to the 1988 campaign helped along this effort. Robertson was among the most vigorous users of videocassettes as well as audiocassettes, but virtually all of the candidates used videos as direct mailers and handouts.[33] Bruce Babbitt, for instance, sent 500 videotapes into New Hampshire as direct mailers, while Bob Dole distributed about a thousand as the focus for house parties.[34] Potential candidate Pat Schroeder also made videos available for showing at 700 coordinated house parties held on one Sunday.[35]

Various special interests prepared videos for the campaign period. The AFL-CIO produced a video that posed questions to the candidates and asked for candidate responses to incorporate into a finished video which would be distributed to various labor groups.[36] The National Right to Life group also produced a "training video" called "1988: If You Care, You'll Be There."[37]

The most famous video (outside of ads) of the 1988 campaign was the "attack video" described in Chapter 3, accusing Senator Joseph Biden of plagerism. Typical of other "attack videos" was one prepared by Massachusetts Republicans and made available to Republican chairmen in every state, telling the "truth" about Michael Dukakis.[38]

Paid TV advertising, which accounted for much of the 1988 candidates' spending, had been escalating in importance over the past several elections, videotaped ads having come into general use during the campaigns of late 1970s and early 1980s. Although video is said to produce a less realistic ad product than film, it has been found ideal for making the (variously called) "instant response," "back-and-forth," or "counter" commercials.[39] Computer technology combined with video technology is necessary to produce the barrage of such ads which the candidates in the 1988 campaign regularly used to criticize each other. *The New York Times* credits the "spirited volley" of ads the 1988 candidates aimed at each other to this new combination of technologies:[40]

> that now allows a campaign to conduct a survey, analyze the effect of an opponent's spot, write a response, shoot it and put it on the air, all within 24 hours.

This back-and-forth technique, used as long ago as 1982 in Senate races,[41] has been greatly aided by upgraded and widely disseminated computers.

USES OF COMPUTERS IN THE CAMPAIGN

Mainframe computers were initiated into U.S. electoral proceedings by the Republicans in the 1970s, being used at that time to keep fundraising lists and to do bookkeeping and word processing.[42] Computers were also used extensively by the Republicans during the two Reagan campaigns. By 1988, the Democrats had more or less caught up with the Republicans. In 1984, the Democrats had taken only 12 PCs along to their convention, while in 1988, they took along, and networked, 300.[43] Besides their first massive use in a presidential campaign, computers were also put to general use for the first time in 1988 Congressional races.[44]

Although still very much in use, mainframes and minicomputers often took a back seat to networks of desktop PCs and hosts of laptops in the 1988 campaign. The types of uses to which computers could be put had in the meantime exploded. As one campaign's computer operations director said:[45]

> Asking a political professional in 1988 how he uses a computer is a little bit like asking a reporter how he uses his telephone.

A few of these uses were for identifying and contacting target groups, tracking delegates, communicating with headquarters, collecting and analyzing information on the opposition, keeping up-to-date via the "Campaign Hotline," as an aid in poll taking, and as a multi-purpose tool in running the party convention.

Identifying and Contacting Target Groups

PCs were used extensively to combine voter lists with information from other data banks, and to break this information down by such things as age, sex, ethnic group, income, or special interests. Computerized voter lists by name, address, and political party drawn up for the various states, and available to campaigns for a few thousand dollars, have been referred to as "one of the most sophisticated new areas of campaign technology."[46] For instance, to target upscale Democrats under age 30, voter lists can be compared with lists of car registrations and drivers licenses to pick out young people who own sports cars.[47] A *Washington Post* editorial remarked, only partly facetiously, that such lists can now be narrowed down to "left-handed dog owners."[48] By combining various computer-generated databases with each other, the possibilities for breadth or pinpointing is nearly limitless. Other mailing lists are available from a wide variety of sources, and special-interest organizations routinely sell or exchange them. Targeting in this way for fund raising and vote getting is part of the larger problem of computer-induced invasions of privacy.[49]

Once targeted, groups involving thousands can easily be barraged with personalized letters, courtesy of the computer. During the Iowa caucus, for example, Missourians sent 16,000 letters to Iowans in support of Richard Gephardt, and Representative Claude Pepper of Florida sent 56,000 letters specifically targeted to Iowa's senior citizens.[50] Gephardt himself used a network of PCs to send personalized invitations for the caucuses to all Iowa Democrats.[51] Similar efforts were made in Iowa and elsewhere for and by the other candidates, with the total computerized messages from the various campaigns numbering in the untold millions. This was not an entirely new endeavor, however, since in 1984, the Reagan campaign had already made "multi-million-copy mailings."[52]

Computerized phone banks can also zero in on targets, and all of the campaigns were thus enabled to make tens of thousands of daily phone calls. Calls to computer-selected people were often made personally by campaign workers with some computer assistance. But, using a programmed script, the computer could also dial and deliver a message, using a human assistant to push the proper response buttons and update the computer files.[53] Richard Gephardt, again, as just one example, sent out a taped message to thousands of Michigan homes via computer.[54] Such telemarketing with computerized messages had already been used to some extent in the 1984 presidential campaign.

Mapping Media Markets

PCs and other computers were used in the 1988 campaign to identify and map special media markets for everything from Super Tuesday's 20 states to various cable TV neighborhoods. Farrell Media, Inc., which had mapped the markets for President Reagan's 1984 campaign, performed the same task for George Bush. *The New York Times* reported that, for all Super Tuesday markets, Farrell's computer was able to estimate prices and time availability "in minutes."[55] The ability to move quickly was absolutely crucial to stay ahead in a race where there was such a variety of political competition.

Tracking Delegates

Both Republicans and Democrats set up computer systems to keep constant track of their delegate support. The Dukakis Campaign reportedly stored useful personal information on delegates in its computer, down to and including the interests and preferences of families. The computer tracked the number of times each delegate was contacted and his or her reactions, and maintained a constantly updated record of probable support level.[56] The Bush Campaign kept much the same sort of computerized information. The Republicans also wooed delegates by sending them certificates, as well as greeting cards for anniversaries and birthdays.[57]

Using Databases to "Get the Goods" on the Competition

Beginning with President Reagan's 1984 campaign, computers have been used to store data useful in defeating the opposition, data often contained in the opponent's past speeches. In 1984, the Republican Opposition Research Group collected innumerable hours worth of videotapes of Walter Mondale's activities, plus 75,000 of his quotations. This and other information, coded and cross-referenced for easy retrieval from a Republican Headquarters computer, was used, among other things, "to insert attack lines into Reagan speeches."[58] Similar materials were compiled and used in the 1988 campaign by the candidates of both parties.[59]

Databases were also much used by reporters during the campaign to investigate the candidates. For example, a *Washington Post* computer analyzed Gary Hart's records as a basis for questions about his campaign finances.[60] Databases that record just about every transaction conducted in daily life are now, in any case, regular resources for investigative reporters.[61]

Aiding Poll Taking

Computers were also used in the 1988 campaign to help speed up the ever-increasing numbers of polls being taken. Although computers were already employed in 1984 presidential polls, 1988 marked the first time they had been fully tested. Following interviews, their "lightning speed and new networking systems" were used "to compile and tabulate data and present the results in graphic form within seconds."[62] The computer also assisted in selecting the areas to be polled and in collecting the necessary information. It could be programmed to randomly select phone numbers, dial them, and keep calling back until somebody answered.[63]

The reactions of selected 1988 groups to candidates were analyzed, using methods similar to those which measure reactions to commercial ads, and also used to measure potential voter response to 1984 political debates. Audiences recorded their responses to speeches or debates through knobs on hand-held devices, or by using digital keypads, with a PC collecting the information. A computer then separated the responses according to various criteria and analyzed the results immediately. Although these analyses were controversial, the method did provide instant feedback, which was said to be useful in attempts to improve candidates' performances.[64]

Communicating With Headquarters

Armies of computers in the field were used to communicate with other computers at campaign headquarters during the 50-state campaign activities. Laptops let campaign assistants write the day's news and reports and ship them off to homebase computers via telephone and modem.[65] Laptops were also the constant companions of campaign-following news reporters.

Computers At The Conventions

Various computerized methods were used at the conventions to furnish the public with information, distribute party-generated news, maintain unity under stress, and supply information to the media.[66] The Democrats linked their network of 300 PCs, which were scattered about Atlanta and connected by Local Area Networks (LANS) and Wide Area Networks (WANs), to a Washington, DC headquarters mainframe. Among other things, the computers issued thousands of delegate credentials daily. Some Macintosh PCs were also brought along by the Democrats, specifically to do some on-the-spot desktop publishing.[67]

The Hotline

The Presidential Campaign '88 Hotline, a computer version of the faxed newspapers described in an earlier chapter, supplied information specifically directed toward the campaign from September 1987 until the election. The Hotline was a private, nonpartisan venture that used computers to collect hot-off-the-griddle political news and information from newspapers, TV news, and the various campaigns, and to ship compilations of this news to specialized subscribers.[68] A PC, a modem, and a subscription fee of up to $350 a month got the information to politicians, campaign headquarters, lobbyists, political funding groups, and members of the news media.[69] Some news media members got a discount for Hotline's services by contributing their own political writings (by computer, of course) to the Hotline.

Each campaign was allowed to contribute 200 words a day of its own choosing to the Hotline. The staffs of several of the presidential candidates were regular contributors, shipping their laptop-produced prose by modem and phone line from wherever they happened to be at the moment.[70] Among other things, campaign staffs sometimes used their 200 words for "damage control," that is, to quickly rebut adverse stories.[71]

By collecting computerized news from sources all over the country, not just the usual few, the Hotline, it was said, made much more varied news available than usual. It also dispersed local news from scenes of intense action more widely and up to 48 hours earlier than traditional means were doing, including that from key states like Iowa and New Hampshire. Hotline was thus praised for serving a democratizing role by giving local reporting and other sources a chance to compete in the national arena. But it was also criticized for providing a single homogenized source of information for all reporters. It made reporting too easy and too similar, said some critics, discouraging independent exploration of sources and encouraging "pack journalism."[72] Because of Hotline's success, similar services devoted to other political activities are very likely to be forthcoming.

POLITICAL USES OF THESE TECHNOLOGIES IN MORE GENERAL SITUATIONS

Variations on the uses described above have been cited in other chapters for many of these new media and there is nothing to prevent all such uses from finding adaptations among the peoples of the world in general. As one example, satellite TV to targeted audiences can lend itself to cross-border political activities, and has been used that way in at least two instances. *U.S. News & World Report* has claimed that, in December 1988, two Hezbollah members came to the U.S. to talk to "American-based Moslem extremist groups." Their contacts, it said, included 2,000 students who met in Tulsa, Oklahoma, and "watched a speech by Iranian President Ali Kameini beamed by satellite from Teheran." The magazine cited U.S. officials who deal with counterterrorism as saying that there is no law to "prevent even the Ayatollah Khomeini from buying satellite-TV time."[73] And *Time* reported that in 1985 Louis Farrakhan, leader of the black Nation of Islam group, invited members of Chicago's El Rukns gang to a rally, the main feature of which was a "watch party" focused on a live satellite broadcast by Libya's Colonel Gaddafi. In this cross-border address, Gadaffi, to whom El Rukns members had pledged their allegiance in a videotape, is said to have "urged blacks serving in the U.S. military to desert and join his forces."[74]

NOTES

1. Andrew Rosenthal, "Politicians Yield to Computers. Campaigns Finally Adopt Technology," *The New York Times*, May 9, 1988, p. D-1.
2. Sidney Topol, Chairman of the Board for Scientific Atlanta, "The Global Impact of Satellite Television," Seminar, Center for International Affairs and Program on Information Resources Policy, Harvard University, Cambridge, MA, October 29, 1990. See also: Oswald H. Ganley and Gladys D. Ganley, *To Inform Or To Control? The New Communications Networks*, Second Edition, Ablex Publishing Corporation, Norwood, NJ, 1989, pp. 58-61.
3. Richard Fly and Frances Seghers, "Campaign '88 Makes a Cable Connection. Lower Costs and Upscale Audiences Draw Candidates' Dollars," *Business Week*, November 23, 1987, p. 74; and Andrew Rosenthal, "Cable TV Playing Key Role in 1988," *The New York Times*, January 16, 1988, p. A-8.
4. Andrew Rosenthal, "Cable TV Playing Key Role in 1988," *The New York Times*, January 16, 1988, p. A-8.
5. For some discussion of the uses of these and other technologies in the 1988 campaign, see Jeffrey B. Abramson et al., *The Electronic Commonwealth*, Basic Books, Inc., New York, 1988, Chapter 3.
6. John Aloysius Farrell, "Stumping Out, Media In As March 8 Nears," *The Boston Globe*, February 29, 1988, pp. 1, 6.
7. Bob Davis, "....So, Candidates Take to Outer Space to Launch Invasions of Local Stations," *The Wall Street Journal*, January 13, 1988, p. 50.
8. "Candidate Dukakis Holding Conference Using 100 Cablers," *Variety*, January 20, 1988, p. 165; Bob Kur, NBC Nightly News, January 29, 1988.
9. "Candidate Dukakis Holding Conference Using 100 Cablers," *Variety*, January 20, 1988, p. 165. See also Diane Alters and Thomas Oliphant, "Dukakis Steps Up Rhythm in Iowa, and a Vigorous Kennedy Pitches In," *The Boston Globe*, January 22, 1988, p. 10.
10. John Aloysius Farrell, "Stumping Out, Media In as March 8 Nears," *The Boston Globe*, February 29, 1988, pp. 1, 6.

11. Dennis Holder, "Local Coverage on Ku. Direct Broadcasting, A Place in History," *Washington Journalism Review*, October 1985, pp. 46-49. See also: Andrew Blake, "Boston Television Won't Skimp on Coverage," *The Boston Globe*, August 14, 1988, p. 23; Andrew Blake, "Byte by Byte, Technology Aids Reporters," *The Boston Globe*, July 3, 1988, p. 12; Gregory Katz, "High-Tech TV Is Top Player in Iowa Race," *USA Today*, February 3, 1988, p. 1-A, and Harry F. Waters with Peter McKillop, "TV News: The Rapid Rise of Home Rule. Local Newscasts are Stealing the Networks' Beat," *Newsweek*, October 17, 1988, pp. 94-97.

12. Keith Bradsher, "Broadcast Wheels. High-Tech Trucks Dish Up News from Seoul to Santa Ana," *Los Angeles Times*, February 22, 1988, Pt. IV, p. 5; Dennis Holder, "Local Coverage on Ku. Direct Broadcasting, a Place in History," *Washington Journalism Review*, October 1985, pp. 46-49; Gregory Katz, "High Tech TV is Top Player in Iowa Race," *USA Today*, February 3, 1988, p. 1-A, and Harry F. Waters with Peter McKillop, "TV News: The Rapid Rise of Home Rule. Local Newscasts are Stealing the Networks' Beat," *Newsweek*, October 17, 1988, pp. 94-97.

13. R. D. Sahl, Co-anchor, WNEV-TV News, Boston, Seminar, The Joan Shorenstein Barone Center on the Press, Politics, and Public Policy, John F. Kennedy School of Government, Harvard University, Cambridge, MA, October 24, 1989.

14. Paul O. Wilson, "Presidential Advertising in 1988," *Election Politics*, Volume 4, No. 4, Fall 1987, p. 21. (Article pp. 17-21.)

15. "An Event-Filled Day in Iowa: '88 Campaigns See the Finish Line," *The Washington Post*, November 9, 1988, p. A-8. (Article begins p. A-1.) See also: Thomas Oliphant, "Democrats Hold Early Revelry in Iowa," *The Boston Globe*, November 8, 1987, p. 28. Andrew Blake, "Byte by Byte, Technology Aids Reporters," *The Boston Globe*, July 3, 1988, p. 12.

16. Mary T. Schmich, "Schroeder Goes Video to Raise Funds," *Chicago Tribune*, September 21, 1987, Section 1, p. 4. See also: Hal Malchow and Fran May, "Television Watch Parties: 1984's Fundraising Innovation," *Campaigns & Elections*, Fall 1985, pp. 18-22.

17. Howard LaFranchi, "Robertson Mix: Satellites and Coffee Klatches. GOP Hopeful Adds Video to His Campaign Arsenal," *The Christian Science Monitor*, December 3, 1987, p. 1.

18. "TV Parties Planned to Aid 3 Hopefuls," *The Boston Globe*, December 2, 1987, p. 26.

19. Gregory Katz, "High-tech TV Is Top Player in Iowa Race," *USA Today*, February 3, 1988, p. 1-A.

20. Ronald Brownstein, "Here's How Coverage Will Change—In Response to Network Budget Cuts, Improved Technology and the Large Field of Candidates," *TV Guide*, October 31, 1987, p. 7. (Article pp. 5-9.)

21. Ibid.

22. Bob Kur, NBC Nightly News, January 29, 1988.

23. Ibid.

24. Andrew Rosenthal, "Candidates Can Land On TV Just By Landing," *The New York Times*, March 3, 1988, pp. A-1, D-23 (quote on D-23).

25. For example, see: Gregory Katz, "High-Tech TV is Top Player in Iowa Race," *USA Today*, February 3, 1988, p. 1-A; and Andrew Rosenthal, "Candidates Can Land On TV Just By Landing," *The New York Times*, March 3, 1988, pp. A-1, D-23. Bob Kur, on NBC Nightly News, January 29, 1988, also mentioned this.

26. Bob Davis, "...So, Candidates Take to Outer Space to Launch Invasions of Local Stations," *The Wall Street Journal*, January 13, 1988, p. 50.

27. R.D. Sahl, Co-anchor, WNEV-TV News, Boston, Seminar, The Joan Shorenstein Barone Center on the Press, Politics, and Public Policy, John F. Kennedy School of Government, Harvard University, Cambridge, MA, October 24, 1989.

28. Bob Davis, "....So, Candidates Take to Outer Space to Launch Invasions of Local Stations," *The Wall Street Journal*, February 13, 1988, p. 50.

29. John Ellement, "On Tapes in N.H. Mailing, Robertson Toughens Talk," *The Boston Globe*, February 4, 1988, p. 24; David Rogers and James M. Perry, "Dole Wins Big in GOP Caucus in Iowa: Gephardt Leads Democratic Contenders. Robertson's Surprise Finish in Second Place Leaves Vice President in Third," *The Wall Street Journal*, February 9, 1988, p. 70; Jonathan Alter with Howard Fineman, Mark Miller, and Patricia King, "Pat Robertson: The TelePolitician. He's Much More Than a 'Christian Businessman,'" *Newsweek*, February 22, 1988, pp. 18-19; James M. Perry and David Shribman, "Robertson's Showing and Dole's Triumph Change GOP Picture. Bush's Lead Could Dwindle in New Hampshire Race, But He Has Advantages. Who Will Stop The Preacher?" *The Wall Street Journal*, February 10, 1988, p. 1; David Nyhan, "Will Rev. Robertson Keep Rolling?" *The Boston Sunday Globe*, February 14, 1988, p. A-23. "Robertson Is Victor in Alaska," *The New York Times*, March 3, 1988, p. D-23; Andrew Rosenthal, "New Hampshire Ponders Robertson," *The New York Times*, February 10, 1988, p. A-22; John Robinson, "A 'Hidden Army' of Christian Soldiers. Robertson's Supporters, Concerned About US Morality, Begin to Emerge," *The Boston Globe*, February 11, 1988, p. 20; Harrison Rainie, with Gordon Witkin, Sharon F. Golden, and Donald Baer, "Robertson's Grand Design," *U.S. News & World Report*, February 22, 1988, pp. 14-18; Walter V. Robinson, "The Stakes Rise in South Carolina Primary," *The Boston Globe*, February 27, 1988, p. 6; and David Nyhan, "Robertson Rides Magic Carpet Into N.H.," *The Boston Globe*, February 10, 1988, p. 19.

30. Harrison Rainie with Gordon Witkin, Sharon F. Golden and Donald Baer, "Robertson's Grand Design," *U.S. News & World Report*, February 22, 1988, p. 18. (Article pp. 14-18.)

31. John Robinson, "How Robertson Outspends Jackson's Shoestring Campaign," *The Boston Globe*, March 1, 1988, p. 12.

32. Diane Cole, "A Hot Medium For the Message," *The New York Times*, November 29, 1987, p. 17.

33. John Milne, "Candidates Reach Out to N. H. Voters—Via Video," *The Boston Globe*, November 2, 1987, p. 1. For Robertson, see also: Michael Kranish, "Robertson Candidacy at Crucial Crossroad," *The Boston Globe*, November 6, 1987, p. 1.

34. John Milne, "Candidates Reach Out to N. H. Voters—Via Video," *The Boston Globe*, November 2, 1987, p. 1. See also: Steven Marantz, "As Iowa Steals the Spotlight, N.H. Tactic is 'Spin Control,'" *The Boston Sunday Globe*, February 7, 1988, p. 23.

35. Mary T. Schmich, "Schroeder Goes Video to Raise Funds," *Chicago Tribune*, September 21, 1987, Section 1, p. 4.

36. James Warren, "Candidates Face Labor's Screen Test," *The Chicago Tribune*, April 13, 1987, Section 1, p. 13.

37. "An Event-Filled Day in Iowa: '88 Campaigns See the Finish Line," *The Washington Post*, November 9, 1988, pp. A-1, A-8.

38. Christine Chinlund and John Ellement, "Republicans Lash Out At Opponents' 'Pastel Patriotism,'" *The Boston Globe*, August 17, 1988, p. 16. (Article begins p. 1.)

39. Paul O. Wilson, "Presidential Advertising in 1988," *Election Politics*, Volume 4, No. 4, Fall, 1987, pp. 17-21. This article is a good review of the history of political ads, from the first presidential radio programs in 1924 and political radio spots in 1928 to the varied uses of videotaped ads at present.

40. Randall Rothenberg, "TV's New Age of Thrust and Parry," *The New York Times*, August 7, 1988, p. 24. For a discussion of back-and-forth ads, see also: Michael Barone, "Is Technology to Blame?" *The Washington Post*, November 2, 1986, p. C-8, and Andy Plattner, "The Key Ingredient. It's the Year of Counterpunch Politics, and TV Ads Will Define the Race," *U.S. News & World Report*, August 29/September 5, 1988, pp. 54-55.

41. The first "back-and-forth" ad is claimed to have been used during the senate race of Harriet Woods in Missouri in 1982. It was then extensively used in the 1984 North Carolina campaign of Senator Jesse Helms. By 1986, it is said to have become

"commonplace" in senatorial races. (Randall Rothenberg, "TV's New Age of Thrust and Parry," *The New York Times*, August 7, 1988, p. 24, and also Michael Barone, "Is Technology to Blame?" *The Washington Post*, November 2, 1986, p. C-8.)

42. Jon Haber, "Waging Political War with Computer Weaponry," *The Boston Globe*, June 27, 1988, p. 29. For a good look at how campaigns are run, and the way computers fit their needs, see: Thomas E. Baker, *Computers and Political Campaigns: A Look At Technology and Social Change*, Program on Information Resources Policy, Harvard University, Cambridge, MA, June 1983.

43. Lawrence J. Magid, "Computer File. Will Hosts of PCs Help Democrats?" *Los Angeles Times*, July 14, 1988, Pt. IV, p. 3.

44. Jon Haber, "Waging Political War With Computer Weaponry," *The Boston Globe*, June 27, 1988, p. 29. See also: Jon Haber, "Computers for Microcampaigns," *Campaigns and Elections*, January 1988, p. 55ff.

45. Andrew Rosenthal, "Politicians Yield to Computers. Campaigns Finally Adopt Technology," *The New York Times*, May 9, 1988, pp. D-1, D-5. Pamela Lowry, Director of Computer Operations for the Dukakis campaign, is being quoted.

46. John Milne, "FEC Reviews 4 Candidates' Methods of Paying For Voter Lists," *The Boston Globe*, January 28, 1988, p. 17. Richard Gephardt's manager in the New Hampshire campaign, Mark Longabaugh, is being quoted.

47. Ibid.

48. "Opening Up Direct Mail," Editorial, *The Washington Post*, September 29, 1988, p. A-20.

49. Among other articles dealing with the general subject of privacy invasion due to new computer powers, see: Mary Lu Carnevale and Julie Amparano Lopez, "Party Line. Making a Phone Call Might Mean Telling The World About You. Number Identification Service Is a Dream for Marketers But a Threat to Privacy. Name, Home, Pay, Car Model," *The Wall Street Journal*, November 28, 1989, p. 1, and Jeffrey Rothfeder with Stephen Phillips, Dean Foust, Wanda Cantrell, Paula Dwyer, and Michele Galen, "Is Nothing Private? Computers Hold Lots of Data on You—And There are Few Limits on Its Use," *Business Week*, September 4, 1989, pp. 74-82.

50. Chris Black, "In Iowa, It's the Best Organization That Counts," *The Boston Globe*, February 1, 1988, p. 12.

51. Jon Haber, "Waging Political War With Computer Weaponry," *The Boston Globe*, June 27, 1988, p. 29.

52. Ibid.

53. David S. Boim, "The Telemarketing Center: Nucleus of a Modern Campaign," *Campaigns and Elections*, Spring 1984, pp. 73-78.

54. Andrew Rosenthal, "Politicians Yield to Computers. Campaigns Finally Adopt Technology," *The New York Times*, May 9, 1988, p. D-1.

55. Ibid., p. D-5.

56. John Aloysius Farrell, "Dukakis Going on High-tech Hunt to Bag Nomination Before Atlanta," *The Boston Globe*, April 24, 1988, p. 19.

57. Andrew Rosenthal, "Politicians Yield to Computers. Campaigns Finally Adopt Technology," *The New York Times*, May 9, 1988, p. D-1.

58. "Secret Reagan Weapon in Race: Computer," *The New York Times*, November 13, 1984, p. A-25. See also: Michael J. Bayer and Joseph Rodota, "Computerized Opposition Research: The Instant Parry," *Campaigns and Elections*, Spring 1985, pp. 25-29; and Jon Haber, "Waging Political War with Computer Weaponry," *The Boston Globe*, June 27, 1988, p. 29.

59. Jon Haber, "Waging Political War With Computer Weaponry," *The Boston Globe*, June 27, 1988, p. 29.

60. Richard L. Berke, "Hart's Advisers Deny New Charges, but Are Fearful of Impact," *The New York Times*, January 22, 1988, p. A-16.

61. Gregory Stricharchuk, "Computer Records Become Powerful Tool for Investigative Reporters and Editors," *The Wall Street Journal*, February 3, 1988, p. 25; Tim Miller, "The Data-base Revolution. A Look at How Reporters are Making Use of a Powerful New Technology," *Columbia Journalism Review*, September/October 1988, pp. 35-38; Tom McNichol, "Databases. Reeling in Scoops with High Tech," *Washington Journalism Review*, July/August 1987, pp. 27-29; and Kathleen Hansen and Jean Ward, "Quantity In, Quantity Out. On-Line With Electronic Information," *Washington Journalism Review*, August 1985, pp. 53-55. For a good discussion of the uses of various electronic technologies by reporters, see: Andrew Blake, "Byte by Byte, Technology Aids Reporters," *The Boston Globe*, July 3, 1988, p. 12.

62. Jerry Ackerman, "Computers Make Polls Speedier," *The Boston Globe*, March 7, 1988, p. 28.

63. Ibid.

64. Andrew W. Rosenthal, "Political Marketing. Campaigning to Instant Responses," *The New York Times*, July 25, 1987, p. A-9.

65. Brit Hume, "Lightweight Tandy Lap-Top Makes It Easier to Write on the Go," *The Washington Post*, Washington Business Section, February 8, 1988, p. 19.

66. Leslie Phillips, "Dems Go High-Tech to Make News in GA," *USA Today*, June 21, 1988, p. 4A. See also: Beth A. Miller, "Hotline Offers Inside Scoop," *First Monday*, August 1988, p. 9.

67. Lawrence J. Magid, "Computer File. Will Host of PCs Help Democrats?" *Los Angeles Times*, July 14, 1988, Part IV, p. 3.

68. Robert L. Turner, "The Political Force is With Us. New Computerized Hotline Links Press, Pollsters, and Presidential Players," *The Boston Globe*, January 31, 1988, p. 73. See also: Mickey Kaus and Eleanor Clift, "Fresh-Baked Political Wisdom. How to Cover a Campaign Without Really Trying," *Newsweek*, November 2, 1987, p. 83.

69. Susan Dillingham, "Business Briefing. Politicians, Media Get '88 Campaign Hotline," *Insight*, November 9, 1987, p. 43.

70. Robert L. Turner, "The Political Force is With Us. New Computerized Hotline Links Press, Pollsters and Presidential Players," *The Boston Globe*, January 31, 1988, p. 73.

71. Eleanor Randolph, "A Hot-Off-The-Wire Service for Political Junkies. Computerized Information Flows Daily from McLean for Morning Digestion," *The Washington Post*, October 11, 1987, p. A-18.

72. Ibid., and also Jonathan Kaufman, "Pace of Politics Quickens. Computer 'Hotline' Keeps Media Moving," *The Boston Globe*, August 24, 1988, p. 1.

73. "Washington Whispers. Greetings From Hezbollah," Charles Fenyvesi, ed., *U.S. News & World Report*, April 3, 1989, p. 16. See also: "The Latest Hezbollah Caper," *Infoscope*, Volume 11, Number 5, May 1989, p. 1.

74. "Gaddafi's Goons. A Chicago Gang's Terrorist Plot," *Time*, December 7, 1987, p. 27.

chapter 12

THE CHINA STORY*

During the first weekend in June 1989, hell literally broke loose in Tiananmen Square in Beijing. The government of the Peoples' Republic of China brutally crushed the 7-week-old nonviolent demonstrations by university students and their supporters which called for more freedom, the so-called "pro-democracy movement."[1] Restrictions were slapped on the foreign mass media, satellite transmission by Western television cut off, China's government-controlled television filled with massive disinformation, the unusual liberties taken for a few weeks by China's press and TV cracked down on, foreign mail and newspapers confiscated at the border, and communications equipment like fax machines removed or put under guard.

But the media cat was already out of the bag, with her kittens irretrievably scattered. For, during the uprising and even as it was being crushed, Chinese students and their sympathizers within and outside China had used personal media—the direct-dial telephone, facsimile machines, personal computers, dry copiers, audio and videocassettes, and camcorders—to gather firsthand information within China, to scatter it through the country and get it across the border, to collect information elsewhere in the world and reformulate parts of it, and to send it back to known and unknown people in multiple cities in China. And, for the first time in history, a large computer network—the U.S. BITNET—was used by dissidents, not only to communicate news and

---

* The uses of various media in China during the period of the 1989 "pro-democracy movement" were many and complex. The mass media played a large role, and the Chinese government used both personal and mass media information to implicate the students. Many fascinating aspects of this period have had to be ignored to focus on the role played by new personal media.

compile casualty lists, but also to coordinate strategies, arrange phone, fax, and letter-writing brigades, swap Chinese fax and phone numbers, raise funds, and mount lobbying and public relations efforts.*

Just as the Shah of Iran had encouraged his own downfall by giving his opposition modern communications technologies to work with, so had Deng Xiaoping. For, in reforming the Chinese economy during the 1980s, Deng had begun to improve telecommunications and to permit the use of many personal electronic media. Deng's partial relaxation of central controls on the economy had not only allowed modernization to begin, but also caused inflation, income disparities, and corruption, and hence, widespread resentment.[2] Like the Iranians, the Chinese students wanted to move the clock, but not backward. Exposed to some freedoms and progress, they wanted more, and attempted to force their government into· faster forward.

The student movement, which received a great deal of nonstudent support, was played out on a global electronic stage set as an "accident of history,"[3] for an unprecedented 1,200-strong international mass media presence and its supporting technology had been allowed to assemble in Beijing to cover the May 15-19 Sino-Soviet Summit.[4] Cable Network News (CNN), for instance, increased its staff in China from 3 to 40 for the occasion, and brought in a fly-away dish and microwave satellite uplink units among other high tech equipment. CNN broadcasts were being

---

* Since 1978, China had been opening up somewhat to the world, importing technologies and attempting to modernize its economy. Thus, for a decade, students had enjoyed some Western media and teachers, tens of thousands of students had gone abroad to study, and there was contact with foreign tourists and businesses. On April 15, 1989, Hu Yaobang, China's ousted Communist Party chief, a martyr to student hopes, died, catalyzing massive student demonstrations. This was followed by government tightening of censorship and bans on protests, with student defiance of the bans and boycotts of classes. After a month of upheaval, Soviet leader Mikhail Gorbachev arrived in Beijing for the first Sino-Soviet Summit in 30 years. With the foreign media present to cover the Summit, a thousand students staged a hunger strike in Beijing's Tiananmen Square, supported by some 300,000 protesters. During the Summit, demonstrations grew to a million Chinese from various walks of life, and protests erupted in nearly all China's provinces. Summit meetings were forced to be rescheduled, relocated, or canceled. Following the Summit, protests escalated in Beijing, with students and their supporters bodily blocking police and troops from Tiananmen Square. Protestors swelled to tens of thousands of all ages, and included some government workers and military. On the night of June 3-4, trucks and tanks rolled into the Square; the crowds were bloodily dispersed, and an unknown number killed. Within a few days, many of the student leaders fled the country, and others went into hiding. Massive Chinese propaganda attempted to undo the story, while protest leaders were rounded up for punishment. For a detailed account of events, see: Stefan R. Landsberger, "The 1989 Student Demonstrations in Beijing: A Chronology of Events," *China Information*, Leiden, The Netherlands, Volume IV, no. 1, Summer 1989, pp. 37-55. Briefer chronologies were given by many newspapers.

distributed in 83 countries at the time, making news available to nations with no news personnel in China.[5]

Between Chinese students in China and around the world, other Chinese citizens, Chinese expatriots, other worldwide supporters, the briefly vocal Chinese mass media, Asian and Western mass media, and the Voice of America, never have so many had such diverse technologies available and used them to scatter so much information of a political uprising so quickly and so widely. As *Newsweek* said:[6]

> It was revolution by fax machine, computer and word of mouth, by photocopier and wall poster, by direct-dialed phone calls, shortwave radio and letters in the mail.

It was also revolution by walkie-talkie, cellular phone, audio and videotape, and satellite television. Traditional means of political expression mixed with new electronic means. Throughout the crisis, those involved within and outside China wrote thousands of letters.[7] Wall posters, handbills, banners, art work, a "goddess of freedom and democracy" sculpture, loudspeakers, and folk songs and spirituals were all part of the demonstrations.

As studied as was the Ayatollah Khomeini's use of both mass and personal media in his revolution a decade earlier, so spontaneous, apparently, was that of the Chinese students. Although they quickly learned to use the mass media very effectively, demonstrators in China are said to have been rather media shy until the arrival of Soviet leader Mikhail Gorbachev a month into the uprising.[8] China's own communications facilities are still rudimentary by world standards. But new means of communications are now so ubiquitous globally and so interlinked that those involved in China's crisis found themselves with a wide range of options.

China has a history of repeatedly suppressing students and intellectuals.[9] But having opted over the last decade to modernize its agriculture, industry, science, technology, and the military, educated people and especially those trained in the sciences have become China's life blood. By 1985, 28% of the Chinese students sent abroad were studying science, and nearly 40%, engineering.[10] At the time of the pro-democracy movement, there were about 43,000 Chinese students and scholars in the U.S. alone.[11]

These human resources, tens of thousands of them, were scattered after the government crackdown: into hiding, into exile, into temporary refuge in Western countries, or into safe, nonadventuresome types of activities. But residual information from the 49-day uprising, including audio and videotapes, had meanwhile been strewn among the Chinese people, and exiled students had undertaken various dissident movements with communications and information as key weapons.

TELECOMMUNICATIONS IN CHINA AND THE ROLE OF THE PHONE IN THE UPRISING

China has a very backward telecommunications system which has been only recently, and so far modestly, upgraded. In the mid-1980s, it had about six phones for every 1,000 people, compared to the Soviet Union with 92, Taiwan with 210,[12] a world average of 120, and the U.S. with more than 920 phones per thousand.[13] Calls in China are said to be completed only about half the time, and placing a call from Beijing to Shanghai can take four hours.[14] By the end of 1987, China had, however, provided local exchanges with 4.64 million lines, and given direct-dialing capability to 30% of them.[15] Since 1987, Hong Kong has also been furnishing a number of Chinese cities with cellular phone facilities.[16]

Throughout the seven-week uprising, and with increasing intensity as it grew, phone lines were busy across China, and between the rest of the world and that country. Many of the Chinese students in the U.S. ran up huge phone bills in an attempt to get information on the situation from student leaders, friends, and family in China, and, when the Chinese government blacked out news, to keep the homeland informed with news from foreign sources. News from China was taped off the phone, then relayed around the U.S. by tape, computer, and phone, played on the phone to Chinese callers, and given to sources that could send it back to other parts of China. After the martial law declaration on May 20th, for instance, one Chinese student in Cambridge, Massachusetts is said to have set up a "Boston-Beijing Hotline" which allowed information to make "a 'giant U-turn.'" In a singlehanded operation, he would call student leaders in Beijing, tape their messages, relay the tape to Voice of America for broadcast into China, give the information to Chinese language newspapers that publish in Hong Kong and distribute in the PRC, and use the information to update the computer bulletin boards on the academic network, BITNET.[17] Students at Caltech did the same sort of thing, not only calling Beijing University several times a day, but direct dialing students in such cities as Wuhan, Shanghai, Nanjing, and Canton.[18]

Chinese students at Columbia University, Berkeley, Stanford, the University of Texas, the University of Maryland, the University of Chicago, and at the Chinese Information Center in Boston—all over the U.S.—participated in similar efforts.[19] The Chinese Information Center's phone number was widely available in China during the crisis period, being broadcast by the Voice of America and, before the crackdown, over Tiananmen Square loudspeakers.[20]

News, scarce for the Chinese after martial law was declared, became more so after the June crackdown. In an attempt to correct the "widespread ignorance" they perceived in China about what was happening, Chinese students in the U.S. redoubled their efforts. One student at the University of Massachusetts said, "I've called everyone I know and told them to tell 100 other people."[21]

During the seven-week crisis period, deficiencies and overloads of the internal Chinese telecommunications system were sometimes compensated for transcontinentally. When people in Beijing, for instance, could not get through to other parts of China on the domestic long distance phone lines, they sometimes direct-dialed people outside the country, who then relayed their messages via direct-dial to the intended recipient in China.[22]

At the height of the crisis, "indiscriminate" or "blind" phone calls to strangers were also made by Chinese students at U.S. universities. Students at Brandeis and Harvard, for example, were reported to be telephoning China around the clock, "reading news reports and messages of encouragement to anyone who answers."[23]

JAMMING THE POSTCRACKDOWN HOT LINES

After the demonstrations had been crushed, China's government set aside 15 phone lines for the Chinese public to call in tips on where student leaders might be hiding. Chinese students in the U.S. responded by attempting to frustrate these efforts, keeping these "hotlines" busy by constantly calling them. A Chinese student at Brandeis told a *Los Angeles Times* reporter that the students had "photocopied all the numbers and have been telling everyone to call."[24]

USES OF FACSIMILE

Every phase of the China story was larger than life, but facsimile was the personal medium that got the most publicity. Chinese students in the United States appear to have been unaware of the use of facsimile nearly two years earlier to send information into Panama, and are said to have discovered its use independently just after Gorbachev's Beijing visit.[25] According to one source, Chinese students in California had been contacting students in China through academic computer links, and decided to use fax when this contact "stopped working" when martial law was declared. The uses of fax in China was probably more varied than they had been in the Panamanian situation. Like the phone, fax was used to get information from specific individuals out of China, to get information from the outside into China, to redirect information either between cities, or, from China to the U.S. and then back again to other Chinese cities, and to "indiscriminately" fax information to unknown people in various Chinese cities. In addition, fax was used to send photographs and other materials for public display and to serve as "documented" evidence to confirm the "truth" of other information. Fax is the ideal medium for transmitting the Chinese language, which poses difficulties for typing.[26]

By the time of the uprising, perhaps as many as 10,000 facsimile machines had been installed in Chinese government offices, universities, businesses, hotels, and hospitals.[27] During the demonstrations, Chinese students at U.S. universities and some centers in the U.S., including the China Information Center in Newton, Massachusetts, faxed copious amounts of U.S. press accounts of Chinese happenings into China. At Berkeley, for example, the students divided into groups to collect information from newspapers, TV, and radio, then combined and summarized it and faxed it to China.[28] Summaries of phone calls and letters received in the U.S. from Chinese family and friends were also faxed to others in China.[29] Chinese students at European universities, and the Chinese in Hong Kong, were doing similar faxing, and information was also faxed between Chinese cities.[30]

Fax numbers for those in China were collected from wherever they could be gotten. At Stanford, for instance, a list was compiled from numbers on the business cards of Chinese company representatives, some of whom were involved in U.S.-China joint ventures and came for U.S. visits.[31] Fax numbers of hotels and other businesses in various Chinese cities were compiled from various sources, including business directories.[32] Fifty-two hundred Chinese fax numbers are said to be listed in Hong Kong directories,[33] but these were apparently not known (or not published) at the time of the crackdown. Lists of available fax numbers were exchanged between U.S. campuses via the computer bulletin boards of the academic computer network, BITNET.[34]

One especially heroic faxing effort was attributed to Chinese students at the University of California in Los Angeles. When they learned that Huo Dejian, a popular singer, was planning to join a hunger strike, two people from UCLA went to China to report on this. There they obtained a two-page statement by the singer and faxed it to UCLA, where Chinese students passed it to the University of Southern California, where students faxed it to at least 40 fax machines inside China.[35] A USC faculty member told a *Chicago Tribune* reporter, "It went back all over China."[36]

Information on the swiftly moving political situation was also widely dispersed from the U.S. and elsewhere to collections of fax numbers of strangers in a large number of Chinese cities.[37] *Newsweek* reported on these "blind faxes," which included clips from U.S.-printed Chinese language newspapers, calling them "the electronic equivalent of a note in a bottle."[38] Chinese students at the University of Michigan, Columbia University, and the University of Southern California were among those said to be faxing pictures and news summaries daily to various Chinese cities. Such "blind" faxing increased in intensity in the last days of the crisis, as it became more dangerous and difficult to get through to the student leaders.[39] Once in China, the messages were collected by students and workers, who made hundreds of photocopies for display and distribution. In Shanghai, for instance, posters made from the faxes were attached to city buses halted by the large-scale demonstrations.[40] Fax-originated posters were indeed so prevalent during this upheaval that NBC News President Michael Gartner called them "the wall posters of this generation."[41]

Photographs taken in China and sent to the West were frequently faxed back as proof to the skeptical in China that information being sent was true. While friends and family would usually believe reports from the U.S., strangers often wanted evidence. Photos of the students fasting in Tiananmen Square were faxed back into China to renew the courage of other students. Photos were sometimes considered more effective than words in mass distributions.[42]

AUDIOCASSETTES AND VIDEOCASSETTES

Tape technologies may ultimately be one of the most important of all the personal media in keeping alive the memory of the Chinese uprising and documenting the story. Despite the heavy controls imposed after the government crackdown, a wide variety of tapes of the crisis have undoubtedly gone underground in China.[43] Tapes of Voice of America and other radio programs were made during the crisis. Taped phone conversations have already been mentioned. And those who read wall posters passed the messages on to others on tape recordings, as well as just by noting them down or photographing them.[44] A Chinese viewer in Shanghai who saw scenes, such as the students' meeting with Li Peng, on Chinese television called them "classics" and, says the *Columbia Journalism Review*, "He duly recorded the television report on a video-cassette machine for posterity."[45]

In a unique use of tapes, pop singers in Taiwan killed two birds with one stone, raising money for the Chinese rebels by selling a taped song about the uprising, and sending copies of the tape into China—by balloon! A ballad called "The Wound of History," taped by about 40 Taiwanese pop singers, became "a popular item in the propaganda packages Taiwan sends by balloon to the mainland."[46]

During the crisis, taped-off-the air TV broadcasts of Hong Kong news programs are known to have been smuggled on videocassettes across China.[47] Thousands of similar videotapes of Western news coverage are no doubt in the hands of individuals. Some students in China had video cameras, and some video cameras were bought by Chinese students in the U.S. and sent into China for the express purpose of recording the political action. Students at CalTech in Pasadena, for instance, are reported to have sent both money and video cameras into China.[48]

Videotapes were also used in concert with other personal media. An American who worked with the Chinese students at the China Information Center said that "it was fascinating how various technologies built on each other," explaining that a picture would be taped from a live broadcast received in California from China, and a print made of a scene. Then the print would be faxed back to China and multiple copies made and posted. After that, broadcasts received in the U.S. would show Chinese people looking at the poster.[49]

VCRs, videocassettes, and audiocassettes have long been smuggled into China, and both official and unofficial video parlors exist there. Audiotape recorders, including large ones, are prevalent, and cassettes are popular black market items.[50] By 1987, there were more than a million and a half audiocassette recorders in China, along with three million TV sets and 75.5 million radios.[51] As a part of upgrading its information structure, China has been producing about 44,000 VCRs a year, with the biggest buyers being schools, media outlets, cultural centers, businesses, and government institutions.[52] But there are also many VCRs in the hands of individuals. As early as 1986, there may have been as many as 2 million videocassette recorders in China, although only about 400,000 were officially acknowledged.[53]

COMPUTERS IN CHINA

During the 1980s, personal computers were both manufactured and imported into China in increasing quantities, and between 1983 and 1987, U.S. companies were licensed to export $7.8 billion worth of computer equipment to that country.[54] But China still has less than 4% of the world's PCs.[55] By the mid-1980s, most of these remained unlinked, and many were unused for lack of trained personnel.[56] Rather than computer-to-computer transmission, computerized information was often delivered by bicycle on floppy disks in Chinese cities, and disks mailed back and forth between countries by foreign companies. Exceptions where networking was to be found at that time were a few government offices, the national airlines reservation system, some large tourist hotels, and research programs in universities.[57] Some of the foreign companies in China installed their own networks, and computers in foreign businesses in China were used for political purposes to some extent during the crisis. The President of a Massachusetts high tech and consultancy group has been cited as saying that:[58]

> her company has been shown packages of messages, authored in China, sent out of the country using computer networks put in place by U.S. multinationals.

The messages were said to give "graphic detail" of both civilian and military activities during the height of the Beijing crisis. Wan Run Nan, founder and chairman of Stone Corporation, a Chinese computer outlet for Computerland Corporation of California, one of the more successful private businesses, reportedly "funneled money and computers to student protesters" during the uprising, and after the crackdown, was fired, as well as expelled from the Communist Party.[59]

COORDINATION, COMMUNICATIONS, AND INFORMATION BY COMPUTER

From the standpoint of advances in political uses of personal electronic media, perhaps the most exciting computer happening of the uprising took place in the U.S., where Chinese students with access to BITNET used it to coordinate their activities, for communications, and for information gathering and dissemination during the pro-democracy movement and after the crackdown. BITNET is the academic computer network that links universities in the U.S., Canada, and Mexico, and which is connected to the EARN academic network in Western Europe and the ASIANET network in Japan and the Pacific Basin. Begun in 1981 to join computers just between City University of New York and Yale, BITNET steadily grew, and now gives high-speed satellite and land-line computer linkage to individual students and scholars on hundreds of campuses. American universities that subscribe to BITNET give their students and faculty unlimited free use of its communications lines.[60]

Via BITNET, Chinese students in the U.S. could access three major bulletin board services: "Soc.Culture.China," ENCS, or the Electronic Newsletter for Chinese Students, and China-net.[61] During the summer of

1989, between 500 and 700 national and international articles a week were posted on Soc.Culture.China, which gave the most freedom for passing messages and was the most popular of these boards.[62] The BITNET boards served, among other things, as exchanges for general emotional outpourings all over the U.S., and "from France to Norway" in Europe, much as computer bulletin boards were used in California after the San Francisco earthquake. Chinese students reportedly used the boards:[63]

> to share transcripts of telephone conversations with relatives in China, rage over atrocities witnessed on television, mourn acquaintances slain

But BITNET's bulletin boards were also used for a wide variety of organizational tasks, from setting up phone, fax, and letter-writing brigades, to supplying and coordinating news and passing on messages, to swapping Chinese fax numbers, to compiling lists of the dead and wounded in China, to lobbying Washington, and to mobilizing U.S. public opinion.[64] They were used for fund raising and to make arrangements to get communications equipment to the protestors in China. A Chinese student at Columbia University is quoted as saying that "A friend at Purdue suggested we use the network to collect donations," and that with this money, the students bought "a mimeograph machine, a Chinese character typewriter and a photocopier for the students in Beijing."[65] Someone else on the network, said the student, had Beijing student contacts, "so we arranged a channel to get the machines into China." Fund raising was also conducted to help defray some of the students' phone bills.[66] According to one source, some funds were raised "using computer generated databases from previous letter-writing campaigns a year or two earlier."[67] Fund raising efforts were reported via BITNET by students outside the U.S.—from Trondheim University in Norway, for instance, while various other messages appearing on the boards came from students in Germany, France, England, and Hong Kong.[68] How-to instructions were also posted on Soc.Culture.China, one electronic entry giving detailed instructions for laser printing and faxing photographs taken in China back into China.[69] And when, in Summer 1989, Chinese students in the U.S. began to feel threatened by Chinese consular visits, harassment by unsympathetic Chinese students, and anonymous phone calls, they fought back by BITNET, posting "lists of the names of children of high-ranking Chinese leaders studying in this country," with, as *U.S. News & World Report* says, "the implied, anonymous threat."[70]

Several months after the uprising was crushed, Wu'er Kaixi, one of the student leaders who fled China and became a leader in the exiled dissidents' movement, was criticized for "high living" in a Taiwan-based

Chinese language newspaper.[71] BITNET was said to be "alive with open letters" from Chinese students, responding to the criticism and chastising Wu'er.[72]

THE AFTERMATH OF THE CRACKDOWN

Many Chinese students who remained abroad in the year after the uprising continued the dissent in the U.S. and elsewhere. Dozens of often competing protest organizations were put together in the U.S. alone.[73] While they varied in the level of Chinese reforms they claimed to seek,[74] all these groups purported to have nonviolent change, mainly through barrages of information, as their goal.[75] Some plans called for setting up radio broadcasts via Australia, Taiwan, or elsewhere, and for smuggling an underground newspaper into China.[76] Some groups effectively lobbied the U.S. Congress[77] and were very active in trying to influence U.S. foreign policy with China. They also organized a steady stream of conferences, meetings, and demonstrations.[78] Several archives were established in attempts to preserve information about the uprising. One at Yale requested items reflecting the many newly available personal media. In addition to pamphlets and clippings, and "personal reminiscences and first-hand observations in any language," it asked for contributions of "tapes, videos, photographs, fax prints, electronic mailings, [and] transcripts of phone calls."[79] The East Asia Library at Harvard preserved many of the Soc.Culture.China postings for the period immediately after the uprising.[80]

The China Information Center in Newton, Massachusetts was one of the very active organizations. It was set up and housed by the Walker Center for Ecumenical Exchange, a missionary group dealing with human rights issues. Active in getting information into China during the crisis period, the group later received extensive donations or loans of telephone and security systems, teleconferencing equipment, computers, computer software, laser printers, and fax machines from various U.S. private and corporate donors.[81] This Center established a reputation as a reliable source of news for the international mass media and for the various groups interested in the ongoing situation in China. The Democratic Front of China, an international "pro-democracy" group, was organized in Paris in Summer 1989, with mainly older, non-student leadership.[82]

Some months after the crackdown, a Paris-based group called The Federation for Democracy in China mounted an international effort to send protest materials into China via fax machines. A manifesto was prepared under the masthead of the *People's Daily*, the official Communist Party newspaper. With contributions from periodicals in many countries and the cooperation of the French magazine *Actuel*, on October 28, 1989, the manifestos were faxed into China. The manifesto, ready to be cut out and faxed, was published in the November issues of magazines in France, Holland, Germany, Belgium, Great Britain, Spain, Portugal, Italy, Greece, Denmark, Sweden, Finland, Norway, the U.S., Venezuela, and Brazil, along with a list of 5,000 Chinese fax numbers. The Chinese police seized the copies as they arrived, except for those sent to embassies and foreign news bureaus. The point was made, however, when the Chinese Government lodged a protest against the "fax attack" with the French Embassy in Beijing, and with the publicity attendant on government protests, quite a few Chinese people learned of the effort.[83]

By use of force, the Chinese government was able, not only to put down the uprising, but also to prevent any resurgence of these activities in the years following, despite the outbreak of "freedom" all over Eastern Europe. It is doubtful, however, whether it will be possible to keep dissidents in check for the long term if China intends to keep pushing for modernization.

More than anything, the employment of new personal media during the pro-democracy movement shows what new personal media are now out there, and readily available for imaginative uses in times of political crisis. It demonstrates how they can be mixed and matched to meet the needs of specific occasions. And it reminds us of just how far these personal media have advanced in the few short years since the revolution led by the Ayatollah Khomeini.

NOTES

1. For some of the student demands, see Robert Delfs, "Students Proclaim Hu Yaobang's Democratic Legacy. Wreathed in Protests," *Far Eastern Economic Review*, April 27, 1989, pp. 11-12. For a background on the downfall of Hu Yaobang, see: Robert P. Kreps, *Buying Hens Not Eggs: The Acquisition of Communications and Information Technology by the Peoples' Republic of China*, Program on Information Resources Policy, Harvard University, Cambridge, MA, October 1988, pp. 84-86.
2. See, for instance: Daniel Southerland, "China's Spring Rebellion: Will The Turmoil Return? Disruptions Affected More Than 80 Cities," *The Washington Post*, August 20, 1989, p. A-2.
3. Mike Chinoy, Beijing Bureau Chief for Cable Network News, said he could not emphasize too strongly the accidental nature of the massive coverage. (Mike Chinoy, "Media Coverage in China," Media Coverage of International Affairs Seminar Series, Center for International Affairs, Harvard University, Cambridge, MA, August 2, 1989.)
4. For student activities during the Gorbachev visit, see: "Upheaval in China. A Tumultuous Struggle Over the Destiny of a Nation," (A series of articles), *Newsweek*, May 29, 1989, pp. 16-26; "State of Seige," (A series of articles), *Time*, May 29, 1989, pp. 36-47; "Four Days that Shook the World," *The Economist*, May 20, 1989, pp. 37-38; Jim

Hoagland, "China's Turbulence Mirrors a New Global Pattern," *International Herald Tribune*, May 19, 1989, p. 1; Charles Mitchell, "Kremlin Roadshow Falls Flat. Summit Seemed More a Distraction Than Milestone," *The Japan Times*, May 24, 1989, p. 16; Scott Shane, "Gorbachev Upstaged by Students," *The Japan Times*, May 24, 1989, p. 16, and Claudia Rosett, "The Creed at Tiananmen Square," Editorial, *The Asian Wall Street Journal*, May 22, 1989, p. 8.

5. Mike Chinoy, "Media Coverage in China," Media Coverage of International Affairs Seminar Series, Center for International Affairs, Harvard University, August 2, 1989. The escalation of new types of technology not only permits real time coverage by the mass media, but also makes it competitively imperative. According to Anthony Hall, Director of BBC Television News, BBC had about 20 people in Beijing for the Summit, where maybe six would have been sent less than a decade earlier. (Anthony Hall, Director of BBC Television News, "The 'Black Holes' of Western Television News," Media Coverage of International Affairs Seminar Series, Center for International Affairs, Harvard University, July 13, 1989.)

6. Larry Martz, with Carroll Bogert, Douglas Waller, Margaret Garrard Warner, and Michael Rogers, "Revolution by Information. China's Students Wage High- and Low-tech War on the Blackout," *Newsweek*, June 19, 1989, p. 28.

7. Melanie Kirkpatrick, "TV: Transponding To and From China," *The Asian Wall Street Journal*, May 29, 1989, p. 8; Constance L. Hays, "Chinese Students Keep the Pressure On in U.S.," *The New York Times*, June 10, 1989, p. A-6; "Throughout the Land, Chinese React With Anger and Action," *The Boston Globe*, June 6, 1989, p. 11; Charles M. Madigan, "Chinese Students in U.S. Find New Role," *Chicago Tribune*, June 6, 1989, Sec. 1, p. 2, and Larry Martz et al., "Revolution by Information," *Newsweek*, June 19, 1989, pp. 28-29.

8. John H. Reiss, "A Producer's Story. The Camera's Red Glare," *Washington Journalism Review*, p. 28. (Article begins p. 27.) Mike Chinoy, in his seminar on "Media Coverage in China," said he had no "sense" that the students had planned to use the media. See also: John Schidlovsky, "A Correspondent's Story. Euphoria and Wu'er Kaixi ... And Then The Killing," *Washington Journalism Review*, September 1989, pp. 20-24.

9. For China's treatment of intellectuals, see: Robert P. Kreps, *Buying Hens Not Eggs: The Acquisition of Communications and Information Technology by the Peoples' Republic of China*, Program on Information Resources Policy, Harvard University, Cambridge, MA, October 1988, pp. 80-87. Kreps notes that "In China, anyone who is a graduate of a middle school or above can be considered an intellectual" (p. 81).

10. O. Schnepp, "The Impact of Returning Scholars on Chinese Science and Technology," in *Science and Technology in Post-Mao China*, Denis Fred Simon and Merle Goldman, Eds., Harvard University Press, Cambridge, MA, 1989, p. 176.

11. Leo A. Orleans, "Chinese in America: The Numbers Game," *China Exchange News*, September 1989, Volume 17, No. 3, pp. 9-10.

12. A 1987 *World Almanac* figure, cited in Richard Baum, "DOS ex Machina: The Microelectronic Ghost in China's Modernization Machine," in *Science and Technology in Post-Mao China*, Denis Fred Simon and Merle Goldman, Eds., Harvard University Press, Cambridge, MA, 1989, p. 370.

13. Robert P. Kreps, *Buying Hens Not Eggs: The Acquisition of Communications and Information Technology by the People's Republic of China*, Program on Information Resources Policy, Harvard University, Cambridge, MA, October 1988, pp. 71, 73.

14. Ibid., p. 73. U.S. Department of Commerce figures cited by *The New York Times* in February 1990 gave the USSR 124 phones per 1000 people, East Germany 233, Poland 122, Hungary 152, Romania 111, Czechoslovakia 246, and Bulgaria 248. ("National Standings," Chart, *The New York Times*, February 18, 1990, p. E-3. See also: "The Editorial Notebook. It's a Wired, Wired World," *The New York Times*, June 13, 1990, p. A-30.)

15. Francis Pearce, "Communications: Vital for Growth," *Far East Business*, May 1989, pp. 39-40. China had also provided Telex to 60 cities. Under a 1984 plan, says Pearce, China expects to invest nearly $22 billion to make 33.6 million phones available by the year 2000. See also: "China's Telecom Strategy," Pyramid Research, Inc., Cambridge, MA, May 1989, p. 55.

16. Since 1987, Hong Kong has been installing transmission towers for cellular phone service in various mainland China cities and routing international calls from the PRC via Hong Kong. (Martin P. Hughes and Sandra J. Langel, "Threats to the Development of the Public Switched Network: Examples and Alternatives," Southwestern Bell Telephone Company, August 26, 1988, pp. 5-6.) Cellular or mobile radio phone systems are being installed in many areas that lack more traditional telecommunications infrastructures. Asia has 18 of the 50 worldwide cellular networks, and this service is being widely used "either to supplement countries' existing telephone networks as in Japan and Hong Kong or as an alternative to expensive cabled telephone systems as in Thailand and Indonesia." ("Mobile Phones Sales Skyrocket in Asia," *Far East Business*, May 1989, p. 44.)

17. Douglas Jehl, "Boston Hot Line: Hope From China by Fax, Computer, Word of Mouth. Electronic Network Speeds News Around Globe," *Los Angeles Times*, May 26, 1989, Sec. 1, p. 20.

18. Ashley Dunn, "Phones, Faxes: Students in U.S. Keep Lines of Communication Open," *Los Angeles Times*, June 6, 1989, Sec. I, p. 8.

19. Constance L. Hays, "Chinese Students Keep the Pressure On In U.S.," *The New York Times*, June 10, 1989, p. A-6; "From the Barrel of a Fax. Part Three of Our Unintentional Series on Unsolicited 'Junk Faxes' Finds That They Have Their Uses, Too," *The Economist*, June 17, 1989, p. 32; Ashley Dunn, "Chinese Students in U.S. Seeking to Foil 'Tip' Lines," *Los Angeles Times*, June 11, 1989, Section 1, p. 9; Marianne Yen, "Across U.S., A Frantic Hunt for News," *The Washington Post*, June 6, 1989, p. A-12, and Paul Katzeff, "Lifeline to China. How a Modest Home in a Boston Suburb Became a Nerve Center For the Students of Tiananmen Square," *Boston Herald*, September 24, 1989, pp. 8-10.

20. Paul Katzeff, "Lifeline to China." *Boston Herald*, September 24, 1989, p. 9. (Article begins p. 8.)

21. Larry Martz et al., "Revolution by Information," *Newsweek*, June 19, 1989, pp. 28-29.

22. Jonathan Kaufman, "A New Foe for Censors: The Fax Machine," *The Boston Globe*, June 7, 1989, p. 3.

23. Steven V. Roberts with Paul Glastris, Pamela Ellis-Simons, Alice Z. Cuneo, Andrew Jack, Scott Minerbrook, Bruce B. Auster, and Sharon F. Golden, "New Diplomacy by Fax Americana," *U.S. News & World Report*, June 19, 1989, pp. 32-34.

24. Ashley Dunn, "Chinese Students in U.S. Seeking to Foil 'Tip' Lines," *Los Angeles Times*, June 11, 1989, Section 1, p. 9.

25. ". . . As Chinese in U.S. Pierce a News Blockade," *The New York Times*, May 24, 1989, p. A-11.

26. See, for instance, Fumio Kodama, "Information Technology Driving Force Behind Global Wave of Political Change," *The Japan Economic Journal*, June 23, 1990, p. 8.

27. Della Bradshaw, "News Smuggled Out of China With High-tech Help," *Financial Times*, June 20, 1989, p. 35, says 10,000. See also: "China's Telecom Strategy," Pyramid Research, Inc., Cambridge, MA, May 1989, pp. 55, 100. This source says that the Chinese fax market grew from $3 million in 1985 to $5 million in 1986, $8 million in 1987, and $11 million in 1988. Prior to 1986, it says, the machines were mainly produced locally, but by 1989, about 65% of the machines were being imported from several Japanese companies.

28. "...As Chinese in U.S. Pierce a News Blockade," *The New York Times*, May 24, 1989, p. A-11. See also: Marianne Yen, "Across U.S., A Frantic Hunt For News," *The Washington*

Post, June 6, 1989, p. A-12; Melanie Kirkpatrick, "TV: Transponding To and From China," *The Asian Wall Street Journal,* May 29, 1989, p. 8; Elizabeth A. Brown, "After Tiananmen Square. Network Links Chinese in US. Student-run Centers Collect Up-to-date Information and Support the Chinese Movement in Exile," *The Christian Science Monitor,* September 29, 1989, p. 12.

29.   Marianne Yen, "Across U.S., A Frantic Hunt For News," *The Washington Post,* June 6, 1989, p. A-12.

30.   "Topics of the Times. China's Fax Invasion," *The New York Times,* June 20, 1989, p. A-22; Jonathan Kaufman, "A New Foe for Censors: The Fax Machine," *The Boston Globe,* June 7, 1989, p. 3.

31.   "...As Chinese in U.S. Pierce a News Blockade," *The New York Times,* May 24, 1989, p. A-11.

32.   Ibid., and also: Ashley Dunn, "Chinese Students in U.S. Seeking to Foil 'Tip' Lines," *Los Angeles Times,* June 11, 1989, Sec. I., pp. 9-11.

33.   "Chinese Sent Police to Seize Copies of Dissident Manifesto Sent by Fax," *International Herald Tribune,* November 3, 1989, p. 7.

34.   Larry Martz et al., "Revolution By Information," *Newsweek,* June 19, 1989, pp. 28-29. "Fax Against Fictions," *Time,* June 19, 1989, p. 32.

35.   Charles M. Madigan, "Chinese Students in U.S. Find New Role," *Chicago Tribune,* June 6, 1989, Sec. 1, p. 2.

36.   Ibid.

37.   Larry Martz et al., "Revolution by Information," *Newsweek,* June 19, 1989, pp. 28-29. See also: "From the Barrel of a Fax," *The Economist,* June 17, 1989, p. 32.

38.   Larry Martz et al., "Revolution by Information," *Newsweek,* June 19, 1989, pp. 28-29.

39.   Ashley Dunn, "Phones, Faxes: Students in U.S. Keep Lines of Communication Open," *Los Angeles Times,* June 6, 1989, Sec. 1, p. 8. Among others who reported on blind faxing were Steven V. Roberts et al., "New Diplomacy by Fax Americana," *U.S. News & World Report,* June 19, 1989, pp. 32-32, Jonathan Kaufman, "A New Foe For Censors: The Fax Machine," *The Boston Globe,* June 7, 1989, p. 3, "Fax Against Fictions," *Time,* June 19, 1989, p. 32, and "From the Barrel of a Fax," *The Economist,* June 17, 1989, p. 32.

40.   Larry Martz et al., "Revolution by Information," *Newsweek,* June 19, 1989, pp. 28-29.

41.   Michael Gartner, "Up Freedom! Faxes to the Rebels, Gunfire Via Cellular Phone," *The Wall Street Journal,* June 8, 1989, p. A-19. Michael J. Berlin, "A Teacher's Story. Chinese Journalists Cover (And Join) The Revolution," *Washington Journalism Review,* September 1989, p. 37, also mentions the faxed wall posters. See the complete article (pp. 32-37) for the use of *dazibao* or wall posters in the uprising.

42.   Larry Martz et al., "Revolution by Information," *Newsweek,* June 19, 1989, pp. 28-29; Frederic E. Wakeman, Jr., "The June Fourth Movement in China," *Items,* Social Science Research Council, Volume 43, No. 3, September 1989, p. 60 (article 57-64); and Elizabeth A. Brown, "After Tiananmen Square. Network Links Chinese in US," *The Christian Science Monitor,* September 29, 1989, p. 12.

43.   Edward Fouhy, former Executive Producer of CBS Evening News With Walter Cronkite and of NBC Nightly News, among others, has suggested this. (Edward Fouhy, "The Whole World is Watching: Television News and Mental Images," Media Coverage of International Affairs Seminar Series, Center for International Affairs, Harvard University, Cambridge, MA, July 6, 1989.)

44.   Michael J. Berlin, "A Teacher's Story. Chinese Journalists Cover (And Join) The Revolution," *Washington Journalism Review,* p. 34. Conversely, Chinese who listened to Voice of America broadcasts sometimes took notes and made them into wall posters. (Larry Martz et al., "Revolution by Information," *Newsweek,* June 19, 1989, pp. 28-29.)

45.   Mark Hopkins, "Watching China Change. Chinese TV Was a Force For Freedom. Then

The Party Took Over," *Columbia Journalism Review*, September/October, 1989, p. 38. (Article pp. 35-40.)

46. Lincoln Kaye, "Smug and Smiling," *Far Eastern Economic Review*, August 24, 1989, p. 18.

47. Rod Nordland, "We Know What Really Happened," *Newsweek*, June 26, 1989, p. 28. This article mentions Hong Kong news videotapes being smuggled to Wuhan, for instance.

48. Steven V. Roberts et al., "New Diplomacy by Fax Americana," *U.S. News & World Report*, June 19, 1989, pp. 32-34, and Jonathan Alter, "Karl Marx, Meet Marshall McLuhan," *Newsweek*, May 29, 1989, p. 28.

49. Paul Katzeff, "Lifeline to China," *Boston Herald*, September 24, 1989, p. 10. Jessica Lipnack, President of Networking Institute of Massachusetts, is being quoted.

50. Gladys D. Ganley and Oswald H. Ganley, *Global Political Fallout. The VCR's First Decade 1976-1985*, Ablex Publishing Corporation, Norwood, NJ, 1987, pp. 14-15, 37-38, 72-73.

51. Xie Wenqing, "China: Narrowing the Technological Gap," *InterMedia*, Volume 16, Nos. 4-6, Autumn 1988, pp. 16-17.

52. "Calls on Industry for VCRs," *South China Morning Post*, May 15, 1989, Business Sec., p. 10.

53. Mark Silverman, "Mainland China Tries Regulating Vid Distribution," *Variety*, March 5, 1986, p. 104. (Article begins p. 1.)

54. Della Bradshaw, "News Smuggled Out of China With High-Tech Help," *The Financial Times*, June 20, 1989, p. 35.

55. Robert P. Kreps, *Buying Hens Not Eggs: The Acquisition of Communications and Information Technology by the Peoples' Republic of China*, Program on Information Resources Policy, Harvard University, Cambridge, MA, October 1988, p. 61. See also: Richard Baum, "DOS ex Machina: The Microelectronic Ghost in China's Modernization Machine," in *Science and Technology in Post-Mao China*, Denis Fred Simon and Merle Goldman, Eds., Harvard University Press, Cambridge, MA, 1989, pp. 347-371, for a discussion of computers in China in the 1980s. Pyramid Research says there are "at least 250,000 PCs in operation and a strong local PC manufacturing base" in China ("China's Telecom Strategy," Pyramid Research, Inc., Cambridge, MA, May 1989, p. 55.) International Data Corporation is said to have estimated that there are as many as 340,000 PCs there. (Della Bradshaw, "News Smuggled Out of China with High-tech Help," *Financial Times*, June 20, 1989, p. 35.)

56. Richard Baum, "Dos Ex Machina: The Electronic Ghost in China's Modernization Machine," in *Science and Technology in Post-Mao China*, Denis Fred Simon and Merle Goldman, Eds., Harvard University Press, Cambridge, MA, 1989, pp. 355, 360.

57. Ibid. Richard Baum (notes, p. 447) cites "A Tour of Computing Facilities in China," *Computer*, January 1985, for bicycle delivery within cities. Robert P. Kreps, in *Buying Hens Not Eggs*, Program on Information Resources Policy, Harvard University, Cambridge, MA, October 1988, pp. 73, 90, cites Lisa Vickery, "Communicating Across the Pacific," *The Asian Wall Street Journal Weekly*, September 30, 1985, p. 6C, for floppy disk mailing by foreign companies.

58. Della Bradshaw, "News Smuggled Out of China With High-tech Help," *Financial Times*, June 20, 1989, p. 35. Jessica Lipnack, President of Networking Institute of Massachusetts, is being cited.

59. Mike Langberg, "Computer Retailer Loses Big in China," *The Boston Globe*, September 25, 1989, p. 9. See also: Howard W. French, "Chinese Opposition Group Plans Secret Parley in West Next Month," *The New York Times*, August 4, 1989, p. A-2.

60. James Flanigan, "The Chip May Prove Mightier Than The Sword," *Los Angeles Times*, June 14, 1989, Section 4, p. 1; and D. D. Guttenplan, "Computer Network Is Student Lifeline," *Newsday*, June 25, 1989, p. 7. Guttenplan says that, while BITNET is not

connected to mainland China, the PRC can be accessed via USENET through a linkup with the University of Karlsruhe, West Germany.

61. Ashley Dunn and Elizabeth Lu, "A High-Tech Version of Wallposter. Computer Network Links Chinese Around the Globe," *Los Angeles Times*, June 9, 1989, p. 1.

62. Ibid., and also "Updating China News on the Electronic Mail Services," *China Update*, An Occasional Bulletin of the China Scholars Coordinating Committee, No. 1, August 1989, p. 19. The latter article, which gave instructions for using the various electronic services, warned users to be prepared to spend a lot of time on Soc. Culture.China listings, which contained "anything anyone wants to post, including personal disputes and musings."

63. Ashley Dunn and Elizabeth Lu, "A High-Tech Version of Wallposter. Computer Network Links Chinese Around the Globe," *Los Angeles Times*, June 9, 1989, p. 1.

64. Ashley Dunn, "Phones, Faxes: Students In U.S. Keep Lines of Communication Open," *Los Angeles Times*, June 6, 1989, Section 1, p. 8; and Larry Martz et al., "Revolution by Information," *Newsweek*, June 19, 1989, pp. 28-29.

65. D. D. Guttenplan, "Computer Network Is Student Lifeline," *Newsday*, June 25, 1989, p. 7.

66. Ashley Dunn, "Chinese Students in U.S. Seeking to Foil 'Tip' Lines," *Los Angeles Times*, June 11, 1989, Section 1, pp. 9-11.

67. Frederic E. Wakeman, Jr., "The June Fourth Movement in China," *Items*, Social Science Research Council, Volume 43, No. 3, September 1989, p. 60. (Article begins p. 57.)

68. Ashley Dunn and Elizabeth Lu, "A High-Tech Version of Wallposter. Computer Network Links Chinese Around the Globe," *Los Angeles Times*, June 9, 1989, p. 1.

69. D. D. Guttenplan, "Computer Network Is Student Lifeline," *Newsday*, June 25, 1989, p. 7.

70. Emily MacFarquhar and Susan Lawrence, "Outside Agitators For Democracy. From the U.S., Chinese Students Fight On," *U.S. News & World Report*, August 7, 1989, p. 35. (Article, pp. 34-35.)

71. Xue Xiao Guang published the article "Does Wu'er Kaixi Get Lost in the Money World?" in *Shijie Ribao* at the end of October, according to *The Boston Globe*. (Charles A. Radin, "Chinese Student Leader Reproached for High Living," *The Boston Globe*, November 4, 1989, p. 5.)

72. Charles A. Radin, "Chinese Student Leader Reproached for High Living," *The Boston Globe*, November 4, 1989, p. 5.

73. Susumu Awanohara, "In The Land of The Free. Exiled Dissidents Split Between Revolution and Reform," *Far Eastern Economic Review*, August 24, 1989, p. 18.

74. Charles A. Radin, "China Activism is Gaining Force on US Campuses," *The Boston Globe*, September 17, 1989, pp. 1, 24. Susumu Awanohara, "Exiled Dissidents Split Between Revolution and Reform," *Far Eastern Economic Review*, August 24, 1989, pp. 18-21.

75. For listing of some of the international groups, see: "Organizations and Activities of Chinese Abroad," and "Directory of Organizations Mentioned in This Issue," *China Update*, No. 1, August 1989, pp. 11-12, 19-20. See also: Emily MacFarquhar and Susan Lawrence, "Outside Agitators for Democracy," *U.S. News & World Report*, August 7, 1989, p. 34, among others.

76. Jeffrey Bartholet with Ray Wilkinson and Dorinda Elliott, "China's New Long March. In Chicago and Beijing, Students Keep the Spirit," *Newsweek*, August 7, 1989, p. 37; Howard W. French, "Chinese Opposition Group Plans Secret Parley in West Next Month," *The New York Times*, August 4, 1989, p. A-2; Marianne Yen, "Students in U.S. Plan Prodemocracy Fight. Young Chinese Convene in Chicago to Continue Movement Begun at Beijing University," *The Washington Post*, July 28, 1989, p. A-32; and Mayfair Yang, "The First Congress of Chinese Students in the USA: A Personal Account," *China Update*, No. 1, August 1989, pp. 13-15.

77. Emily MacFarquhar and Susan Lawrence, "Outside Agitators For Democracy," *U.S.*

News & World Report, August 7, 1989, p. 34. See also: Susumu Awanohara, "Exiled Dissidents Split Between Revolution and Reform," *Far Eastern Economic Review,* August 24, 1989, pp. 18-21.

78. Charles A. Radin, "China Activism is Gaining Force on US Campuses," *The Boston Globe,* September 17, 1989, pp. 1, 24; Tracy Thompson, "In D.C. 3,500 Chinese Students March in Sorrow, Resolution," *The Washington Post,* October 2, 1989, p. A-10, and Jay Mathews, "Chinese Students' Audiences Thin Out. Democratic Movement Faces Flagging Interest Among Americans," *The Washington Post,* October 7, 1989, p. A-11.

79. Jonathan D. Spence, "China's Witnesses," Letter to the Editor, *Asian Wall Street Journal,* July 14, 1989.

80. "Updating China News on the Electronic Mail Services," *China Update,* No. 1, August 1989, p. 19. Items on the uprising being sought by archival collections at Harvard University, University of Chicago, Columbia University, Stanford University, University of Toronto, and University of Leiden and Amsterdam International Institute for Social History, along with some descriptions of exhibits and documentary collections, are listed in "Archives, Exhibitions, Documents: a Survey," *China Update,* No. 1, August 1989, pp. 17-18.

81. Elizabeth A. Brown, "After Tiananmen Square. Network Links Chinese in US," *The Christian Science Monitor,* September 29, 1989, p. 12, and Paul Katzeff, "Lifeline to China. How a Modest Home in a Boston Suburb Became a Nerve Center for the Students of Tiananmen Square," *Boston Herald,* September 24, 1989, pp. 8-9.

82. Susumu Awanohara, "Exiled Dissidents Split Between Revolution and Reform," *Far Eastern Economic Review,* August 24, 1989, p. 18. See also: Jay Mathews, "Chinese Students' Audiences Thin Out. Democratic Movement Faces Flagging Interest Among Americans," *The Washington Post,* October 7, 1989, p. A-11, and Howard W. French, "Chinese Opposition Group Plans Secret Parley in West Next Month," *The New York Times,* August 4, 1989, p. A-2.

83. "Arriva in Cina Via Fax Falso Giornale del PCC," *Corriere Della Sera,* October 27, 1989, p. 4; "Chinese Sent Police to Seize Copies of Dissident Manifesto Sent by Fax," *International Herald Tribune,* November 3, 1989, p. 7; "China Lodges Protest Against France," *International Herald Tribune,* November 1, 1989, p. 2; "Exiles to Flood China With Faxed Appeals," *International Herald Tribune,* October 24, 1989, p. 8; "Computer Fraud Booms in China," *Financial Times,* October 24, 1989, p. 3; and John Maxwell Hamilton, "Everybody's A Diplomat," *The Boston Globe* Magazine, April 1, 1990, pp. 26, 28. (Article begins p. 23.)

chapter 13

FREEDOM AND DESTABILIZATION

What can you say about a decade that begins with one old man using audiocassettes to lead a host of followers, and ends with hosts of young students using a computer network to guide each other? The decade that ended dramatically with young East Germans and their babies breaching the Berlin wall, and East European Communist parties falling like tenpins. And then, the unbelievable beginning of the next decade, with Germany reunited.

Shortly after the pro-democracy movement in China was crushed, Michael Blumenthal, former U.S. Secretary of the Treasury, appeared on the David Brinkley show and was asked his opinion of what "was going on in China," and Blumenthal answered, "The same thing that is happening throughout the communist world...the computer revolution." "The tremendous power of that little chip," said Blumenthal, now governs "everything that we do and that the communist countries have had to learn to do."[1] James Reston said of the overwhelming changes in the communist countries of Europe in the last months of 1989:[2]

> "In the days of Goebbels, they could enslave a people....But then along came these new instruments, and they vault over boundaries and Iron Curtains

The new personal media have been a vital part of the communications and information revolution of the past few decades. It is these media, and especially the tape technologies, that have at least partially pried loose the grasp of hundreds of years of censorship. Facsimile has opened an instantaneous self-service window in virtually every national wall. Satellite television, new uplinks, and growing numbers of satellite dishes and cable television stations are letting all sorts of individuals address targeted audiences and tune into and tape specialized programs. Computer bulletin boards and videocassettes permit people of like minds in diverse locations to exchange ideas, seek kindred spirits, and, if they choose, plot revolutions.

Single incidents of a given kind carried out with the help of a single medium are important in themselves. But the real importance lies in the piling up of varying incidents involving multiple types of media, often in the face of political controls that theoretically should never allow these things to happen. The real importance is that events propelled by new personal media are interacting with overall world changes. The real importance is that the new personal media have brought globalization, with all its shifting power structures, opportunities, and problems right down to the level of the individual.

Personal media have provided a powerful force for freedom, but "freedom" comes in many flavors. If the status quo in communist states can be eroded by these new forces, it should be remembered that so can the status quo in democratic countries. Power so generously dispersed among the individuals of the world can not only draw people together, but can also fragment the world into multitudes of power centers. This can remove the glue of social cohesion until recently provided by a limited number of organizations and governments.

Loosened cohesion could be even more destabilizing in democratic countries than in those where systems are more rigid. People in democratic countries are used to great personal freedoms, and under yesterday's terms of engagement, their infrastructures were built to withstand them. Today's terms of engagement are different because the weapons are different, and democracies may not be attuned to see changes occurring in the givens.

A world where information flies across borders on the wings of computer networks and facsimile and satellite TV and videocassettes is not a world we are accustomed to live in. Nor is a world where access to information, and the means of creation, production, and dissemination have edged over into the hands of countless millions of people. The big question is, now that the people have these means, what are the people going to do with them? That big question is no longer entirely addressable to centralized sources or amenable to good, dull, rational bureaucratic answers. Because *the people* armed with these new media are spread throughout the world, each literally following his or her own agenda. One constant remains among all the changes—not every individual is a responsible individual. Nor is every individual an adherent to your particular political agenda or my particular political agenda.

With the tremendous scarcity of personal media that formerly prevailed, it was possible for only limited numbers of individuals or small groups to achieve a critical mass of followers who made changing things possible. Now it is possible for many groups to effect a wide variety of different changes and to do so simultaneously. These many individuals and groups with varied ideas and goals can impact, influence, and reshape things in ways that are politically uncertain. Thus, any political situation is liable to upset, and how this plays itself out will surely be different from anything in our past experience. What appears to be desirable from a democratic point of view may create such unsettling shifts that in the end, it may not really be desirable.

The uses of the new personal media by governments have not been discussed here, but rest assured they are being implemented. Databanks of frightening breadth are being assembled. Police departments and even cars are equipped with more and more sophisticated equipment for surveillance and compliance. Listening and recording devices are used regularly, and propaganda is created and distributed. While personal media have provided governments with better ways to govern, they have not neglected to supply better means of suppression. Businesses are also using these new media in ways that are detrimental to individuals, for example, collecting and selling long lists of information about them.

Nor should individuals feel secure in accepting the new power of personal media as a given. While the tide is running with more individual power and freedom today, a political crackdown could come if vested interests become too threatened. This has already happened, at least temporarily, in China, which has been willing to sacrifice some of the thrust of its modernization to the control of the flow of information. These new freedoms are not just at risk in restrictive countries. They could also be threatened in democracies where laws or regulations are imposed that are poorly thought through or are too stringent. Old laws and institutions could simply catch up, putting various brakes on the uses of personal media. Novelty and the element of surprise have played important roles in the successful political uses of these media, but these could lose their impact with repetition. Overuse creates bordeom, and this is happening with mass mailings, telephone barrages, and videotaped advertising. Where political repression has lessened, as it miraculously has to some small extent in parts of the world, some types of needs for these media could also lessen. But the need for political power by individuals is not likely to go away, and neither are these new media. And these machines do have a certain staying power. For all their newness, they have already become part and parcel of how the world now lives and makes its living.

Five weeks after the Berlin wall was breached on November 9, 1989, and two weeks before the 1980s ended, U.S. Secretary of State James Baker and East German Prime Minister Hans Modrow met in Potsdam. One of the subjects under discussion had been taboo for 44 years—the possible reunification of East and West Germany. President Bush had outlined a rational, political step by political step plan for such a reunification. But the East Germans were in no mood to go slow. For, as Modrow told Baker:[3]

> the push for unification from East Germans is being driven not so much by nationalist impulses but by consumer impulses, not by visions of a grand Germany but visions of videocassette recorders.

This book is called *The Exploding Political Power of Personal Media*, and the emphasis ought to rest on exploding. By definition, explosions are only partly controllable, with fragments going off in every direction. And, all over the globe, that is exactly what is happening.

NOTES

1. James Flanigan, "The Chip May Prove Mightier Than The Sword," *Los Angeles Times*, June 14, 1989, Sec. IV, p. 1.
2. R. W. Apple, Jr., "Reston, Retiring at 80, Still Looks Up the Road," *The New York Times*, November 5, 1989, p. 34.
3. Thomas L. Friedman, "Europeans Praising Baker Blueprint," *The New York Times*, December 14, 1989, p. A-22.

AUTHOR INDEX

Subject Index